The Art of
Autobiography
in 19th and 20th Century England

A.O.J. Cockshut

Yale University Press
New Haven & London
1984

For Charmian and Timothy

Designed by Stephanie Hallin
and set in Compugraphic Bembo
by Red Lion Setters, London.
Printed in Great Britain
by the Pitman Press,
Bath.

Library of Congress Cataloging in Publication Data

Cockshut, A.O.J.
The art of autobiography in 19th and 20th century England.

Includes index.
1. Autobiography.
I. Title
CT25.C63 1984   808' .06692   84-40183
ISBN 0-300-03235-8

How often in the overflowing Streets,
Have I gone forward with the Crowd, and said
Unto myself, the face of every one
That passes by me is a mystery.
Thus have I look'd, nor ceased to look, oppress'd
By thoughts of what, and whither, when and how,
Until the shapes before my eyes became
A second-sight procession, such as glides
Over still mountains, or appears in dreams;
And all the ballast of familiar life,
The present, and the past; hope, fear; all stays,
All laws of acting, thinking, speaking man
Went from me, neither knowing me, nor known.
And once, far-travelled in such mood, beyond
The reach of common indications, lost
Amid the moving pageant, 'twas my chance
Abruptly to be smitten with the view
Of a blind Beggar, who, with upright face,
Stood propp'd against a Wall, upon his Chest
Wearing a written paper, to explain
The story of the Man, and who he was.
My mind did at this spectacle turn round
As with the might of waters, and it seem'd
To me that in this Label was a type,
Or emblem, of the utmost that we know,
Both of ourselves and of the universe;
And, on the shape of the unmoving man,
His fixed face and sightless eyes, I look'd
As if admonish'd from another world.

Wordsworth, *The Prelude*, 1805, Book VII, II, 594–622.

No man is given to see his work through. Man goes forth unto his work and to his labour until the evening, but the evening falls before it is done. There was One alone who began and finished and died.

J.H. Newman, *The Reformation of the Eleventh Century*, 1841.

From the dread Watch tower of man's absolute Self.

Coleridge, Letter to Wordsworth, 30 May 1815.

An autobiography, alone of all books, may be more valuable in proportion to the amount of misrepresentation which it contains.

Leslie Stephen, *Hours in a Library*, 1892, III, p.237.

If you do not want to explore an egoism you should not read autobiography.

H.G. Wells, *Experiment in Autobiography*, 1934, Chap. VII.

It is misleading to talk of the 'self-love' of autobiographers; most of us love ourselves too dearly to be autobiographers.

Roy Pascal, *Design and Truth in Autobiography*, 1960, p.187.

Contents

Chronological Table   ix

I Introduction   I

II The Halfway House   15

III Childhood   35

  (i) Memory   36
  (ii) Bereavement   38
  (iii) The Transmission of Values 43

IV The Child Alone   53

  (i) Conflict: W.H. Hudson 55
  (ii) Regression: Forrest Reid 60
  (iii) Reconciliation: Edwin Muir 66
  (iv) Paradise Shared: Eleanor Farjeon 70
  (v) Paradise to Order: Christopher Milne 73
  (vi) Emotion Recollected in Cynicism: Lord Berners 76

V The Child at Home   81

  (i) The Dominant Father: Victor Gollancz 82
  (ii) The Dominant 'Mother': Augustus Hare 88
  (iii) A Fluid Background: Stephen Spender 92
  (iv) Deprivation: Winifred Foley and Neville Cardus 95

VI   The Dedicated Child   99

   (i)   Ruskin   100
   (ii) Edmund Gosse   108
   (iii) Daughter of Bertrand Russell   114

VII Defined by the World   119

   (i)   Beatrice Webb   120
   (ii) H.G. Wells   129
   (iii) Bertrand Russell   135

VIII The Quest   147

   (i)   The High Quest: Kathleen Raine   149
   (ii) The Quest in the World:
      (a) De Quincey   155
      (b) Benjamin Haydon   161
      (c) John Cowper Powys   164
   (iii) The Low Quest: J.R. Ackerley   170

IX   Conversion   177

X   Conclusion   215

   Index   219

Chronological Table

	Born	Date of Autobiography	Age in year of publication
J.R. ACKERLEY	1896	1968	posthumous
Enid BAGNOLD	1889	1969	80
Patricia BEER	1924	1968	44
Lord BERNERS	1883	1934 & 1945	51 62
James BOSWELL	1740	None	
John BUNYAN	1628	1666	38
Lord BYRON	1788	None (destroyed)	
Neville CARDUS	1889	1947	58
G.K. CHESTERTON	1874	1936	62
Richard CHURCH	1892	1955 & 1957	63–5
Cyril CONNOLLY	1903	1938	35
Thomas DE QUINCEY	1785	1822 onwards	37 onwards
Havelock ELLIS	1859	1940	posthumous
Eleanor FARJEON	1881	1935	54
Benjamin FRANKLIN	1706	1817	posthumous
Winifred FOLEY	1914	1974	60
Eric GILL	1882	1940	posthumous
Victor GOLLANCZ	1893	1952–3	59–60
Edmund GOSSE	1849	1907	58
Bede GRIFFITHS	1906	1954	48
Augustus HARE	1834	1896–1900	62–6
Benjamin HAYDON	1786	1876	posthumous
W.H. HUDSON	1841	1918	77
Leigh HUNT	1784	1850	66
Douglas HYDE	?1911	1950	?39
Vernon JOHNSON	1886	1929	43
Sheila KAYE-SMITH	1887	1937	50
Ronald KNOX	1888	1918	30

	Born	Date of Autobiography	Age in year of publication
C.S. LEWIS	1898	1955	57
Gavin MAXWELL	1914	1965	51
J.S. MILL	1806	1873	posthumous
Christopher MILNE	1920	1974	54
Edwin MUIR	1887	1954 (incorporating shorter version 1940)	53–67
Priscilla NAPIER	1908	1966	58
J.H. NEWMAN	1801	1864	63
J.C. POWYS	1872	1934	62
Kathleen RAINE	1908	1973–7	65–9
Gwen RAVERAT	1885	1952	67
Forrest REID	1875	1926	51
John RUSKIN	1819	1885–9	66–70
Bertrand RUSSELL	1872	1967–9 (some extracts earlier	95–7
Dora RUSSELL	1894	1975	81
Elizabeth SEWELL	1815	1907	posthumous
Stephen SPENDER	1909	1951	42
Katharine TAIT	1923	1975	52
George TYRRELL	1861	1912	posthumous
Beatrice WEBB	1858	1926 & 1948	68 & posthumous
H.G. WELLS	1866	1934	68
Blanco WHITE	1775	1845	posthumous
Harriette WILSON	1786	1825	39

I
Introduction

As in my former books, *Truth to Life* and *Man and Woman*, the method of this book is selective, and no general historical survey is attempted. The choice is made from works in English only. Bunyan's *Grace Abounding* is the only work written before 1750 discussed in any detail, while the great majority of examples are taken from the nineteenth and twentieth centuries. Choice must be to some extent arbitrary; but the principle has been to select both from well-known and comparatively little-known works those that best illustrate certain broad general types of character and personal history. What these are will be seen in the chapter headings. Some autobiographies have been omitted because I have written about them before, others because I did not think I had anything new to say about them, others because they did not illustrate the categories that most interested me, others because there was not space for them, and yet others (probably) simply because I had not read them. Those who find that their favourites are omitted or given cursory treatment will forgive me, I hope. At least I would claim that, though much fascinating material is omitted, nothing that is included lacks interest. (I speak, naturally, of the original works, not of my discussion of them.)

I adopt as my own the broad and sensible distinction made by Roy Pascal between autobiography and memoir or reminiscence: 'In the autobiography proper, attention is focused on the self, in the memoir or reminiscence on others.'[1] Autobiography and memoir may be mixed in the same book, and sometimes on the same page, but they are still theoretically distinct. As my title will indicate, my concern is exclusively with the first. The question proposed by this book is: how do people perceive their own nature and development, and what literary forms do they find to convey them to their readers? There are a few cases (very few, I think), like Newman's *Apologia*, of works which are equally notable both as memoir and as autobiography. Then I ignore the memoir as far as I can, as falling outside my subject.

The arrangement of examples according to similarities of character type and subject matter has entailed one important sacrifice—of chronology. The reader may find himself going from the eighteenth to the twentieth century and back again. I try to compensate as far as possible for this by giving detailed chronological lists[2] which show the date of birth and death, and the age at which the author published his autobiography. The handicap, though real, is perhaps less than it would be in an account of

[1] Roy Pascal, *Design and Truth in Autobiography*, Routledge & Kegan Paul, 1960, p.5.
[2] See p. ix.

poetry or prose fiction. Doubtless most autobiographers have read auto-biographies of others before they begin work. But they seldom refer to them or reveal their influence. If there are 'schools' of autobiography (which is perhaps doubtful) they are determined more by similarities of character and experience than by literary fashion. The epithets that we apply to poetry, 'Augustan', 'Romantic', 'Pre-Raphaelite' and the like, have no equivalents in the study of autobiography. My own categories, such as quest and conversion, seem to me equally applicable over the whole time-span with which the book deals; and it is obvious that books far removed from the period and the language of which I write would fit into them too. Conversely, autobiographies published at about the same time may have almost nothing in common. So it is that the sacrifice of chronology seemed much the lesser evil when the alternative was to sacri-fice close comparisons between works with real similarities and interest-ing points of difference.

Though the example of St Augustine is alone enough to show that a great autobiography could be written many centuries before the begin-nings of self-consciousness in its modern forms, it is still significant that autobiography was not identified as a separate form with a name of its own until the early nineteenth century. (The earliest example given by OED comes from Southey.) Dr Johnson, who quotes freely and with obvious interest from autobiographical writings, is still content with the single word *biography* to cover both types. We may suppose that this was because more interest was felt in the actual record of a life and in the facts shown than in the point of view from which it was written. When the question of point of view becomes crucial for the reader, then only comes the awareness of autobiography as a separate form.

When this stage is reached—and it is hard to imagine any going back from it after it has been reached—we are likely to be more aware of the strong contrast between biography and autobiography than of the more obvious similarity. First, the time scale is utterly different. Biography commonly hurries rapidly over the first fifteen, twenty or twenty-five years of life, concentrates on the active middle years, sketches old age, and then gives a special emphasis to death. People with or against whom the subject worked in his active years, husband or wife or lovers are apt to figure much more strongly than parents or siblings. In autobiography childhood is often the most important time of all, and my sense of this will be found reflected in the proportion of pages assigned to it. Parents and siblings are often central, friends sometimes important (but often not). Wives and husbands are as a rule shadowy figures. This may be due to reticence and good taste; but perhaps more often they are too near to be seen. And though the distinguished autobiographer may equally be celibate or happily married or sexually promiscuous, there is something inherently virginal about his aim. He is retreating from life, temporarily, to find something in himself that the ordinary round of life, both domestic and professional, ignores or pushes to one side. It is a fair guess, I think, that wives, husbands or lovers who read the partner's autobiography are surprised both by what is included and by what is omitted, unless they too are potential or actual autobiographers; when they may reflect that they might behave similarly themselves. Some of the exceptions to this, like J.S. Mill, may be thought to 'prove the rule'. Mill's Harriet Taylor is a person that neither those who knew her in life nor those who have studied her since could recognize. The necessary absence of death and the common absence of old age from the autobiographical account need no stressing.

The autobiographer has more power over the evidence than the responsible biographer. Thus Elizabeth Sewell can convey all the tone of her home, and of early religious and moral life by two sharp instances. She says that it seemed as if she was marked for life when detected in a frightened lie; and when she read the story of Jephthah's vow, she wondered whether she was not bound in conscience to kill her mother because she thought she had made a vow to do so. She can omit or pass lightly over all the background which a biographer would be likely to give, about family discipline, about Protestant attitudes to the Old Testament, about the duty of truth-telling. The vividness of a memory overshadowing all that lies near it, carrying its own unanswerable guarantee of significance, can never quite be equalled even by the most striking piece of evidence among a biographer's materials.

Autobiographers may and often do make use of documents, diaries and letters. Nevertheless, the balance of importance between written and spoken is in most cases entirely different from that in biography. Written materials are used, commonly, to resuscitate memories, whether of inner feelings or of people speaking. The inner feeling and the spoken word are the natural masters of autobiography. What reader of St Augustine's *Confessions* has not a more vivid impression of the two words 'Tolle, lege' than of all the texts of the Manichees or Neo-Platonists?

Just as a wife or husband may be too near to be seen in autobiography, so an event may be too near in time to the writer to be caught. Edwin Muir, such a wonderful recorder of childhood, is comparatively unconvincing when he writes of the most stirring public event in all his experience, the Communist take-over of Prague. Is this because it was a public event? Partly, perhaps, but we have the feeling that if he had seen it at the age of ten he would have had more of interest to say about it. No doubt this is because the autobiographical process begins with a long, barely conscious process of inner assimilation. A journalist, even if he happened also to be a gifted autobiographer, could hardly write a convincing autobiographical account of the incident which he reported brilliantly yesterday. But thirty years later perhaps he might.

So there is a particular interest in knowing the age at which the autobiographer wrote. No doubt it is an obscure sense of the autobiographer's need for these years of assimilation that makes the idea of an autobiography written by a very young person seem faintly ridiculous. When Beverley Nichols published a book entitled *Twenty-five Years*, it was greeted either as a typical undergraduate jape or, by those who took it more seriously, as a pompous absurdity. But no one considers it absurd for a biographer to produce a long book about Keats, who died at about the age Nichols was at the time of writing. No one doubts that much interesting experience could be concentraed into twenty-five years; but could this experience be comprehended so soon? If a man of sixty-five chose to write only of his own first twenty-five years, no one would open his book with a presumption that it must be worthless and silly.

Some old men leave their autobiography too late, when fading powers and loss of memory deprive it of the sharpness it might have had earlier. Some like G.K. Chesterton and Eric Gill write in their fifties or sixties, while at the height of their powers, and then die shortly after. But any autobiographer who survives his book by many years is leaving a poignant hostage to fortune. H.G. Wells was nearing the term of the ordinary human span when he wrote his jaunty, optimistic conclusion, in which the Wellsian Utopia, due to be ushered in by devoted 'disciples', was almost visible coming over the horizon. More than ten years later he wrote one of the most despairing brief general studies of human life in all literature.[3] If he had died in 1936, instead of 1946, how damaging to our understanding of Wells would the lack of this contrast have been? Perhaps less than at first appears; for *Mind at the End of Its Tether* (it might well be thought) only provides explicit confirmation of what the attentive reader of the autobiography would be inclined to guess. Wells's sense of society and of the world's political prospects was in large part a gigantic projection of his ego. While he was rich, successful, praised by

[3] H.G. Wells, *Mind at the End of Its Tether*, Heinemann, 1945.

reviewers, and attractive to women, the world seemed a wonderful place, with all its pains and injustices due to disappear as easily as he had emerged from the draper's shop. When his vigour was gone, pain a constant companion, and death imminent, things looked different. Or perhaps it may be felt that there is some hindsight and special pleading in this account; and it is certainly true that *Mind at the End of Its Tether* still has the power to surprise by its unlikeness to all Wells's other books. The general point is this: there are two ways of reading autobiography. The first, which with momentary exceptions like this paragraph, is the one adopted here is to take it as a work of art, to judge it from within by the standards which an actual reading of it suggests. Thus one may note interior inconsistencies or falsities of tone, but relegate external evidence of untruth or exaggeration to mere scholarly footnotes. Or one can read as a historical record, which it is right to check and criticise in the light of the available evidence from all sources. It would seem, on the whole, that autobiography lends itself naturally to the first kind of reading, and memoir to the second.

Occasionally, and these are moments of special interest, the reader is guided to his second thoughts by the direction of the autobiographer himself. Thus Bertrand Russell[4] writes of his feeling in 1918 that love and intellect were for him placed in two separate worlds that could never meet; and this theme is found to be a most important guide to his whole three-volume work. But at the age of ninety-five, in the happiness of his last attachment, he added the telling footnote: 'This and what follows is no longer true.' We might argue for a long time about the true interpretation of this; but no one will deny its interest or relevance; and no one could have predicted that just this would be the effect of extreme old age.

Sometimes the leading characters mentioned in an autobiography are themselves autobiographers. If, for instance, we read Gavin Maxwell's *House of Elrig* (1965) in conjuction with the longer and more important work of Kathleen Raine, in which an unrequited passion for Maxwell is a leading theme, the main impression is favourable to both works. Strikingly different as their view of the same events is bound to be, we are not inclined to accuse either of falsifying. Rather the dominant impression is of the private nature of each person's world; and of how some aspects of this privacy are incommunicable in life, but are capable of imaginative recreation in art. The sense of their inevitable failure to understand or

---

[4] Bertrand Russell, *Autobiography*, I (1872–1914), 1967; II (1914–44), 1968; III (1944–67), 1969. All pub. George Allen & Unwin.

satisfy each other is already a strong presence in each book taken separately. When the books are read together the poignancy of this is more than doubled. There is nothing in either book tending to refute the other. They are contrary as balancing colours are, not in the way that incompatible propositions are.

Rather different is the effect exercised on our understanding of Bertrand Russell's work by Dora Russell's *The Tamarisk Tree* published after his death. The easy free love principle, upon which they first came together, takes on a more sinister guise, when we see how it invariably worked to his advantage and against hers. We see a woman struggling to believe that she was acting on modern theories, when really all her emotions were ordinary, traditional feminine ones. She tries hard to exclude jealousy, but the effort to exclude it makes it all the more apparent when we come to passages like this: 'He told me that Colette was coming down and that I must go away. So it had only been an amusing summer incident. I packed up and went.' When Bertie slept with the governess, she bravely transferred her natural feelings to a theoretic plane of educational endeavour, where, it might be supposed, he would find it hard not to concede that she was right: 'I could not help being upset. I felt let down over all the work I was doing for the school.'[5]

However, she combines this with an admission that about the same time she slept with a young man far away in London. She is rather vain of the way she turns the tables, and adopts the traditional masculine excuse for treating a woman's infidelity as more serious than a man's. She, as it were, was spitting out of the window, and he in the bedroom. This is in accord with the theory upon which they both professed to be acting— that the two sexes were essentially the same in their emotional life, and differ only in unimportant physical ways. But whether she wishes it or not, her book (especially if read together with his) shows exactly the opposite, that the theory which worked so conveniently for him was deadly for her. And yet, it would be wrong to say that her book throws an entirely new light on his. If we pause while reading his book to imagine the sensations of the women of whom he speaks, we might arrive at something recognizably like the picture she gives. Similar comparisons might be made between Russell's work and that of his daughter Katharine Tait.

Different again is the case of Osbert Sitwell. His long autobiography gives a particularly sharp contrast; his relation with his father is portrayed as an endlessly prolonged misunderstanding, which, despite its comic

---

[5] Dora Russell, op. cit., Elek/Pemberton, 1975, p.198.

character, is extremely frustrating and time-consuming. More surprising perhaps, adulthood brings scarcely any relief. His relation with his brother and sister is unclouded by the slightest touch of selfishness or disharmony; and these two seem to be the predestined friends who alone understand the author's aesthetic life. A reading of the family biography will suggest that Osbert projected all the quarrels and dissatisfactions of a difficult, touchy character onto the single figure of his father. But isn't this really what a reading of the autobiography alone already suggests? We are simply not convinced that a talented young man living an active social and artistic life far from the family home would really have been so much obsessed with his father; and if we could not guess the precise nature of the conflicts with brother and sister, we are hardly persuaded by the bland presentation of them. In cases like this the literary experience gives at least some pointers towards relevant truths an author neglects, and we go to history for confirmation and detail.

We need to distinguish sharply between falsification and omission. An autobiographer, we may feel, has more right to omit than a biographer has. If he has an orderly mind and composes his work upon an intelligible principle, his process of selection will be inherent in the plan of his work. Thus Newman sticks exactly to the brief he wrote for himself in his subtitle, (or title of Part III in the original) 'History of My Religious Opinions'. Naturally he does not mention many things, such as playing the fiddle or reading Trollope, which engaged his enthusiastic attention and are mentioned in his letters, but which had no effect on his stated theme. But he does mention other things such as his early conviction that he would be celibate, or the stain on his imagination in supposing the Pope to be anti-Christ, about which he would rather have been silent. The form of the work is exactly determined by the proposed limitations of subject.

But it is rare for autobiographers to be so precise as this. Are we prepared to blame Mill for not mentioning his mother, when his father bulks so large in his narrative? Various answers might be given. We might say that, while it was a blemish in Mill the man that he felt such an amazing disproportion in the influence of his parents, yet it was no blemish in the autobiography. For it furthered the truest aims of autobiography by helping to show what manner of man he was. The great inner theme of the early chapters is the complete absence of emotional life when the intellectual life was being so precociously developed. The brooding presence of the father and the total absence of the mother are symbolic equivalents of this.

Yet it may be felt that this is altogether too neat a critical construction. Emotion was not killed in Mill's life; it was only delayed. And when it does appear in his book, in the account of his twentieth year, he writes as if it was generated entirely from within. We are not entitled to require that he connect it with his mother, because that may not be the truth. But is it not a sign of the blindness (in some directions) of this man who was also so perceptive that he does not even ask himself whether his neglect of his mother and obsession with his father was significant? Does not even wonder whether the question will be in the reader's mind? Does not even raise the question if only to dismiss it? He admits, a little unwillingly, that he was unusual in the age at which he read Plato; but he does not appear to see that he was equally unusual in having no discernible feeling at all about his mother. If he had disliked her, we could understand it. But not to notice her!—and this especially when we know from his letters that his mother and siblings occupied a good deal of his attention after his father's death.

A third approach might be to praise the sturdy independence and scrupulous truthfulness of a man so free of convention that he did not need to apologize for lacking feelings that anybody else would have had. And then we might add that he was acting in the very spirit of the autobiographical form; what the form aims at is to show the uniqueness of each case. Generalization may be left to philosophers and poets. Mill's absence of reaction to his mother's affection was (almost) unique; therefore it is a precious aspect of his work.

I put all these three approaches side by side because none of them entirely convinces me, and each seems to have something to be said for it. One point, at any rate, is clear. Something which Mill never mentions, and (as far as we know) never considered, becomes one of the most fascinating issues in the judgment of his work.

There is a more elusive type of omission, which is perhaps better called an absence; and this, too, may be illustrated from Mill. Sometimes there is a long gap between our sense of what we are told and our sense of the person telling us. Thus, Mill describes, with patent truth and sincerity, his enormous debt to Wordsworth. What he says about Wordsworth's power to restore his lost sense of purpose and interest after his acute depression of 1826 is of the highest value. It is an essential part of the story; and it is told in Mill's customary lucid and modest prose, with his habitual exactness in the use of words. He satisfies our curiosity at an important point; and yet the literary experience is vaguely unsatisfying. Why? Because Mill's prose, formed by the writing of innumerable analytical and expository essays, possessed of so many of the virtues of the tradition of English empirical philosophy, cannot give us any equivalent for the sensation of an intense response to Wordsworth. We do not doubt that he had it, but we have to rely on our own memories to guess its impact; and we may not have the right memories. Mill here is a man plainly telling the truth, but he ceases to be recognizable. The intimate link between an autobiographer and his material, between the author and the self, is lost to view, and almost broken. The man is great, but the writer is not equally great.

Different again is the case where something is omitted which would, if it had been mentioned, have altered our interpretation of what is given.

Joseph Blanco White, the Spanish ex-priest, who became a member of the Oriel Senior Common Room in the days of the Oxford Movement, was an Anglican for some years, and finally a Unitarian. Most of the early part of his book is devoted to a vigorous attack on the Catholic Church in Spain, and he shows his parting from it as motivated by a desire to do the will of God. In the English part of his narrative, he speaks proudly of his son holding a commission in an English regiment. He says nothing of the boy's mother, and the reader may suppose that he had married after giving up his priesthood. Actually, the boy was born of a Spanish mother and there was no marriage. We naturally wish to know the connection in his own mind and feelings between his change of faith and his rejection of celibacy. It makes a great difference which came first; whether he felt that he had weakly broken a vow, or whether he supposed himself to have rejected the vow on grounds of principle before he broke it. All this is omitted; but he does not go on to take the easy course of omitting all mention of the son as well. Those who knew him (including Newman) believed him to be a scrupulously truthful, though a prejudiced and one-sided witness. He may not have intended to falsify; he may have thought the general outline of the facts was known; and have thought it indelicate to speak of details. His reputation for honesty may thus be saved. But there can be no question of the damage done to his book as autobiographical art. However much we deplore the omission of Mill's mother, we can agree that his story is intelligible without her. Blanco White's story without his mistress is hopelessly incomplete. He is denying us the very evidence we need to judge him. As autobiography the book must fail; as memoir it remains of considerable interest. The point to notice is that the failure is on his terms. He had chosen that the giving up of the priesthood should be central, and that his book should be mainly a religious history. It is not our irrelevant curiosity, but our very sense of the

book's form of art that requires us to censure the author's failure to maintain it. It is on these grounds alone, I believe, that we are entitled to
blame an autobiographer for what he has not said.

If this is true of intimate and personal issues, it is even more obviously
true of public ones. It is possible to imagine, though perhaps not to
name, an English autobiography of merit which dwells on the year 1940
without mentioning the Battle of Britain. All the same, the external
world has its important part. It may be in the form of public events
simply, as the death of Robespierre creates one of the most memorable
scenes in *The Prelude*. More often it will be in the form of the daily life of
a given milieu, a family, a trade, a class, a religious or political group.
Autobiography is admittedly among the most inward and personal of
literary forms. But if it is to convince it must deal with the real man; and
the real man cannot but be part of the world, will always have neighbours. The best autobiographies achieve a balance between inner and
outer. It need not be an even balance. The work may be as inward as
Grace Abounding, where the subjective is so dominant that solid objects
like church towers acquire a phantasmagoric, intensely personal character.
Or it may be as factual and detached as Benjamin Franklin's work. But
these are extreme cases; and perhaps each comes near to the limit, the
overstepping of which would deprive a book of true autobiographical
character. Neither a simple record of feelings and reflections, nor a simple
recollected milieu would count as autobiography. On the whole, with
due respect to Bunyan and Franklin, we may say that the classics of autobiography tend towards the centre of this pendulum swinging between
subjective and objective. To be free and to be constrained are both necessary human experiences; much of the interest lies in the conflict between
this freedom and this constraint. One who is aware of no constraints on
his freedom is omitting too much; one who is aware of no area of free
choice is abdicating his humanity and forfeiting all sympathy.

In between freedom and constraint lies a no-man's land often disputed
by both, the territory of habit and custom. The following quotation is
whimsical and not wholly sincere, and yet throws a sharp light here:

> I certainly think little of the habit of swearing, however idle, if it be
> carried no further than is done by many gallant and very good men,
> wise and great ones not excepted. But the fact is ... an oath has not
> escaped my lips from that day to this.
> I hope no 'good fellow' will think ill of me for it. ... I look upon
> Tom Jones, who swore, as an angel of light compared with Blifil,

who, I am afraid, swore no more than myself. Steele, I suspect, occasionally rapt out an oath; which is not to be supposed of Addison. And this again might tempt me into a grudge against my nonjuring form of colloquy . . . But habit is habit, negative as well as positive. Let him that is without one cast the first sarcasm.[6]'

Where Hunt speaks lightly of a comparatively trivial matter, many great autobiographers have found great issues.

Finally, we should not forget that there is one fundamental respect in which autobiography is just like other literary forms, from sonnet to historical novel. Reading it intelligently involves two kinds of judgment, a judgment of the author's idea in writing and of the formal principle upon which he composed it, and judgment of the degree to which the finished work embodies the idea. In autobiography one may find minor works which perfectly embody a simple idea of limited interest (like *The Importance of Being Earnest*) and major works with obvious faults (like *Macbeth* or *Rob Roy*). And, as in the study of other literary forms, to find the idea and formal principle of the work, one cannot rely solely on what the author may have said about it, useful evidence as that may be. There is only one final court of appeal, the work itself, whose aims may not be identical with the author's intentions. In reading any literary work we have the right, and sometimes the duty to introduce considerations ignored by the author. But in autobiography especially so, for the last thing any person, however truthful, learns to treat with perfect fairness is the self.

I am aware that my chapter-divisions are arbitrary; but I can sketch some of the considerations that led to them. Over a quarter of the book is devoted to childhood; this reflects both the enormous space which it occupies in autobiography, and my sense of its importance in the formation of adults. With respect to Dickens and a few others, we may say that this is the only literary form which shows its full importance.

Of the other chapter-subjects, two (*The Halfway House* and *Defined by the World*) were chosen in an attempt to mark the limits of the subject. The authors discussed in the first are just beyond the borders of autobiography, the second group near it on the hither side. The latter encountered the world in such a way that they had to look inwards, were driven to discover and define what they were. In the finest of them external events, perhaps trivial ones like bicycle rides, became the objective correlative of inner states.

[6] Leigh Hunt, *Autobiography*, 1850. Quoted from Cresset Press ed. 1948, p.38.

The last two chapters deal with the purest (which does not invariably mean the best) autobiographers. Both the questers and the converts were trying to penetrate to the point where the deepest choices are made. Opposite in the direction of their search, they were alike in needing to strip away many habits and easy assumptions, many worldly precepts of parents and teachers, to find, or at least to seek with persistence, what they held the *unum necessarium*, the pearl of great price. For those of them, like De Quincey, Haydon and Newman, who were also greatly gifted as writers, autobiography became their most natural form of expression, in which they achieved their masterpieces.

II

The Half-Way House

in many cases it would not be altogether absurd if a man were to thank God for his vanity among the other comforts of life.

(Benjamin Franklin, *Autobiography*, ed. Max Farrand, 1949, p.4)

The thing we believe to be our self is as ephemeral and automatic a product of external circumstances as the form of a sea-wave.

Simone Weil, *Gateway to God*, ed. David Raper, p.92.
Translated from her *Pensées sans Ordre*.)

As we have seen, the true autobiographers are those who answer, though they may not always consciously ask, the question: 'How did I become what I am?' There is, however, an intermediate group, who do not answer this question, who lack a sense of their own being in development; who have, nevertheless some of the most important autobiographical qualities: articulateness, fidelity to experience, sensitiveness to small currents of feeling, and, above all, curiosity. Writers of this type can hardly achieve high classic status as autobiographers; but they may produce a set of self-portraits of distinction. At the same time, by their likeness in some ways, and strong contrast in others, to the true and complete autobiographer, they can sharpen understanding of classic works which they cannot rival. I propose to discuss three members of this type, Boswell (1740–1795), Harriette Wilson (1789–1846) and Byron (1788–1824). For Boswell, the source is his voluminous journals, for Harriette Wilson her *Memoirs*, and for Byron his letters and journals.

In his entry for 29 January 1780, Boswell wrote:

> It is unpleasant to observe how imperfect a picture of my life this journal presents. Yet I have certainly much more of *myself* thus preserved than most people have.[1]

There can be no doubt that he was right on the second count; on the first he may have been partly wrong, but the comment is interesting as showing the faint, unanalysed dissatisfaction of the gifted diarist at not being a true autobiographer.

Most readers come to the journals when already familiar with the *Life of Johnson*. Certain differences are immediately apparent. The *Life* is official and public, the journals unbuttoned, scurrilous, and, at times, obscene. Johnson's more outspoken phrases like 'You can find a wife in the streets' recorded in the journal,[2] are omitted in the *Life*, and sometimes Boswell's own words, recorded in the journal, are left anonymous in the *Life*. In part, the journal, though full of sincere expressions of admiration for Johnson, is written in reaction from the strain of his presence, from the severity of his intellectual and moral demands, which Boswell was so often unable to meet. There is even, perhaps, an unspoken undercurrent of feeling 'At least I can be the hero of *this* work, though a weak and foolish one, as I freely admit.' Though the *Life* had not yet

---

[1] *Boswell, Laird of Auchinleck*, Yale ed., p.174. All references are to this edition, which will in future be indicated by date and page number alone.
[2] 1766–9, p.67.

been written, the intention to write it seems already to be a factor in Bos-well's view of himself. But different as the journals and the *Life* are, there is a vital link between them; they are both created out of the author's negative capability. The chameleon character in Boswell—he is perhaps as extreme case of this as any on record—allows him to adapt with equal facility and equal felicity to every unexpected quirk and turn of both characters, Johnson's and his own.

Boswell must, we suppose, have developed, since it is in the nature of human beings to do so; but the journals will provide little evidence of it. No entry taken at random could confidently be placed as early or late except by outward circumstances. If there is a change he is somewhat more fluent and analytical when he is very young than he is later. In the very first volume (1762–3) the Louisa episode reads almost like a novel at times, and he holds back the crucial piece of information, his infection with venereal disease, as a novelist might, to the moment when it will tell as a literary effect. Yet even here he can descend into a crass egoism which interrupts the artistic flow of the story and tells us only (without at all meaning to) how incorrigibly self-centred he is. He writes:

> Thus ended my intrigue with the fair Louisa, which I flattered myself so much with, and from which I expected at least a winter's safe copu-lation. It is indeed very hard. I cannot say, like young fellows who get themselves clapped in a bawdy-house, that I will take better care again. *For I really did take care.*[3]

For all Boswell's lively, questing intelligence,[4] the pervading impres-sion of the journals taken as a whole is of the omnipotence of feeling. This goes far beyond living in the moment and obliviousness of conse-quences, fairly common human traits. Boswell is most exceptional because at times he actually comes to adopt the omnipotence of feeling as a theory in defiance of all experience. Thus he writes:

> I have a torpidity of mind that I have not often experienced. I have not 'a lively hope of immortality'. It occurred to me today that perhaps a man is immortal or not as he happens to die in a dull or lively frame. I

[3] 1762–3, p.161. My italics.

[4] Macaulay called him a 'great fool', and thus involved himself in a lot of unconvincing paradoxes. Boswell was almost the Platonic idea of the egregious ass who is anything but a fool.

have often been an immortal soul. At present it seems to me that I am not of celestial fire.[5]

And, on another occasion, with entirely unconscious bathos, of a quiet evening at Auchinlech Manse:

Life was a good thing. We passed our time agreeably. That . . . is enough. For what else shall we do in Heaven?

Such a man in incapable of having a settled opinion, except on those very few subjects, such as Dr Johnson and the aristocratic principle, upon which his feelings do not oscillate. Hence all his argumentative and 'philosophical' passages are worthless. Thought, too, is only sensation in the end.

He must have had a good memory, else he could not have written the conversation-pieces in the *Life of Johnson*. Yet, in the journals, he recalls the past only seldom. After recording innumerable sudden shifts of feeling, he still does not seem to recognize his changeableness as a personal characteristic with implications for the future. As late as 4 July 1782, more than twenty years after his impulsive and temporary conversion to Catholicism, he is still asserting: 'I am calm. I am heavenly-minded' and asking himself 'Shall I end my days in a convent?'[6] and a few months earlier he had been asserting: 'A profane clergyman is contemptible as a fool and detestable as a cheat.'[7]

The naive severity is sincere; he judges others confidently without any awareness, for the time, of the evidences for the weakness of the human will he had so abundantly recorded in telling his own story. For nearly twenty years before he had written for his own frequent perusal an 'Inviolable Plan' full of dignified Augustan and Anglican sentiments, where the stress was on steadiness, persistence in doing good, the careful avoidance of excitement and dissipation.[8] (Apart from a certain insipidity of style Johnson himself might have written this.) It is a safe guess, though, that Boswell never connected that 'profane clergyman' with himself.

Not that he is entirely cut off from memory of his past. But the rare moments when the journals return to earlier scenes are all marked by that

[5] 1778–82, p.412.
[6] 1778–72, p.454.
[7] Ibid., p.253.
[8] 1763–4, p.376.

same inability to learn from experience, an extraordinary lack of *resonance*. Thus he boldly writes on 1 April 1773: 'The satisfaction which I feel from the comparison of my present with my former self is immense.'[9] He looks back with pitying wonder at his dissipated life in London in 1762–3 like a lunatic in a lucid interval contemplating a mad spell. But 1762–3 is likely to seem to the reader a comparatively coherent phase.

He is frequent and sometimes vehement in self-reproach; yet this hardly serves to modify our general impression of immense self-satisfaction. When he has made a feeble pun he is as pleased with himself as ever Mr Pooter was. For his innumerable falls into drink and whoring after renewed good resolutions he is usually content with poor excuses about the legitimate demands of sociability. After his marriage, his constant praise of his wife does not seriously affect either his infidelities or his later reflections upon them. Even when he records that he was violent and threw things at her, or that after a debauch he breathed so ill that she feared he might die, and could not sleep for worrying about him, these are still isolated incidents. Marriage, being a continuing and developing relation, is beyond his imaginative grasp; for him it is only a jumble of domestic episodes.

No doubt his utter lack of any sense of continuity, scale and proportion is the key to his immense verve and talent as a journalist. At the same time, the incongruity of his comparisons is sometimes breathtaking. Recording the languor he experienced after three months in the continual company of Johnson on the Highland tour, he writes:

> My mind had been kept upon its utmost stretch in his company. I had exhausted all my powers to entertain him. While he was with me, his noble exuberance of genius excited my spirits to a high degree, so that I did not feel at the time how much I was weakened. I was like a man who drinks hard and is kept in high glee by what is wasting his constitution, but perceives his enfeebling effects as soon as he lives without it.[10]

Who could possibly guess from this passage what we all know so well— that his admiration for Johnson, both intellectually and morally, was as high as possible? Yet we hardly need to be surprised. For languor after stimulation is such an intense experience for him that the obvious inappropriateness of the comparison could never come into his mind.

9 1769–74, p.164.
10 Ibid., p.207.

His principles are almost as quick to change as his moods and habits. Thus:

> In the evening [after he had dallied with a fifteen-year-old at dinner who allowed him 'luscious liberties' to his wife's displeasure] I met an old dallying companion, now married. She willingly followed me to a field . . . She seemed to wish to have me to press her to let me enjoy her fully, for she was big with child. But I thought it wrong, so only indulged a lesser lascivious sport.[11]

At another time he would have taken a different moral view, which might probably have been laxer but possibly more severe. But since he is in this comparatively moral vein, he cannot deny himself a sage reflection on the slackness of feminine adherence to principles: 'struck, however, with the insensibility to the moral doctrines of their country which some women have'. The most inconsistent of men, he hardly deserves to be called pharasaical when he rebukes the inconsistency of others; he has simply forgotten his own. Indeed, our sense of his wavering weakness of character needs to be balanced, in reading the journals, with a sense of an endless series of subjective stabilities, Boswell is like Constable who said that 'light never stands still', but bequeathed us a set of timeless moments of monumental stillness; but with the very important difference that Constable understood the paradox and Boswell did not. Indeed, one could with equal truth call him the most self-conscious or the most unselfconscious of men. His intense vision can comprehend only one thing at a time; if it is not, for the moment, himself, then he forgets self altogether until the next time.

When he argues with himself, he is incapable of arranging his reasons on any plan. In 1774, he was worried that he might be required to take an anti-Catholic oath when he went to vote in a Parliamentary election. All kinds of considerations derived from different layers of thought and feeling tumble pell-mell into his mind. He might pretend to be ill, he might have to go into exile, perhaps the oath would not be required (it seldom was), he could not see that Catholic doctrine on purgatory was incompatible with Scripture, or if it was, he couldn't recall the relevant passages, he might get a friend to arrange to have the oath waived.[12] Embarrassment, fear, theological reflection, and the sense of his own social position are flung into the pot together like the ingredients of a

[11] 1776–8, p.107.
[12] 1774–6, p.26.

stew designed to finish up what is in the house on the day before the holidays.

Perhaps there are times when a faint self-irony pierces the carapace of complacency. Is he laughing at himself, just a little, when he writes:

> I have often determined to be strictly sober, and have often fixed an era for the commencement of my proper conduct. I have a curious inclination to have an era for almost everything. The period of my being strictly sober has been advanced from one time to another.[13]

But then we are inclined to answer 'No', when soon afterwards we come upon the following prize piece of uncritical inconsistency:

> I was cheerful and happy . . . being very well established as an agreeable companion, and being a married man. Life is like a road, the first part of which is a hill. A man must for a while be constantly pulling that he may get forward, and not run back. When he has got beyond the steep, and on smooth ground—that is, *when his character is fixed*—he goes on smoothly upon level ground. I could not help indulging Asiatic ideas as I viewed such a number of pretty women.[14]

At another time he is eager to show us a Boswell whose aesthetic sensibilities are so pure that he is half above the flesh:

> A beautiful, gentle, sweet maid . . . In one of the garret rooms I kissed her, and she curtsied. I was charmed with her for the moment as with a rose or some pleasing object which makes a slight but very vivid impression.[15]

His occasional musings on complete moral reform or on preparation for death have a childish air. He toys with the idea of burning all his journals, with a vague anticipation that the bonds of habit would dissolve with the destruction of memorials of the past. Or he wonders whether incessant travelling, by accustoming him to change, might not make the change of death easier to bear. A conversation with the Socinian, Sir John Pringle, gives him doubts about the Trinity, and he immediately transfers this into a moral doubt.[16] So he goes off to 'dally' with two whores, but is 'restrained' from completion by his habitual fear of disease. He

---

[13] Ibid., p.35.
[14] Ibid., p.65. My italics. *Asiatic* is Boswell's standard euphemism for promiscuity.
[15] Ibid., p.293.
[16] Ibid., p.139.

never recollects how often he had done similar things when not under any sceptical influence. Perhaps, unconsciously, he desires as many different kinds of excuse as possible for his lapses, like the 'alternative defences' which his legal training would have made familiar.

His impulses of reform are sometimes as wayward as his lapses:

> I swore solemnly neither to talk as an infidel nor to enjoy a woman before seeing Rousseau. So I am bound a month at least.[17]

Was this a superstitious bargain with fate? Or a childish attempt at atonement for his strong desire to meet a man regarded as a prophet both of infidelity and promiscuity? He gives us no clue. Perhaps it was neither, but merely an attempt to conquer the languor and depression he always dreaded by having an entertaining bet with himself. His intense excitability, his wayward enthusiasms are balanced by inability to feel greater things in full measure. He is almost perfunctory in recording the death of an illegitimate child, mentioned with rather less emphasis than the 'severe cold' he complains of in the very same sentence.[18] The lack of a sense of scale and proportion, one of his most strongly marked characteristics, works both ways. When he says of the dead child, 'I mourn for an idea', we are inclined to wonder whether this is not a rare moment of insincerity, whether he does not really mean that he is surprised at himself for feeling nothing. This is unexpected because we have become accustomed to a Boswell whose curiosity about himself conquers all shame; and there might have followed a passage probing the strangeness of his own insensibility.

As a rule, though, the self remains an object of admiring contemplation through every shame and every contradiction. Sometimes the contradiction is simply the outcome of very rapid oscillations of feeling:

> I was in the humour of gallantry tonight. I was pleased with the romantic idea of making love to a Turk. However, I talked morality at last and thought myself a Johnson. She seemed too indolent in body and too vivacious in mind to be a very rigid lady. Besides her ideas were quite different from mine. Her religion was of a very different kind from mind. Bless me! what are mortals?[19]

At other times, the contradiction springs from an unperceived illogicality;

[17] 1763–4, p.146.
[18] 1763–4, p.189.
[19] 1763–4, p.18.

as when he argues that his mistress has no duty to her husband, but 'were she to be unfaithful to me, she ought to be pierced with a Corsican poniard'.[20] He concludes this passage, like so many others, with ardent self-congratulation: 'I am safe and happy and in no danger either of the perils of Venus or of desperate matrimony.' We are not surprised to find him married soon after.

In the end we may be left with the impression that Boswell loved his own inconsistency because it ministered to his insatiable need for surprise. He reads himself like a man reading an exciting thriller and stopping his ears as he says: 'Don't tell me what happens next.' Many people have wondered what could have drawn him and Johnson together. The contrasts between them are important and obvious. But perhaps they shared one characteristic that has not often been noticed. They were both terrified of a void. For Johnson unlimited pain was better than insentience; for Boswell any degree of sin and folly.

*   *   *

Harriette Wilson's motives for writing about her own life were very different. A fashionable courtesan with expensive tastes, she was driven, as her fortieth birthday approached, to consider less obvious ways of making money. She thought that if she wrote her memoirs she could gain in two ways, by profits from sales, and by accepting bribes from men who preferred not to be mentioned. She was proved right. It is probable that she gave little thought to the self-portrait she would almost accidentally be drawing. Her very first, often-quoted sentence shows at once that she belongs in this chapter and not among the true auto-biographers:

I shall not say why and how I became, at the age of fifteen, the mistress of the Earl of Craven.[21]

In fact she does not think it would interest us to know about her parents, her early training, her motives or her moral struggles, if any. She assumes that the reader will take her for granted and want to hear

[20] 1766–9, p.26.
[21] Harriette Wilson's *Memoirs* of herself and others, 1825. All quotations from James Laver's ed., 1929.

about the raptures, the regrets and the follies of famous men. She is very unlike Boswell in not being, at the conscious level, curious about herself at all. Her self-portrait is all the more convincing for being drawn in a fit of absence of mind. Yet she is like Boswell in this: she separates out the various roles she sees herself playing. She never tries to harmonize herself as saucy girl, or as wild romantic creature of impulse, or as tender sister. Like a real-life actress who will not want to remember how she looked and spoke as Desdemona when she is playing Cleopatra, she is complete and adequate to every occasion, but never allows one occasion or one role to influence the next. There is however—here she differs again from Boswell—a common thread, of which she was probably not aware. She always comes off best; she is always one up on every rival, man or woman. If the contest is about sexual attractiveness, she wins; if about wit and intelligence, she wins; if about magnanimity and self-sacrifice, she wins again. She is a kind of perpetual duellist asking everyone she meets, lover or beloved or feminine rival to choose their weapons, and proving, to her own satisfaction, if not to ours, her superiority with rapier or pistol or bludgeon.

One of her commonest and perhaps her favourite role of all is that of the saucy girl[22] who invariably triumphs in a contest of repartee. She delights to tell how she interrupted a heart-broken man telling her how his wife had left him with: 'I would not be so very demonstrative as to touch my forehead, if I were you.'[23] She clearly enjoyed provoking him. And the following is very characteristic of her desire to turn every occasion into a context: '"Do speak louder, Marquis," I answered, provoked that he should be afraid of any woman but myself.'[24]

She is equally fond of the idea of herself as a wild creature of impulse, 'ever ready to sacrifice more than life for those I loved'. In this way thoughtlessness becomes a kind of virtue because it is a proof of intensity of feeling. When she was in love with Lord Ponsonby she believes she could have renounced him at once if she had thought just once of his 'young, innocent and lovely wife'.[25] But she declares that Lady Fanny never once entered her head. As if to prove her sincerity in saying this,

[22] Walter Scott, who seems to have met her only once, described her as 'far from beautiful . . . but a smart saucy girl . . . with the manners of a wild schoolboy'. Journal, 9 Dec. 1825. The meeting, which Scott recalled when the *Memoirs* were published, was some twenty years earlier, when she was twenty or less.
[23] Wilson, *Memoirs*, p.103. The reference is to cuckold's horns.
[24] Ibid, p.37.
[25] Ibid., p.81.

she describes how she tore up unopened his letter offering her a financial provision.[26] And with art, conscious or unconscious, she makes their first assignation a chaste one, full of fine sentiments and protestations, as a change from the beddings it is so often her serious business to describe.

When she had seen Lady Ponsonby in the street, and could no longer maintain that she had never entered her head, she is still able to offer herself a study in magnanimity:

> If ever our intimacy is discovered, so as to disturb her peace of mind, on that day we must separate for ever.[27]

Perhaps, however, it struck her that the disinterestedness of a girl who consorted so largely with the rich and titled might be suspect. Then she is ready with an account of the deep attraction exercised upon her at a distance by a handsome hussar, a simple uneducated lad who had never attained promotion. The beauty of his face reminded her of Lord Byron; and a week or two after she saw him he died.

> The man had stood before me, with all his godlike beauty, but a few days past! Methought I yet saw that mantling blush, and the fine expressive curve of that quivering lip!
> Feeling the tears again rushing to my eyes, I ran out of the room.[28]

It is interesting to notice how the style varies to suit the role she is playing. This is the language of the novels of sensibility in which she may have sought distraction from the serious business of being an earl's mistress and craving out further conquests.

Having established her susceptibility to male beauty and manly pathos, she now begins 'to grow in love with mind', and demonstrates her superiority to the common run of women by professing her love for an ugly man of superior attainments.

But it is not enough to show her unusual discrimination; she must also show her firmness. The role of the proud, disdainful beauty—we remember that Scott thought her plain, and she may have feared that others thought the same—was too good a form of superiority not to figure in her repertoire.

My carriage was soon surrounded by trotting beaux, whom I could

[26] Ibid., p.45.
[27] Ibid., p.97.
[28] Ibid., p.366–7.

not listen to, because that adored, sly, beautiful face of Ponsonby's was fixed on me *à la distance*. With all my rudeness and inattention I could not get rid of Lord Frederick Beauclerc.[29]

And near the end of her book she rubs the lesson in by telling how a Guards officer 'insisted on falling in love with me, merely to prove himself a fashionable man'.[30]

At the same time she certainly does not wish us to forget that though sex may be the serious business and the hard work and even part of the excitement and interest of life, there are other things. She wishes to be admired also for feminine qualities not usually associated with women of her stamp. She can be the shrewd, well-judging, sisterly friend who consoles men with tea and sympathy for the loss of their worthless wives. She records with satisfaction that they chose her for this service because 'I was a woman of such acute feelings.'[31] At such times she can enjoy the role of the serious moralist, who does not judge as the world judges but sees that it is a vulgar error of the Protestant world to equate chastity and virtue. And this, not because she is (for the time) sneering at chastity, but because she is entertaining a deeper and more spiritual conception of virtue.

But these recipients of her sisterly charity were still men; and she is ready to forestall the conventional reproach that women of her type are devoid of natural affection and are hostile to their own sex. She is able to rebut any such charge with a splendid tableau of three sisters, one being herself, watching the death of the fourth.

My readers will believe that my poor sister's death affected me deeply, and my health suffered seriously from anxiety and want of rest.[32]

Those last three words, unobtrusive in the context, are inserted with conscious art. For we soon learn that 'the night-watching devolved entirely upon me'. But as if remembering that magnanimity towards the surviving sisters is also necessary to obviate any suggestion of cattiness, she offers this carefully-considered mixture of generosity and belittlement:

I am glad, I can, with truth, affirm that Sophia did her duty *in this instance*, and Amy also, *in the daytime*.[33]

[29] Ibid., p.123.
[30] Ibid., p.440.
[31] Ibid., p.602.
[32] Ibid., p.637.
[33] Ibid. My italics.

Her own superior devotion is attested by the greater arduousness of watching at night, and her goodwill to the surviving sisters by her kindness in omitting to mention it. She does not need to, since she has already in a previous chapter established for us a view of one sister:

> 'You surely must be in love with his large property?' said I to Amy.
> 'In love with his property! Why, is he not an Adonis?' Amy's Adonis is a short, thick man, almost a mulatto, with little purblind eyes and straight, coarse, black hair; and his age at least five and forty.[34]

And earlier we had been told that Amy 'ever made it her particular study to wound my feelings',[35] while Sophia, when she married Lord Berwick, had callously agreed to cut her sisters dead, though previously she had been leading the same life as they.

But natural feeling and sympathy are not enough. She must also have credit for pure, disinterested virtue and principled renunciation. She achieves this especially in the eloquent letter she wrote to the Duke of Beaufort, solemnly renouncing the prospect of marriage to his heir, Lord Worcester, simply out of concern for the parental feelings of the Duke and Duchess. To add to her self-sacrifice, she will not leave the young man she refuses to marry, because he could hardly live without her. She is careful to obtain a lawyer's opinion that the letters are worth at least £20,000 before returning them gratis. All she asks in return for this notable act of generosity is that they should 'feel some confidence in the goodness of my heart'.[36]

On the other hand, she does not wish us to think that this heroic goodness concerns itself only with grand, quixotic gestures. She is able to balance this picture with a humbler and more touching one. She befriends a poor prostitute, unconsciously revealing by the strong sense of condescension in this her rigid sense of class-consciousness within the same profession, and she gives 'from my own pocket' a five-pound note to a poor Italian beggar 'who seemed absolutely overcome by excess of gratitude'.[37] Indeed her warm-heartedness has become a by-word:

> I am, as I believe all my friends will admit, so warm-hearted, naturally, that my mere friendship is quite a match for many women's love.[38]

[34] Ibid., p.569.
[35] Ibid., p.115.
[36] Ibid., p.431.
[37] Ibid., p.553.
[38] Ibid., p.440.

She rightly senses, though, that the reader will want something unexpected, something that would never come into a novel about a frail beauty with a heart of gold. On at least two occasions she is able to provide that also. She has her scholarly period, when she is working so hard at serious books that she can only allow herself a few minutes for dinner. And her encounter with Byron has an interesting unexpected character because they were not and did not wish to be lovers. Byron was so relieved by her absence of passion that he:

> threw off all reserve, and wrote and spoke to me with the confidence of easy friendship and good-will, as though he had been delighted to find a woman capable of friendship, to whose vanity it was not at all necessary to administer by saying soft things to her.[39]

When they part with an affectionate kiss, she offers 'a short ejaculatory prayer to heaven, for this interesting young man's better health'.[40]

And so, with an ample gesture of triumph, she scores with a single stroke off Byron, off all the women who could not resist his charm, and off the reader, who was expecting a tender or a sensual episode with the most famous lover of the age.

*   *   *

To unravel Byron's idea of himself is a far more difficult task. We are confronted with a resourceful adversary, whose obsessive interest in himself is matched by his love of appearing in multiple disguises of the spirit, and by a pervasive sense of mischief which makes it hard to tell when he is in earnest. It is difficult, too, to distinguish the actual vagaries and inconsistencies of character from his delight in presenting himself as the most fascinatingly inconsistent of men.

It is not true, though, as one may at first be tempted to think, that Byron never maintains a consistent view of anything. He never wavers in admiration for Pope's poetry, and it is a subject on which he will not permit levity, his own or other people's. Though often inclined to make fun of his own poetic reputation ('damn it, Tom, don't let's get poetical' he said to Moore once) he is never inclined to trifle about the supposed

---

[39] Ibid., p.249.
[40] Ibid., p.595.

excellence of his Venetian tragedies. He was always firm, too, against her mother's wishes, in demanding a Catholic education for his natural daughter, Allegra.

In all the vagaries of sensuality and the unpredictable changes of passionate feeling, we find a few enduring landmarks, and one in particular. From October 1821 to May 1822 he jotted down what he called *Detached Thoughts*.[41] These show, on the whole, a greater reflectiveness and less disposition to clown than his letters and his other journal entries.

There is a rare note of solemnity in his remarks about his Harrow friendship with Lord Clare:

> My school friendships were with me passions (for I was always violent) but I do not know that there is one which has endured (to be sure some have been cut short by death) till now—that with Lord Clare began one of the earliest and lasted longest . . . I never hear the word 'Clare' without a beating of the heart—even *now* & I write it—with the feelings of 1803–4–5—ad infinitum.[42]

A few pages later, he writes:

> I had alluded to my friend Lord Clare in terms such as my feelings suggested.—About a week or two afterwards I met him on the road between Imola and Bologna—after not having met for seven or eight years. . . . This meeting annihilated for a moment all the years between the present time and the days of *Harrow*. It was a new and inexplicable feeling like rising from the grave to me.[43]

The persistence of this feeling through some eighteen years is particularly striking for Byron's rapid changes and his strong sense of living his life at a more rapid rate than others made him feel at twenty-nine as if he was sixty, and in his thirties he constantly wrote as if he was old, as if he foresaw his own early death.

Though just as curious about himself a Boswell, he differs from him in having areas of reticence. Thus he writes:

> My passions were developed very early—so early—that few would believe me—if I were to state the period—and the facts which accompanied it.

---

[41] Byron's *Letters and Journals*, ed. Leslie A. Marchand, IX. All Byron references are to this edition, which will in future be indicated by volume and page number alone.
[42] IX, p.44.
[43] IX, p.49.

He may mean here very precocious schoolboy friendships with overtly homosexual acts. But given the frankness of his other references to these friendships, the probability seems to be that he is speaking guardedly of something earlier still, perhaps connected with his mother or a female servant. We cannot know. But it is very characteristic that he goes on to connect this hidden experience with his melancholy, his constant sense of having anticipated life. What began perhaps as not much more than the conventional knowingness and cynicism of the precocious schoolboy ended by becoming a real burden of premature senility, an entirely subjective sensation, which friends and observers could not understand.

He is often worrying away at the paradox that one of the most passionate and feeling of men should have been also one of the most promiscuous, and, at times, one of the most cynical about women, capable of referring to a mistress as 'carnal baggage'. He records how in one of his early love encounters a separation of even twelve hours was felt as intolerable. Perhaps he comes nearest to an explanation when he writes of the time immediately after leaving Harrow:

> I took my gradations in the vices—with great promptitude—but they were not to my taste—for my early passions though violent in the extreme—were concentrated—and hated division or spreading abroad. I could have left or lost the world with or for that which I loved—but though my temperament was naturally burning—I could not share in the common place libertinism of the place and time—without disgust. —And yet this very disgust and my heart thrown back upon itself— threw me into excesses perhaps more fatal than those from which I shrank—as fixing upon one (at a time) the passions which spread among many would have hurt only myself.[44]

The analysis is convincing up to a point—certainly intelligent, yet characteristically wavering and incomplete. The frequent use of the dash, always in his prose writings a sign of hurry, and often of indecision or changing emotion, corresponds to the incompleteness of the analysis. Why for instance does he not tell us what impulse was so much stronger than the disgust to make him share in the 'common place libertinism'? Knowing him as we do from all his letters, we may guess that the strongest factor was his ingrained need to be accepted in every company in which he found himself, and to excel according to the standards of the given group, even if these were alien to him. (Thus though lame and not much

44 IX, p.38.

liking the game he played cricket for Harrow against Eton.) But if he is aware of this feature of his character, he does not show it.

Writing to his wife from Italy, too, he shows a sense of the connection between a brooding passion for a woman now unattainable (though his wife) and the rackety inconstant life he was leading. With tender reproach he tells her that three hours have not passed, even in the most incongruous and dissipated company, when he has not thought of her.[45] But this tone coexists uneasily with his sweeping denunciations of her as his 'destroyer', and his favourite term for her, both in prose and verse, is 'Clytemnestra', the murderer of her husband. The mixture of frustration, humiliation, longing, resentment and sheer blank surprise is there for us to analyse but is never seriously analysed by him. At times he seems genuinely at a loss to explain the strength and the contradictoriness of his own feelings about her. And he seems unable to grasp clearly one element in the tissue of feeling which is most obvious to us—the sheer uncomprehending frustration at getting no response to all his argument, his pleading, his anger, his tender reproaches. With his genius, his charm, his rank and his unique combination of fame and notoriety, this was for him unprecedented and incomprehensible. Silence is the unanswerable repartee.

Intelligent and reflective though he can be in analysing parts or aspects of his life, he is incapable of drawing them into a unity. If he is writing of Augusta or of Mary Chaworth, or of Lord Clare or of his wife, this one for the time crowds out all consideration of the others. He is almost prepared to explain his whole history by reference to one of them, and then, in discussing another, to forget that he has done so.

At the same time he keeps returning to something unstated in his early life. He titillates us with its strangeness, its uniqueness, its incredible character.[46] Is this the hidden key? Or, more probably is it felt to be so only in one mood, just as in other moods Lord Clare or his wife was the key. Indeed when he writes, 'I must not go on with these reflections—or I shall be letting out some secret or other to paralyse posterity,' we may be inclined to suspect him of deliberate mystery-mongering. He certainly enjoyed being inscrutable, the Hamlet of the bohemians. But whether we take him at his word here or not, the fact remains that he centres his own interpretation of his life on a void. He explains everything as a consequence of what he cannot or will not say. Either he is afraid or he is kidding; and either hypothesis limits him as an enquirer into the self.

[45] VI, p.260-1.
[46] e.g. IX, p.38.

And indeed, the extraordinary volatility of feeling in him must have made it very difficult to arrive at any clear view. Thus on the same day, 23 August 1819, we find him writing one letter to Hobhouse bemoaning the weak effeminacy of 'this Cicisbean existence' with Teresa Guiccioli and writing in the tenderest and most feeling tone to Teresa herself.[47] In another man this might be hypocrisy or simple deceit. In Byron it may be neither, but only a very rapid change of mood. Fond as he is of giving opinions, often intemperately, on every subject, he showed a shrewd touch of self-knowledge when he wrote to Murray: 'You are of *every man's* opinion . . . and I of *no* man's.—Both extremes are bad.'[48] This letter accompanied the *Detached Thoughts*, often quoted above; and there is an emblematic fitness, so often found in Byron's life and not least in the manner of his death, in the fact that they were delivered to Murray by Lord Clare.

This volatility of mood affected his serious thoughts just as much as his passions and follies. Thus he writes to Hobhouse in April 1817:

> I do not know what to believe—or what to disbelieve—which is the devil—to have no religion at all—all sense & senses are against it—but all belief and much evidence is for it—it is walking in the dark over a rabbit warren—or a garden with steel traps and spring guns.[49]

He is so confused here that it is not clear what kind of contrast is intended between 'sense' and 'evidence' or how the metaphors of the rabbit warren and the steel traps apply to the argument. 'It' grammatically, is religion, but perhaps in Byron's mind is more the dangerous process of living either with or without religion. At other times he will lace his habitual ribaldry with religious references which are perhaps more than half-serious:

> I never wrote nor copied *an entire scene of that play*—without being obliged to *break* a commandment;—to obey a woman's, and to forget God's. Remember the drain of this upon a Man's heart and brain—to say nothing of his immortal Soul.[50]

A little over a year later, in the more coherent tone of the *Detached Thoughts*, he writes:

[47] VI, pp.214–6.
[48] IX, p.168.
[49] V, p.216.
[50] VII, p.195 (Oct. 1820).

Of the Immortality of the Soul—it appears to me that there can be little doubt—if we attend to the action of Mind.—It is perpetual activity;—I used to doubt it—but reflection has taught me better . . . I have ventured upon the question without recurring to Revelation—which however is at least as rational a solution of it—as any other.[51]

He could not make up his mind about the great questions, though one is always inclined to think that belief, often in resentful or rebellious form, predominated. This is not capable of proof; the evidence is too shadowy and too contradictory. But I take this view because his remarks in favour of religion are generally written in a serious tone, while his attacks on it are flippant or exasperated and closely intertwined with his own accounts of his sensuality or his pride or his weakness of will. Even though steeped in the Augustan classics, and often quoting them, he is immune to the influence of the calm, philosophic, sceptical tone of Voltaire, Hume and Gibbon. But, once again, he is too uncertain and inconstant to analyse the development of his thought. And characteristically, when he asks himself whether he regrets anything, the only thing he finds is that he was ever born at all.[52]

[51] IX, p.45. The part omitted contains an account of ancient Stoic speculation.
[52] IX, p.45.

III
Childhood

In that first onrush of life's chariot-wheels,
We know not if the forests move or we.

(E.B. Browning, *Aurora Leigh*, 1856, Book I)

The process of living seems to consist in coming to realize truths so ancient and simple that, if stated, they sould like barren platitudes. They cannot sound otherwise to those who have not had the relevant experience: that is why there is no real teaching of such truths possible and every generation starts from scratch

C.S. Lewis, *Letters*, ed. by W.H. Lewis, 1966. To Bede Griffiths,
8 May 1939)

(i) *Memory*

It is a commonplace that the early chapters of autobiographies, which describe childhood, are the best. Like most commonplaces, this is a half-truth. It is more nearly true of less distinguished works than it is of the greatest. Only people of imaginative and intellectual power can recreate adult experience in a pattern both truthful and satisfying. But almost any-one can interest us for the time in a vivid glimpse of earliest memories.

Memory in childhood is more arbitrary and unpredictable than it is later. The adult mind gradually and unconsciously trains itself to recognize the important and reject the inessential, though doubtless in most cases the attempt is never completely successful. But in childhood the natural vagaries are untouched by discipline. Walter de la Mare[1] has an interesting quotation from Charles Babbage:

> I resolved that at a certain hour of a certain day I would go to a certain room in the house, and that if I found the door open, I would believe the Bible; but that if it were closed, I should conclude that it was not true. I remember well that the observation was made, but I have no recollection as to the state of the door.

He must surely at the time have noticed and remembered the state of the door. But later mental processes (how much later? there is no means of guessing) will have suppressed a fact seen to be insignificant and retained what is significant, the state of mind in which religious awe was masked by a wilful and trivial superstition. It is always this 'edited' version of childhood memory that we have to deal with in reading autobiographies written by adults, though it is seldom that the traces of editing are as obvious as they are here. That, no doubt, is part of the reason why so many people can truthfully claim that their very first memory is in some way emblematic of the whole situation in which they were placed as children. For instance, a friend informs me that her earliest memory of all was of being jumped along by both parents each holding one hand on either side of her. As her father had just returned from the war, and she had previously been used to living with her mother alone, this experience represented to her the surprise (and shock) of realizing that she had two parents and two authorities over her. It is to be supposed, in this and many similar cases, that even earlier memories had long since been blotted out because they lacked such significance.

[1] Walter de la Mare, *Early One Morning*, Faber & Faber, 1935, p.197.

Sometimes we are privileged to observe the process of suppression at work. Thus Gavin Maxwell[2] records how, at his preparatory school, he obtained a trivial score over a senior boy, and then felt guilty when he heard that the other boy's father had just died. He brooded sorrowfully over an imaginary image of the dead man, but entirely failed to make any connection with his own case. His own father had been killed in the war when he was three months old. Later in the same volume we find an account of a veiled sexual advance made to him by a master, which was unnoticed by him, though obvious to all his contemporaries.[3] The link between the two cases seems to be the deep-seated reluctance found in many male adolescents to think of themselves as persons, perceptible to others exactly as they perceive others. As this tendency is precisely the opposite of the one which leads people to write autobiographies, it can be a formidable obstacle to a clear presentation of this period of life. And this is one of several reasons why the adolescent period of an autobiography is so often less convincing either than childhood or adulthood.

Many, in writing about their own childhood, stress not the significance of early experience but the discontinuity between experience and meaning. Or, to put it another way, the experience is powerfully memorable for its intensity, but the ostensible cause is trivial. Thus George Tyrrell[4] writes:

> Terrors are my earliest recollections, the speechless terrors of infancy that could not be explained or alleviated—the wall-eyed ghastly bust of Shakespeare in the lobby, that used to drive me into convulsions unaccountable to others; the train rushing over the bridge under which I was wheeled . . . giving an impression of a procession of bodiless heads.

Children acquire very early, whether by nature or training, a sense of the secret and forbidden, a point well brought out by Enid Bagnold:[5]

> there he was . . . holding something terrible and strange in his hand, a piece of his body. I jumped back, shocked, and filled with hatred. I was too old to be so innocent. I thought he was at some nameless practice, some devil's work. It never occurred to me the poor man wanted

[2] Gavin Maxwell, *The House of Elrig*, 1965. Quotations from Penguin ed. 1976, pp.102–3.
[3] Ibid., p.151.
[4] G. Tyrrell, *Autobiographies*. Edited posthumously by M.D. Petre, 1912, I, p.10.
[5] Enid Bagnold, *Autobiography*, Heinemann, 1969, p.22.

to pass water.... As we rode I forgot in five minutes. But I have remembered all these years.

She was approaching eighty when she wrote this.

Just as there can be a great gap between the emotion and its occasion, so there can be between childish belief and imagination. Walter de la Mare[6] quotes an interesting passage from Burns, in which he says he owes much as a poet to the 'ignorance, credulity and superstition' of an old woman who told innumerable stories of the praeter-natural. They had their effect though 'nobody can be more sceptical'.

It is characteristic of memory in general to retain both moments— sudden, surprise events—and a general distillation of long periods of time with their routines and habitual associations. But in childhood this tendency is stronger than it is later. Children seldom have much sense of gradual change and development. Their perceptions move from one pole to the other, from a timeless, unchanging world to the unique moment, which may be preserved for its own sake, or because, like the death of a parent, it introduces an irrevocable change.

Many examples could be given. A typical one is Richard Church,[7] who offers a lovingly timeless picture of a closely-knit, lower-middle class family in the 1890s and 1900s. For chapter after chapter, everything is typical, everything is what *used* to happen, until eventually we reach a unique and unexpected event, as his dying mother rejects all female attendance at her sickbed and requires her son to perform the most intimate services. All good autobiographies preserve, in some way or other, this sense of contrast between the habitual and the unexpected.

Children do not write autobiographies, and young adults very seldom. As well as the unconscious suppression already discussed, we have to reckon with the deliberate shaping of childhood material by the autobiographer, who wishes to see it as forming or adumbrating a more recent past. Events which have seemed trivial at the time may be stressed if they are found long after to have been prophetic.

(ii) *Bereavement*

Bereavement is not necessarily a more intense experience in childhood than it is later. But it is usually more formative, partly because it may

---

[6] Walter de la Mare, op. cit., p.272.
[7] Richard Church, *Over the Bridge*, Heinemann, 1955.

include ideas of death and change apprehended for the first time, while every reflective adult, suffering bereavement, is aware of something which he has long known to be possible, and which he has witnessed in the suffering of others. No one brings home this unrepeatable quality of bereavement in early years better than De Quincey. He suffered the early loss of two sisters, and so is able to present in strong relief the contrast between very early childhood, where experience is separated from any reflection, and a slightly later time when the precocious childish mind strives to find a coherent meaning in apparently contradictory events.

The first sister died shortly after being ill-treated by a female servant. De Quincey had a stronger memory of this than of the death:

> I did not often see the person charged with this cruelty; but when I did, my eyes sought the ground; nor could I have borne to look her in the face; not, however, in any spirit that could be called anger. The feeling which fell upon me was a shuddering horror, as upon a first glimpse of the truth that I was in a world of evil and strife . . . that incident had a lasting revolutionary power in colouring my estimate of life.[8]

But he goes on in a surprisingly different vein, which in its contrast to the foregoing well illustrates the extreme egocentricity of early childhood. His thoughts on the event were more important than the event.

> I knew little more of morality than that Jane had disappeared. She had gone away; but, perhaps, she would come back. Happy interval of heaven-born ignorance . . . Summer and winter come again—crocuses and roses; why not little Jane?

The second loss, that of his sister Elizabeth, which occurred when he was six, was felt as the loss of a distinct person, whom De Quincey believed to have been amazingly gifted, and destined to be his guide through life, if she had lived:

> the night which for me gathered upon that event ran after my steps far into life; and perhaps at this day I resemble little for good or for ill that which else I should have been. Pillar of fire that didst go before me to guide and quicken—pillar of darkness, when thy countenance was

[8] De Quincey, *Works*, edited by David Masson, I, pp.34–5. All quotations from De Quincey are from this collected edition.

turned away to God, that didst too truly reveal to my dawning fears
the secret shadow of death.[9]

He is eloquent about his secret scheme to view her body on the
day after death. It becomes one of those timeless moments which he was
later to find as one of the greatest attractions of the poetry of Wordsworth:

> I imagine that it was about an hour after high noon when I reached the
> chamber-door; it was locked but the key was not taken away. Enter-
> ing, I closed the door so softly, that, although it opened upon a hall
> which ascended through all the storeys, no echo ran along the silent
> walls. Then, turning round, I sought my sister's face. But the bed had
> been moved, and the back was now turned towards myself. Nothing
> met my eyes but one large window, wide-open, through which the
> sun of midsummer at mid-day was showering down torrents of splen-
> dour . . . the blue depths seemed the express types of infinity; and it
> was not possible for eye to behold, or for heart to conceive, any sym-
> bols more pathetic of life and the glory of life.

When he turned to look at the dead face, he thought he was aware of a
step on the stairs, so he kissed her hastily and hurried away, afraid of discovery. His regret at the interruption seems out of proportion:

> thus mutilated was the parting which should have lasted for ever; tainted
> thus with fear was that farewell sacred to love and grief, to perfect love
> and to grief that could not be healed.[10]

But the feeling, though excessive, may well have been real. He is obliquely
expressing the pain and confusion so often felt by those who are capable
of this experience of timelessness, at the intrusion of the workaday world
and the inexorable time process. De Quincey's romanticism is always
infused with a strong measure of realism. He is not satisfied, as a lesser
writer might have been, with his recreation of the timeless moment. He
is no less concerned with the sequel, which inevitably drags him down
from these heights:

> now, therefore, began to open upon me those fascinations of solitude,
> which, when acting as a co-agency with unresisted grief, end in the
> paradoxical result of making out of grief itself a luxury; such a luxury

[9] Ibid., I, p.36.
[10] Ibid., I, p.42.

as finally become a snare, overhanging life itself, and the energies of
life, with growing menaces.

As a final stage, he is able to generalize the experience, and see it as a
type of the solitariness of all human life, and especially of death, and to
link it with religious consolation in the thought of immortality. In all
this, he rivals his master Wordsworth in the power to present the timeless moment as being also, paradoxically, part of the time-series, and as an
influence on the long development of the self. And if he is more rhetorical,
even at times histrionic, than perhaps we like, he balances this by his
shrewd awareness of the self-dramatising powers of childhood and of
their roots in unthinking egoism. This last is stressed once again in the
casual way he speaks of the loss of his brother, which did not touch his
feelings, so that he thinks it sufficient to mention in a footnote that 'for
many a year he has been lying at the bottom of the Atlantic'.[11]
By his very different ways of treating these three deaths he is able to
convey both the experiencing and the inexperiencing mind. At the same
time as he finds an appropriate image for the majesty of death in the
second case, he gives, in the eccentricity of feeling in the first case, and in
the failure to feel at all in the third, an impressive witness to the vagaries
of childhood, and especially to the absence in children of any sense of the
scale of events, and of any attempt to mould feelings in proportion to
their relative importance.
Many examples could be given of the waywardness of childish feeling,
its refusal to adjust to the scale of events. A striking one is given by L.E.
Jones:

Our parents had been invited to spend a fortnight with some French
acquaintances . . . and had decided to take my elder brother with them.
He and I had never . . . spent a night apart, but in my ignorance of the
working of the human heart, I had no forebodings about the coming
separation. The day of departure came, and I stood on the gravel and
cheerfully waved them away . . . loneliness, a strange and unknown
horror, overwhelmed me like a tidal wave. I crawled upstairs . . . on
his side of the bed lay his felt land-and-water hat and his leather belt.
The sight of these familiar belongings of the Lost One tore me to
pieces. I lay on the bed and sobbed, clasping the belt.[12]

[11] Ibid., I, p.67n.
[12] L.E. Jones, *A Victorian Boyhood*, Macmillan, 1955, p.55.

Not long after the elder brother died, when the younger was thirteen, but the shock was felt less than the earlier brief parting had been. It was as if parting had already been felt with maximum intensity and could never be felt so again. And, indeed, the account that follows of his school years is a happy one.

Both De Quincey and Jones write of loss as personal; their curiosity about the feelings of parents (and in De Quincey's case of siblings also) is slight. Patricia Beer, whose very close-knit family will be more fully treated in the next section, sees loss and mourning in more traditional and more social terms. The rather early loss of the mother, who had been completely dominant over both husband and children, was something, she thinks, which should have been a shared experience. She is quite as interested in her father's last conversation with her mother, about which she can only guess, as she is in her own.

Mother's death, instead of quickly making us older, made us, in our own eyes as well as everybody else's, even younger. It was decided that we were not to go to the funeral; it would be too upsetting for us.

We should have gone to the funeral. We should have stayed with Mother while she was dying. When we last saw her she was thinking and talking and even planning, if one can use that word for the anticipation of a reunion in Heaven, and imagination could supply us with the final stages of her approach to death. We should have seen her in her coffin, if only because she had thought it right for us to see a great many people dead in theirs. She should not have been deprived in all these ways, and neither should we. She was robbed of her due, and we were forced into a helplessness and inexperience that made it impossible for real grief to begin.[13]

The contrast of feeling between Patricia Beer and the other two may be largely due to a difference of personalities. But it may also be that it reflects a social and religious difference. De Quincey and Jones both belonged to families that lived very much as their neighbours expected of them, and were accustomed to the Anglican liturgy. The Beer family were much more inward-looking and belonged to a small Protestant sect, of which the mother at least was a devoted adherent. De Quincey and Jones thus had no need to dwell on the social aspects of grief; they could take them for granted, and were supported by venerable traditions. In the Beer household all authority derived directly from the mother; and if she

[13] Patricia Beer, *Mrs Beer's House*, Hutchinson, 1968, pp.236–7.

was taken away, though her fundamental principles might remain enshrined in the more hesitating, less certain minds of the survivors, the actual power of decision on specific issues was lost. Accordingly, the children felt rudderless; they obscurely felt the need for traditions they had never had.

(iii) The Transmission of Values

All children are trained in innumerable beliefs, attitudes, judgments and customs. The training may be formally given or only implied; but in most cases both methods are used. But many parents (and guardians, relatives and schools) unconsciously give guidance which is inconsistent with itself. Many accounts of childhood throw a pitiless light on this.

The simplest and clearest instance is that described by L.E. Jones, where there are two separate authorities (parents and school in this case) which inculcate different standards.

> We learnt from her [his mother's] authoritative lips how much we loved our parents and each other; how much we loved nature; how much we should, some day love Matthew Arnold, and Ruskin, and Emerson . . . Life could be all sweetness and light, if we would but take the mould she had in mind for us . . . but the strain . . . the unacknowledged oppression from which Eton proved to be so glorious a liberation, was the insistent exaction of signs and gestures and words of affection, the tokens of a surrender for which I had no mind. I could be happy without smiling, but smile I must; I could love without hugging, but hug I must.[14]

At Eton it became a matter of adverse comment that his trousers did not exactly match his coat and waistcoat. 'I can remember thinking that happiness—true peace of mind—could be mine if only my change-trousers could match my change-coat.'[15]

He goes on:

> It might be thought that this pressure to conform . . . would have damped by satisfaction in being liberated from that other pressure to conform, at home, with my mother's exacting standards of behaviour,

[14] L.E. Jones, op. cit., p.117–18.
[15] Ibid., p.165.

taste, and affections. But it was not so. The pressure at home had been
on head and heart; one had to think, and to love, to order. At Eton
you could think and love what you liked: only in external matters . . .
need you do as others did.

Jones expresses here a personal view, and a different personality exposed
to the same two influences, might have judged them in an opposite way.
But hardly any inner conflict resulted from different kinds of training
here. Different though they were in spirit they could with a little tact, be
taken as complementary. Only Eton made him feel uneasy about the
strength of his filial affections. And yet, when he writes, of the time
following his brother's death, 'I was frightened because my mother did
not cry', we know that though Eton had submerged, it had not drowned
his more tender sensibilities.

In Gwen Raverat's case, the lucid distinctions she makes between
three systems of value is her own; and she is making them with conscious
analytical effort to penetrate the confusions in the minds and the conduct
of the surrounding adults. System A was the official moral system inculcated by parents. System B was her own private code, which 'overlapped
and agreed in disapproving of dishonesty, cruelty and cowardliness; but
otherwise they had little in common'.[16]

In Code B an honest admission of theft of lumps of sugar removed any
feeling of guilt. She minded being dishonest, but not being disobedient.
She writes rather as if she had invented System B for herself, and so perhaps in some of its little quirks, she did. But in its main lines it was surely
derived from a subtle sense of the unspoken convictions of those who
inculcated System A, only half-believing in it, or at most, thinking it
inappropriate for children. Obedience, which adults of the élite, donnish
type to which her family belonged, generally repudiate for themselves,
was strongly inculcated as a virtue for children; and would not her father
or mother have popped a lump of sugar in their mouth as they passed, if
they had happened to feel like it? The child, in inventing System B was,
in part, at least, responding, as children habitually do, to what their
parents really meant and would not say, and ignoring what they said but
did not mean.

But the ways in which the two codes were identical are also revealing:

Of course, all kinds of goodness, in both systems, were hampered by

---

[16] Gwen Raverat, *Period Piece. A Cambridge Childhood*, 1952, p.214. Quotations from
Faber paperback ed. 1971.

being, by definition, something that you did not want to do. If you did want to do it, then it wasn't goodness. Thus being kind to a person you liked didn't count at all[17]

Here, casually, and without noticing it, she puts her finger on a central weakness of the Protestant tradition, and the élite high agnostic tradition, which derived from it (the Darwins seem to have inhabited a disputed borderland between the two). It never occurred to them that though it is better to do good unwillingly than to do evil willingly, it is best of all to do good willingly and joyfully. They were far from the insight of the old monk in the story, who when asked whether it was easy or difficult to love God, replied, after a silence, 'It is easy to those who do it.' As a consequence even the generous virtues became stained, in the imaginations of those reared in this tradition, with thoughts of prohibition, negation and frustration.

And then there was Code C. This was the code incumbent upon those who considered themselves *Ladies and Gentlemen*:

Ladies are always polite to servants; Gentlemen never show they are afraid; No lady would wear a hat like that; Gentlemen are always generous with money.

Gwen Raverat's comment is a characteristic mixture of incisive shrewdness about other people's motives and real feelings with a weak grasp of the principles involved:

But the grown-ups were not candid in being unwilling to admit that Code C was quite as important as Code A. They believed in it profoundly; much more passionately than in Code A (though they did not know this); and yet they would not say so openly, or let you say so either.[18]

Gwen Raverat likes Code C much better than Code A, and is therefore impatient with the refusal of her elders to admit that it was really dominant in their lives. But they could not really have done so without admitting that they had no general principles at all. For Code C applied only to a tiny minority of a small minority of countries. In the accepted Darwin view, Africans and Indians and Americans, and English plumbers and ticket-collectors couldn't be gentlemen if they tried, though they could,

[17] Ibid., p.214.
[18] Ibid., p.217.

conceivably, be good (Code A). Her elders had a need, which she does not understand, for universal principles and so they held them, sincerely, if tepidly.

The Darwins seem to have had the tact to avoid any serious clash between the codes. But in other households the torrent of precept and traditional wisdom could be experienced as lacking all discrimination. Priscilla Napier, in a most interesting passage, summarizes it thus:

> Don't care was made to care, Don't care was hanged. Take off your hat, William, to Mr and Mrs Dallin. Spare your breath to cool your porridge. And he would fain have filled his belly with the husks that the swine did eat. This little pig went to market, this little pig stayed at home. Blow bugles, blow, set the wild echoes flying, And answer, echoes, answer, dying, dying, dying. Say please, say yes, say thank you, say sorry, say how do you do? For thine is the kingdom, the power, and the glory. Once upon a time there were four little rabbits whose names were Flopsy, Mopsy, Cottontail and Peter. Fold your vest, and clean your teeth, and say your prayers. Nobly, nobly, Cape St Vincent to the North West died away; Sunset ran, one glorious blood-red reeking into Cadiz Bay; Love me, kiss me, Hug me tight. Never kiss a lady with your hat on, William! It's no use grumbling, it's no use fussing, it's no use crying over spilt milk.[19]

Her comment is apt:

> A mingling of folk-lore, impatience, platitude, affection; a jumble of eternal verity and country precept and temporary slang pours out daily over minds half-hearing, half-differentiating, alternately open as a sieve or retentive as clay.

But two questions remain, which cannot be answered with certainty. How far in such cases is an unspoken guidance, offered with the precepts and proverbs, to help the young to discern their relative importance? And, if there was no such guidance, or if it was very weak, was the effort to discriminate for oneself salutary? Perhaps many people, including many autobiographers, would be unsure how to answer them.

But some people felt that only one part of the instruction they were receiving was seriously meant; the rest was only decorative. Cyril Connolly writes:

34 Priscilla Napier, *A Late Beginning*, Michael Joseph, 1966, p.26.

The true religion I had learnt at Eton and St Wulfric's [his prep school] had not been Christianity nor even Imperialism but the primitive gospel of the Jealous God of phthonos...Human beings, it taught, are perpetually getting above themselves.... when they reach the state of insolence or hybris, they are visited with some catastrophe ...though some accounts are allowed to run on longer than others, everything in life has to be paid for.[20]

A very different teaching from that experienced at Eton by L.E. Jones. And I think it would be naive to point to the difference in their ages of about eighteen years as an explanation. The contrast should remind us of the subjectivity of all impressions, even when an honest effort is made to recall everything and to record it in the round.

Patricia Beer, one of the most acute analysts of inconsistency in parental training, brings out very well the power that may sometimes lurk in unstated assumptions, so that their being stated at last may actually lead to their weakening:

My mother had, naturally, trained us in the belief that make-up was wicked. That is to say, she had hardly ever said so. It was such a basic belief that even to state it was to weaken it, seeming to admit other possibilities. I realized this on my own account when I was reading a book that was supposed to be edifying and a man in it said to his daughter, 'Don't let me ever catch you putting on rouge.' I was horrified; it suggested that somebody might.[21]

There is a lesson for parents here, which, to judge from the evidence of autobiographical accounts of childhood, very few of them heed.

Evidently Mrs Beer's successful tactics over make-up were the result of luck, or perhaps of a genuine personal distaste for speaking of it. Another episode shows her making just the mistake she had previously avoided:

in The Scarlet Pimpernel there was the key line, 'That demmed elusive Pimpernel'; and of course 'demmed' would never do, so Mother substituted 'awful'. I think she deliberately chose a word which did not scan and which obviously was not the original one. We knew perfectly well it was 'demmed' ... He [father] also knew it was 'demmed' and must have realised from our self-conscious voices that we knew it too.[22]

[20] Cyril Connolly, Enemies of Promise, Routledge, 1938, p.255.
[21] Patricia Beer, op. cit, p.72.
[22] Ibid., pp.100–1.

Trivial though these issues are in themslves, Patricia Beer (it seems to me) is right to stress them, because, for children, the very fact that something is not to be mentioned gives it an artificial importance, and may in the end contribute powerfully to the end-result, the remaining influence of early training on mature adults.

The Scarlet Pimpernel happened also to provide a good illustration of a much more fundamental disharmony in Mrs Beer's system. Like many another she was totally confused about the connection between her deeply-held religious beliefs and the English class system and her own place in it. Her husband was a railway clerk; she had been trained as a teacher. Clearly, the family was a long way, socially, from any connection with the aristocracy, just as it may be supposed that their fellow-members of the Plymouth Brethren congregation were.

But in reading *The Scarlet Pimpernel*, they all delighted in the aristocratic status both of the authoress and the hero. 'It seemed not to occur to one of us that had we lived then we should by reason of our social status have been *sans-culottes* dancing round the guillotine, rather than *vicomtes* escaping in carts.'

This may be allowed to be a harmless romantic dream; but more serious were the occasions when a clash occurred between religious principles and worldly ambitions. The local school considered by the mother to be the best was run by a Roman Catholic. 'As always, when there was a clash between my mother's religious principles and her plans for our education, the latter won.' Patricia Beer goes on to record how at this time her mother used to speculate that possibly a few Roman Catholics might get to heaven. One would like to think this was due to a broadening of theological sympathies. But the author evidently considers that it was no more than worldly salve for a bruised conscience.

At other times religious principle and worldly considerations gave, fortuitously, the same answer to a question, as when both forbade playing with other children on Sunday, because playing on Sunday was bad, and because the other children were socially unsuitable. But if the children had been of a higher class, the two sets of precepts would have clashed.

One cannot help being sorry for Mrs Beer, and for many like her. Saints are rare, and everybody else is worldly in some degree. Those who profess a demanding other-worldly moral code are particularly vulnerable to charges of inconsistency. The accusing children may have been no less inconsistent. But in a case like this we find, not so much a conflict of values, but a contrast in the ways in which values can be perceived. Mrs Beer had developed all her beliefs, attitudes and aspirations into a comfortable fit, like favourite old clothes. If they are comfortable, it doesn't seem to matter that they are all of different origins and ages. But if the children make up for their lack of experience by keen logical analysis, if, instead of asking whether things are a comfortable fit, they everywhere demand a reason, if they demand that distinctions be made between deep convictions and convenient prejudices and habits, the attitudes of many parents will begin to look threadbare. The accusing tone of many memoirs on this point should be accepted (usually) as a true report of actual feelings, but often rejected as an unjust judgment on members of a race well characterized by Dr Johnson when he said: 'Nothing is too little for so little a creature as man.'

It may happen, too, that children take some precepts more literally than they are meant. Patricia Beer has an amusing account of her revulsion against stage make-up when they did amateur dramatics. She was astonished and shocked when her mother said easily, 'Oh, go along.' Sometimes the children are judging the parents not by their actual standards but by a hypothetical ideal construction that the parents have not contemplated. And this is especially likely to be true if, as in this case, the children are cleverer and more logical than the parents.

If Patricia Beer's account has the value of an extreme, and exeptionally well-articulated case, of something very typical of England in the nineteenth and part of the twentieth centuries, Gavin Maxwell's has the appeal of something unrepeatable. His religious background, his class position and his personal circumstances were all unlikely, and particularly unlikely to be combined as they were. He was able to run free in an apparently limitless world of nature, and to begin that special relation with animals and birds that was to be so important in his adult life. He was the nephew of a Duke, but also the son of a not very prosperous widow. The family, the Percys, were perhaps the only family of their rank who adhered to the Catholic Apostolic sect founded by Carlyle's friend, Irving. The sense of sectarian separateness clashed oddly with the aristocratic confidence. Then he was confronted at school with a different conception of religion, that appeared equally authoritative. The headmaster's first sermon took him aback;

'Religion is a thing of reason and not emotion,' he announced in his clear, harsh voice. 'We must beware of any sort of feeling of uplift—such as you may experience when hearing or singing a beautiful hymn—and try to avoid it at all cost. Religion is a set of rules by which we live, and in a state of emotional uplift we can no more hope to keep a

set of rules than a drunk man can walk in a straight line . . . I thought
of the hymn, 'Far, far away like bells at evening pealing' that used to
fetch tears to my eyes at Heddon Court, and of Vivian singing *Adeste
Fideles* on the moonlit rooftops of St Wulfric's, and felt sad that my
source of beauty was suspect.[23]

Not long after being confronted with two opposite religious authorities, he became aware of the social gulf between his ducal family and
those who were paid to instruct him. This occurred when the headmaster
showed him a book which contained somewhat impertinent criticisms of
his great relations.

When I gave the book back to him his mischief positively crackled
from the harsh sallow face and great grey eyes. He said: 'Well—what
did you think of it?'
  'How much of it is true, sir?'
  'That is a strange question. The answer is what I had hoped you
were going to tell *me*. What did you come to Hurst Court for?' (He
must have rehearsed this in advance.)
  'To learn to think, sir,' I replied dutifully.
  'Good. Well, you must keep the book if it helps towards that end.
But perhaps it would be tactful not to tell your mother how you came
by it.' And, to me, incredibly, he winked.[24]

This cunningly chosen anecdote suddenly shows us the situation from the
other side of the educational fence. The headmaster knew that in a few
years the boy would have outgrown his present awe of schoolmasters,
but that he would never outgrow the effects of his aristocratic birth. He
was aware of a class difference to which his imposing personality and
unlimited authority in the school setting had blinded the boy. He was
helping the boy to see, for the first time, how temporary the present
situation was. He felt confident enough of his own personal authority to
draw attention to its lack of any lasting basis.

The effect seems to have been to intensify the boy's natural tendency
to solitary pursuits and intensely private thoughts. Opposing precepts,
assumptions and social standards tend to cancel out. He was solitary in
any case, and perhaps the headmaster had not considered how little contact he was likely to have with his great relations, brought up by a widow

[24] Gavin Maxwell, op. cit., p.117.
[25] Ibid., p.131.

living in a remote place. In the end one has the impression that, beyond
all these conflicting educational influences, the solitary adventures in pursuit of animals and birds were the most influential factors of all.

   Maxwell is one of many who recall, too, the almost unlimited egoism
of childhood, and so remind us that all efforts to train and mould may fail
to affect some central core of being. The positive or what might be called
the Wordsworthian aspect of this will be considered at some length in
the section that follows. Here we can breifly recall something less interesting but probably, in most cases, stronger. Maxwell tells us that his
chief feeling on learning of the death of his uncle at an early age was
regret at the loss of future presents. Walter de la Mare records how when
as a child he was thought to be near death, and realised the depth of his
mother's anxiety he blamed himself for whistling because 'now they
know I'm better they won't be anxious any more'.[25] And Enid Bagnold
records how at the age of three she engaged in a ruthless contest with her
grandmother for the possession of her mother. Whether egoism declines
with time, or simply learns to disguise itself better, is a question which
each must answer for himself.

[25] Walter de la Mare, op. cit., p.295.

IV
The Child Alone

More fools at twenty years than ten.

(Thomas Traherne, *The Apostasy*)

longing for an Eden from which each one of us is exiled.

(Forrest Reid, *The Apostate*, p.3)

Time was cyclic, not linear.

(Kathleen Raine, *Farewell Happy Fields*, p.35)

CHILDREN HAVE COMMONLY TWO OPPOSITE NEEDS, to communicate, to belong, to be dependent, to be accepted, to conform, to imitate, and, sharply in opposition to this, and sometimes contemporary with it, to be separate, secret, private, to find or imagine or create a solitary world. The second impulse is the subject of this chapter. And, though we often speak of a 'childhood paradise', and though some writers have been able to convince us that they actually experienced this for a time, yet it is well to remember that there is also a contrary state of solitude, perhaps a commoner one. Many children have created their own kingdom of dread in a dark corner of the stairs or an empty wardrobe.

All inwardness and introspection come from looking outwards. If a child attempts directly to know himself, he can find nothing. Instead, he finds external images, things seen and heard, or imagined by combining in a personal pattern things seen and heard, which represent, and bring to consciousness otherwise inarticulate depths of the mind. Without knowing it the dreamy child becomes a subtle theorist of the relation between inner and outer, and, in his own way, retraces the path described by Wordsworth in *The Prelude*.

The paradise of childhood can be made out of almost any material. Often, it is made out of things beautiful in themselves, gardens, woods, birds and wild animals. But Neville Cardus was able to make one from the streets of Manchester, and others have been made from books of little intrinsic merit. Even the one essential feature, separateness, does not need to be an objective fact. It may be that orphans and only children have a stronger tendency to this kind of dreaming, but it is still possible to create the dream of huge imaginary spaces in a crowded nursery or a busy throng of adults.

For the student of autobiography, the most important point will be the relation between the childhood dream and the formed adult being. My first three examples have been chosen to illustrate three different states. W.H. Hudson shows what may happen when there is a prolonged (perhaps lifelong) conflict between the ideas and values suggested by the solitary world and those of society in general. Forrest Reid shows the persistence of the childhod world into the adult, leading to a rebellious rejection of the latter, and an attempt to regress into childhood. Edwin Muir achieves in the end, after many struggles, a reconciliation; for him, unlike the other two, the childhood paradise is finally in harmony with all other formative influences, so that his autobiography achieves a wholeness, and convinces us that his personality achieved a wholeness that the other two lack.

(i) *Conflict: W.H. Hudson*

'It was never,' Hudson begins, 'my intention to write an autobiography.'
And he was late in doing it. It appeared in 1918, when he was well over
75 years old, and was written when he was recovering in London from a
long illness which he may well have expected to be fatal. The lapse of
time, distance, and the strangeness of an England engaged in total war
must have made his Argentinian childhood seem inconceivably remote.
Also, like Muir, but unlike Reid, he had left the scene of his childhood
experience for good at an early age, so that the sense of contrast between
childhood and adult life, strong in all early dreamers, will have been
intensified. His title, *Far Away and Long Ago*, is expressive of all this.
And, like Muir again, he feels an extra sense of separation, because the
world of his childhood is not only lost to him, but has actually disappeared from the earth. He writes:

> And when I recall those vanished scenes, those rushy and flowery
> meres, with their varied and multitudinous wild bird life—the cloud of
> shining wings, the heart-enlivening wild cries, the joy unspeakable it
> was to me in those early years—I am glad to think I shall never revisit
> them, that I shall finish my life thousands of miles removed from
> them, cherishing to the end in my heart the image of a beauty which
> has vanished from the earth.[1]

I quote this passage both because it tells something Hudson deeply felt,
and also to meet at once something unsatisfactory in Hudson's prose,
easily parodied[2] and reminiscent of the weaker side of Georgian poetry. It
should not be allowed to detract more than it must from the great interest of what he has to say.

Most autobiographies begin with a confined world, with a memory of
mother or nurse, or a visual impression of nursery or garden, or sometimes with facts about parentage and ancestry. Hudson begins with illim-
itable space, and with the absence, felt more by the reader than by the
childish subject, of all human surroundings. The first characters are
twenty-five enormous trees, and Hudson is able to use his later expert
knowledge of natural history to give us their Latin name and to tell us
that the leaves are poisonous, and each tree more than a century old. Also
there is another solitary tree which local inhabitants maintain is the only

[1] W.H. Hudson, *Far Away and Long Ago*, 1918. Everyman, 1967, p.230.
[2] See, for instance, Evelyn Waugh's *Scoop*.

one of its kind in the world. The next character is a ghost in a traditional story of passion and violence which Hudson heard of, but never saw. Several remembered scenes follow, before, at last, his mother is introduced, and then in a peculiarly Hudsonian way. She is a distant figure in the landscape, seen as if by a detached portrait painter. And he follows this immediately with a whimsical and surprising image, which is the key to the book's whole structure. Saying that his parents never punished or chided him or his siblings, he compares them to a hen who finds herself in charge of ducklings:

> she . . . is satisfied that they know best what is good for them; though, of course, their ways seem peculiar to her, and she can never entirely sympathize with their fancy for going into water. I need not be told that the hen is after all only stepmother to her ducklings, since I am contending that the civilized woman—the artificial product of our self-imposed conditions—cannot have the same relation to her offspring as the uncivilized woman really has to hers.[3]

The assumption that the absence of civilization is the natural and best state is too deeply-rooted to need arguing. And the book's imagery throughout reverses the normal process of attributing human characteristics to animals or inanimate things. For Hudson humanity is a latecomer on the scene and it is natural to him to attempt to understand it by reference to the non-human. Thus, without any self-consciousness, when, much later, he encounters the upper class of native society dressed in silk hats, suits or black broadcloth and scarlet waistcoats, it occurs to him to see them as a flock of military starlings, with black plumage and scarlet breast.[4] And he compares a mother pleading that her son be not forced to become a soldier to a wild animal trying to save her offspring from hunters.[5]

Yet Hudson does not give us a simple contrast between nature and humanity. If he did, since we all in the end have to live in the human world, he would be bound to fail in imposing his spacious childhood world as a true image of life and a genuine formative power on himself. There is a human presence, besides his own. But, like his childhood self, the man he calls 'the Hermit' seems far remote from society, from civilization and from the other members of Hudson's own family. He is a

[3] W.H. Hudson, op. cit., pp.9–10.
[4] Ibid., p.82.
[5] Ibid., pp.99–100.

beggar who refuses money and cooked food, and makes his own clothes, which are strange enough to terrify the house-dogs.

> It was commonly reported that he had ... committed some terrible crime ... and had adopted his singular mode of life by way of penance ... A terrible wrath would disfigure his countenance and kindle his eyes with demoniac fire; and in sharp ringing tones, that wounded like strokes, he would pour forth a torrent of words in his unknown language.[6]

We feel at once that this figure is central to the author's memory and to his literary intention in a way that his own relatives are not. He is more than a memory; he is an image of isolation in which the writer's deepest experiences occurred. Appropriately, too, he soon provides the book's first death. Although he died more than twenty years later, Hudson presents us with this death immediately because in death as in life, the hermit is offered as the incarnate terror, the image of all that is disturbing for the child in the solitude of the pampas, and in the desired, but also feared, separation from society. Characteristically, he dies alone, so far from mankind that his body has wasted to a skeleton before it is discovered. By placing joy and terror, both in extreme forms, together in his first chapter, Hudson has ensured that his childhood paradise is an image of life as we know it, not of a lost Eden. And almost immediately there is a contrasting image of punishment, that is of society's rejection of parts of itself, in the figure of a murderer bound with thongs of raw hide to a post. We believe that Hudson is speaking the simple truth when he says: 'the image is plain to me now as if I had seen him but yesterday'.[7]

Near the end of the book, when a serious adolescent illness is being described, and Hudson has been told that he is likely to die very soon, the bound murderer reappears in his narrative:

> the dreadful thought that I must soon resign this earthly life which was so much more to me, as I could not help thinking, than to most others. I was like that young man with a ghastly face I had seen bound to a post in our barn; or like any wretched captive, tied hand and foot and left to lie there until it suited his captor to come back and cut his throat.[8]

[6] Ibid., p.13.
[7] Ibid., p.18.
[8] Ibid., p.264.

It is a pity that no one told Hudson then that people whose imminent death is prophesied by doctors normally live, as he did, some sixty or seventy years more. But perhaps we should not regret this, for we should have lost one of the most characteristic and revealing passages in the whole book. He leaves out of account the enormous difference, to most sensibilities, between misfortune and punishment. Once again his idea of nature has come before his idea of society and has determined it. Both the young murderer and he himself on his sick-bed are simply victims of the unexplained, unmotivated, arbitrary painfulness of the world. An underground current of feeling connects them and surfaces here with extraordinary surprising force.

Returning to chapter II, we find, as perhaps we would by now expect, a natural image of mysterious horror, 'big, old, grey rats with long, scaly tails . . . I had not known that the whole world contained so many rats as I now saw congregated before me'.[9] And so, very early Hudson has shown his solitary world of nature as containing images of guilt, pity, fear, horror and mystery.

The next important figure is a tentative link between the private and social worlds. He is another beggar, but very different from the first. Like Scott's Edie Ochiltree, he is a link between the two worlds of solitude and society. He comes with prayer, he appeals to human solidarity, and speaks of the rewards from Heaven that generous giving ensures. He rides a horse, which connects him with a settled, social world. It is characteristic of Hudson's method to make this person rather than his mother, or his four siblings (who throughout are shadowy figures) the first link between his first and second worlds.

But just as the first world contained conflicts, so did the second. A tutor, later dismissed for striking the children with a horsewhip, takes the occasion of the death of a dog to proclaim his belief that men and dogs die in the same way. In answer to this, his mother tells the six-year-old child of the Christian conception of Resurrection, and he immediately believes her: 'I had been in prison and had suffered torture, and was now free again—death would not destroy me!'[10] Shortly after, a servant dies, and he is unable to face the body. Belief in immortality cannot for him tame the fear of death.

By now Hudson has shown how unusual his situation was. It combined in a unique way the characteristics of two opposite kinds of childhood and

9 Ibid., p.19.
10 Ibid., p.33.

thus of autobiography. He has both a settled and affectionate family and a private world of nature. At the same time he has from the first dawn of understanding the doubts and conflicts about life's meaning which more often strike adolescents or young adults. Everything he sees and hears is capable of becoming a symbol of ambivalence. Thus the serpent with a cross is treated as deadly and killed at once;[11] but later he learns to handle similar snakes alive without harm. And the dangerousness and ruthlessness of nature, which terrify him, attract and fascinate him at the same time.

When he comes to the violence which civilized life contains and regularizes, in the sight of two gauchos fighting a duel with knives, he feels the same thrill that he felt at the destructive power of the snake, or later feels at the falcon's cunning method of hunting pigeons. But here again there is conflict. He is puzzled by the contrary tender and feeling aspects of civilized life. He is ashamed when rebuked by an 'ignorant ruffianly gaucho' for his hunting of 'God's little birds'[12] and shows how much he is impressed by comparing him to St Francis. He is deeply puzzled when some women hold a man back from killing a snake, and his mind is troubled by the question: 'Why should you kill it?' This taught him to consider 'whether it might not be better to spare than to kill; better not only for the animal spared but for the soul'.[13]

It is entirely characteristic that he should have received his first strong impression of the real nature of morality and civilization through the medium of dealings with animals. Although he had believed his mother's Christian teaching to be true, it had made little impression on his heart. His sense of awe and mystery, his potential for religious feeling had been restricted to the natural order of plant and beast, while doctrines and religious ideas had come to him sharply defined like the truths of mathematics, without the slightest penumbra of mystery, or the least power to inspire devotional feeling. Just as the normal order of apprehension of the human and the non-human world was reversed, so was the formative function of facts and ideas. Facts gave him awe and mysterious longings; ideas and doctrines only gave him a basis for logical deduction.

At the same time what was religious, civilized and kindly in the human society (which he began to approach so unusually late) seemed to him like an anomaly, while the elements in it of violence and ruthless competition

[11] Ibid., p.45.
[12] Ibid., p.151.
[13] Ibid., p.182.

seemed natural, almost homely and comforting, since they reminded him of his first animal teachers. Growing up naturally alters the perspective; he becomes a civilized man, eventually a learned man. But there still remains a curious uneasy equilibrium between opposite sets of lessons. As his way is, he subsumes all these deep conflicts in a single vivid memory. He was struck on the head a heavy blow by another boy and fell from his pony. He plans an exact retaliation, and after many plots and plans achieves it.

> Would it have been better, when I went out with the bamboo cane, and he asked me what I was going to do with it, if I had gone up to him and shown my face with the broad band across it . . . and had said to him: 'This is the mark of the blow you gave me . . . now take the cane and give me another blow on the left side'? Tolstoy (my favourite author, by the way) would have answered: 'Yes, certainly it would have been better for you—better for the soul.' Nevertheless, I still ask myself: 'Would it?' and if this incident should come before me half a second before my final disappearance from earth, I should still be in doubt.[14]

So we are left with a drawn battle—we may call it a battle between nature and grace, or between the primitive and the civilized, or between the fact and the ideal, or between passion and reason. Whichever we choose to call it, we are left with the indelible influence of childhood to the end of a long life. The shy, never-repeated mention of Tolstoy, the apostle of non-violence, who was also a soldier and the author of the greatest of all war-books, is a fitting reminder that his adult life was as deeply divided as his childhood.

(ii) *Regression: Forrest Reid*

It is characteristic of Forrest Reid that while his account of childhood in *Apostate* is vivid and memorable, its successor, which deals with his adult years possesses little interest. Reid is one of those whose history throws an ironical, even a sinister, light on Wordsworth's line 'The child is father of the man.' If we apply it to Reid, we shall mean almost the opposite of what Wordsworth meant, not a harmonious development with the recurring rainbow as pledge of continuity, but a perpetually

[14] Ibid., p.233.

frustrated, at times angry, exile from the childhood world. His childhood paradise centred round the figure of Emma, his nurse and governess, who suddenly left the family, never to return, when he was six years old. When she read to him from a magazine called *Early Days*:

I saw . . . the dark summer sea widening out and out till it melted into a golden haze that hid yet suggested an enchanted land beyond. The light turned to bright burnished gold where it caught the top of a remote mountain, but here, close at hand, in the rich deep drowsy afternoon, was a smooth green lawn dropping down gently to a white sandy bay where dark waves toppled over in foam and music.[15]

The magazine from which Emma read was intended to have a pious, Protestant tendency, and she herself was 'deeply religious, and she is the only deeply religious person I have met with whom I have been able to feel quite happy and at ease'.[16]

Well aware, then, that Emma would have repudiated his interpretation of the story she was reading, he says bluntly—and it is really the key statement of the whole book—'It [this imaginary world] was the only heaven I wanted, or ever was to want.'[17]

But a man cannot remain a child for ever, however much he wants to, and the passage quoted above (note 15) contains, perhaps without the author's awareness, evidence of this. It is, after all, a very 'literary' passage; and I think we shall be safe in assuming that its literary flavour is not derived mainly from the actual story which he heard when he was six. He has recreated the experience with the help of later adolescent or adult reading—it may be from Keats or Tennyson, or William Morris, or French symbolists. So in a way his dream of childhood is an adult dream. He has partly transposed his sense of the loss of childhood, felt much later, into the different though in some ways cognate experience of childhood yearning. The reader, who may well decide that no child of six could be quite as romantic as that, will also feel that the author's evident unconsciousness of the process of recreation adds to its interest and its poignancy.

The departure of Emma, who was snatched away without warning, left him with his mother still living and present in the house, in the emotional condition of an orphan, but with one important difference.

---

[15] Forrest Reid, *Apostate*, 1926, pp.28–9.
[16] Ibid., p.18.
[17] Ibid., p.28.

His parents, not death, had deprived him of his mother-figure. So very early on an element of bitterness against the parents, and, through them, against the whole adult world, enters to intensify this yearning for perpetual childhood, for time to have a stop.

His mother was remote and proud, intensely aware of her own aristocratic superiority to her husband and to their neighbours. For her he felt 'admiration'. He shared in her feelings of pride in aristocratic poverty, when her social inferiors rode in carriages she could not afford. He was proud of her beauty and distinction. But all these were abstract, cerebral sentiments, hardly connected with his deeper memories of Emma or his private dream-world. When Emma left: 'I do not remember whether my mother came to me or not. If she did, I did not want her.'[18]

His mother alienated him further by lumping all his intimate playmates together under the heading of 'street-boys'. His sympathy with his mother's social attitudes (a superficial but nevertheless real sympathy) shows a deep division of feeling. The different levels of feeling in him could not communicate or influence each other. This is well shown in his attitude to religious teaching. He must be one of the youngest of the innumerable Victorian rebels against the Protestant ethic and the Protestant Sunday. But he did not, until much later, actually disbelieve the religious teaching he received. Thus he can say, casually and without undue emphasis, speaking as if of an accepted and well-known fact:

> they [his mother's relations] stirred my imagination in a way my father's so much more approachable people quite failed to do. Even the fact that some of them were Roman Catholics appeared to me romantic: it was romantic, for instance, to know they were going to hell.[19]

The word *know* here is deeply significant, and reminds us of Hudson's early acceptance of the gentler religious teaching of his mother, accepted like a mathematical formula. In the case of what we *know*, pleasantness or unpleasantness has nothing to do with the case. I know that if I bang my head hard against the wall, I shall injure it, but I shall not injure the wall. To wish that the opposite were true would simply be absurd. But one might combine this realism with a dream-world in which walls parted like magic casements at a touch. Reid was an extreme, but to some extent also a typical, case of many subjects of Protestant upbringing, in regarding the doctrines taught as so many very disagreeable but unquestionable facts.

[18] Ibid., p.30.
[19] Ibid., p.41.

This separation between the public and the private world continued, and even grew deeper, when he was old enough to feel the influence of a prurient adolescent friend. An English boy—ironically his mother's choice to be made his friend—told him how one of his girl cousins had stripped by his bedside in the early morning, and followed this story with a minute explanation of sexual phenomena. Reid says:

> I had heard it all before, though now for some reason I felt impelled to declare that I didn't believe a word of it.[20]

We have little difficulty in understanding what the 'some reason' was when a few pages later we read of his recurrent dream of a deserted garden where he was waiting for someone who had never failed to meet him, 'who was infinitely dearer to me than any friend I had on earth'. The sense of perfect and innocent communion with this beautiful boy, effortlessly attained whenever the dream recurred, naturally caused the rejection of the real boy, so much less pure and so much less satisfying. Once again, as in early childhood, the real failed to match the imagined. But there is also a new element, of which Reid does not choose to speak directly. The real boy was making an appeal to that shared sense of crude masculinity which many sensitive spirits have found boring or oppressive or intolerable, at school, in barrack rooms and at work. The imagined boy was the object of desire; and, though the dream experience was entirely chaste, its potentially homosexual character is plain.

The time came when a real boy, Alan, partly took the place of the imagined one. He half desired to introduce Alan into his dream-world, because his sense of its real existence was strong enough to allow a half-belief that another could enter it. Alan was a dare-devil seeking out dangerous ledges and reckless adventures. Soon he proposed a raid on an empty house. When they found nothing of special interest on the ground floor, Alan suggested going upstairs: 'I didn't want to go upstairs: I never wanted anything less.' But he followed, and was rewarded with the horror of seeing a human foot protruding from under a bed. It turned out to be only an empty boot. An altercation about the legitimacy of stealing follows, and Reid is left with a disillusioned sense of the complete separation between the real friend, now rejected, and the ideal dream one.

All I felt now was an obscure unhappiness—a sense of loss, though I

---

[20] Ibid., p.65.

did not know what I had lost, for surely I could never really have confused my dream-boy with this other boy.[21]

We may prefer to put it rather differently. What he had really hoped
for was that the real boy would prove to be the fulfilment of a prophecy
made in the dream; and so, both his solitude and his emotional dependence on the dream would have been relieved. The two never met again.
And, though he was becoming bookish, literature gave him little help in
closing the gap between the ideal and the real. *Paradise Lost* he found
dull, and his enthusiasm was reserved for works that try to preserve the
childhood paradise intact.

The remainder of the book, which takes the story into the early stages
of his adult life, is reminiscent of a person balancing on a see-saw he can
only half control. Not only is the process of growing up inevitable, but
for an intelligent boy who is an avid reader, the maturing of literary taste
is almost inevitable. But it is possible to regret this, and Reid does. Miss
Corelli's *Ardath*, by which he was 'rapt into the seventh heaven of
romantic poetry',[22] left a memory which causes him to be petulantly dis-
satisfied with the literary pleasure (strong enough, no doubt, in its own
way) later afforded by Henry James and Flaubert. But he casually admits,
without giving a reason, that he has never re-read *Ardath*. Here was a
glittering part of his childhood paradise which he could recapture just by
stretching out his hand. But he will not take the risk of doing so; because
he is too sensible not to know that he would find it cheap and embarrassing. Instead, he indulges in a defiant gesture of loyalty not so much to
the book as to what it once had the power to do for him:

> It filled my mind with beauty. A barbaric, apocalyptic beauty I dare
> say—streaked with lust and blood and flaming strident colours—but
> still beauty.[23]

A little later, perhaps without being aware of it, he explains why he
would not trust himself to re-read *Ardath*:

> Through all beauty there sounded for me a note of sadness. Though
> I loved it, it made me sad. If I wanted to dance and be happy I had to
> turn to games . . . but beauty invariably awoke in me that old endless
> home-sickness, that old longing for a heaven that was not heaven, for

[21] Ibid., p.114.
[22] Ibid., p.181.
[23] Ibid., p.183.

an earth that was not earth, for a love that I knew I should never find either in heaven or on earth.[24]

In fact, unattainability was the necessary condition for the persistence of the magic. No doubt he would have felt more secure if all copies of *Ardath* could have been mysterious removed from the world. As the story reaches late adolescent and early adult years the struggle between dream and realism continues in a curious Fabian manner, with both sides avoiding a pitched battle. Thus when he tried to write a masterpiece describing his visions, he had only to re-read his first chapter to convince himself that his 'fairy-gold was trash'. After what has gone before, the bluntness of this comes as a distinct surprise. But he is still prepared to say that his longing for the visible appearing of the gods of the Greek pantheon 'very nearly came true'. The phrase is mere bravado, since no precise meaning can be attached to it.

I *knew* that the green woodland before me was going to split asunder, to swing back on either side like two great painted doors . . . And then —then I hesitated, blundered, drew back, failed. The moment passed, was gone, and at first gradually, and then rapidly, I felt the world I had so nearly reached slipping from me, till at last there was all around me only a pleasant summer scene.[25]

Just as some have believed that their failures at roulette were due to lack of invincible will to win, Reid believes, or at least says, that the failure to summon Pan was his own; the magic was not quite strong enough. And yet, as we read, we know very well that we are dealing with a sensible man, who is being obstinate, but is not really deceiving himself.

Reid gives the charm of the childhood paradise with unusual directness and force, and hence the interest of his book. But it is in the end a strictly limited interest. And this is because he is only writing about a temperament; indeed he is hardly aware that anything other than temperament and external circumstance form human life. Fortunately we have what scientists call a control. C.S. Lewis in *Surprised by Joy*[26] reveals an early romanticism which is almost indistinguishable from Reid's. But he came to understand it differently, and used it for purposes of which Reid did not dream. Furthermore, since Lewis had no leaning at any time to

---

[24] Ibid., p.190.
[25] Ibid., p.213. My italics.
[26] Discussed below—Chap. IX.

homosexual feelings, we are enabled to identify this element in Reid's vision as accidental, not central. At the most, perhaps, this element in Reid's temperament made his determination to revert to the childhood dream, when he had really outgrown it, more intractable than Lewis's was; so it may have helped to make his domination by his romantic temperament more complete. Lewis was able to find a friend who could partly share his vision, and this in the end would help him to grow beyond it. For Reid the real friend would remain a useless travesty of the imaginary one.

(iii)   *Reconciliation: Edwin Muir*

Edwin Muir's *Autobiography*[27] shows us at once that he he had certain advantages in the task of reconcilition in which Hudson may be said to have failed, and which Reid did not know how to attempt. Born in the Orkneys in 1887, he experienced an archaic civilization there, so that the contrast which everyone feels between childhood and adult years involved for him a real contrast of civilizations. Also, without at that time leaving the Orkneys, his family moved to a new place at a moment which marked off his earliest memories sharply in a single setting. His own sense of time standing still, of each day being in a way identical with every other, was nourished by a growing awareness of a way of life immemorially old:

> Not a tree anywhere. There were only two things that rose from these low, rounded islands; a high, top-heavy castle . . . standing by itself with the insane look of the tall, narrow houses in flat, wide landscapes, and . . . a black chapel with a round, pointed tower, where St Magnus had been murdered in the twelfth century.[28]

From the first, then, the images of religious and secular history are associated with a troubled past. Nor is there anything ideal about the images of the present. One of the first people outside the family he meets is a General, shooting birds, who gave him sixpence. But he was a bad landlord who drove the family out by his exactions. And soon we meet Muir's cousin, Sutherland, who is the father of many illegitimate children, of whom Muir's father said: 'Why the man canna look at a woman,

[27] Published 1940, revised ed. 1954. My references are to Methuen paperback ed. 1964.
[28] Muir, op. cit., pp.15–16.

it seems, without putting her in the family way!' It is interesting that Muir should have remembered these words, which he did not understand, until the time when he did understand them. The lore acquired from his father's stories included the press-gang in the Napoleonic wars, keelhauling and stories of witches and devils.

Thus Muir's childhood dream was like Hudson's and unlike Reid's in a certain realism. However inspiring the vision it was interpenetrated with ordinariness, with pain, fear and human error. But it was unlike Hudson's in being constructed out of the actual life of the society and the family in which he lived, and not from a wild alternative to it. And so, even when the way of life had disappeared from the world, it could retain in memory a perfect solidity. To recall it was not to attempt to escape the present.

It was in this setting, humdrum and familiar no doubt to his elders, that Muir had his experience of the timeless:

> I was lying in some room watching a beam of slanting light in which dusty, bright motes slowly danced and turned, while a low murmuring went on somewhere, possibly the humming of flies . . . The memory has a different quality from any other memory in my life. It was as if, while I lay watching that beam of light, time had not yet begun.[29]

Soon, this experience widened to include parents and siblings: 'they had always been there and I with them, since I could not account for myself'.[30]

And he speaks of being 'not in time (for time still sat on the wrist of each day with its wings folded), but in a vast, boundless calm'.

There can be little doubt that this sensation of timelessness was an experience very unusual both in its intensity and permanence, fostered, though probably not caused, by the old society of the Orkneys. But Muir is inclined to generalize from it, and attribute something similar to the early years of everyone. Though unable to accept this as literally true, we may feel it as part of the sanity and attractiveness of Muir's self-portrait. He was reluctant to see himself as specially gifted. His powerful sense, so well communicated to the reader, of the monumental remoteness of the social world of his childhood is balanced by a genuine unawareness of his own rare vision. By painting in a clear light what he saw he reveals what he was; and at times he seems to do so directly without awareness, like a man passing on a folded message.

[29] Ibid., p.18.
[30] Ibid., p.25.

At the very end of the book, after recounting many bitter times in Glasgow or Prague, he reverts to the scenes of childhood and says:

> I think that if any of us examines his life, he will find that most good has come to him from a few loyalties, and a few discoveries made many generations before he was born, which must always be made anew . . . we receive it from the past, on which we draw with every breath, but also—and this is a point of faith—from the Source of the mystery itself, by the means which religious people call Grace.[31]

The harmony between the beginning and the end of the story may seem effortless. Objectively, though, there have been great changes. He had experienced an early religious conversion in Kirkwall, which he calls 'equivocal', he had become a socialist in Glasgow in his twenties under the influence of Blachford, he had found his life restored in his thirties by a happy marriage, and then had come to believe in immortality, then years later had discovered that for years he had been a Christian without knowing it. Through watching the spontaneity and self-forgetfulness of Catholic life in Italy, he 'discovered . . . that Christ had walked on earth'.[32] All this has involved a vigorous rejection of an important apect of his upbringing, its Protestantism which he found mawkish and unreal in its devotion, narrow, bitter and divisive in its social effect.

There is a whole literature describing reaction against these aspects of Protestantism, some examples of which are to be found in this book. But Muir does not really belong with the others. A history, which, judged by its events and decisions, seems full of sudden changes of direction on fundamental matters, is experienced both by narrator and reader more as a fulfilment. The bitter Protestant temper surrounding his childhood seems no more harmful than the earth surrounding a nutritious vegetable when it is taken from the ground. It will wash off.

It is the same with the early horror induced by watching spiders. Though troubled by dreams of them, he finds the lasting effect of impressions of horror and fear strengthening. They widen the early vision of life so that the shock of later disillusionments is less. And he is helped in mastering panic fears by the variety of their sources. Those that come from books or from his own imagination are balanced by others that derive from practical matters, and can therefore be shared by adults and (often) conquered by their help. When a herd of cows charge in panic aggressively against a

[31] Ibid., p.281.
[32] Ibid., p.280.

strange cow newly introduced into the field, he is comforted when his father and the farmer 'philosophically discussed the incident as two anthropologists might discuss the customs of strange tribes'.[33] Anything which is intelligible becomes less terrifying, and so he is gradually able to overcome fears that he cannot explain or share with adults, such as one induced by a story of a murderer hidden in a sack. It was, indeed, in many ways, an unhappy childhood. He is troubled by irrational guilt about having touched a sack of sheep dip after being forbidden. The interesting thing about this is that he seems certain that he had not in fact touched it. So the fear that he had is part of a general fear of loss of memory and all sanity. At this point the extreme solidity of the world of childhood memory and the timeless quality is challenged by something opposite and potentially destructive of it, a dissolution of all common-sense certainty about familiar things.

He explains the conflict thus:

> Children live in two worlds: in their own and that of grown-up people. What they do in their own world seems natural to them; but in the grown-up world it may be an incomprehensible yet deadly sin. A child has to believe things before he can prove them, often before he can understand them; it is his way of learning about the world, and the only way. Accordingly he can believe that he is sinning without feeling that he is sinning; but the sin, accepted at first on trust and made plausible by make-believe, may later take on an imaginative reality, and guilt may fall upon him from an empty sky.[34]

This experience came at the age of seven; and it is interesting that he is inclined to connect it with the mysterious unknown world of sex. It is as if he is anticipating adolescent experiences. When he emerges from this cloud of guilt, 'the world my eyes saw was a different world from my first childish one, which never returned again'. One can easily imagine that the brevity of his experience of the first childhood world, coupled with the accident of being early removed from its scene, endowed it with a persistent intensity in later memory. Muir's childhood is at once the shortest and the most dominant of all those known to me in the literature of autobiography.

When his father is forced to take a bad farm in place of the good one he had had in Edwin's early childhood:

33 Ibid., p.24.
34 Ibid., p.35.

I had lost my first clear vision of the world, and reached the stage when a child tries desperately to see things as his elders see them, and hopes to grow up by pretending to grow up . . . Under that compulsion I could not see things with my own eyes . . . I eagerly falsified them, knowing that the falsification was expected by every one.[35]

The remainder of the book has great interest in its own way, and considerable variety. But for our present concern, the relation of later experience to childhood memory, all the later scenes tend to merge, until we come to the last. Whether he is having a vision of men as dressed animals, or viewing the dead body of his brother, or witnessing the Communist terror in Prague, or undergoing temporary and, as he came to think, false, religious or political conversions, his busy, active life is that of a sleep-walker. And he is a sleep-walker who dreams of waking—of waking into a restored adult version of the childhood dream, or rather of the childhood reality. Sometimes he comes near to waking, as when he looks on the dead face of his brother:

It was a deep, momentary impression, filling me with dread and peace, a peace too annihilating to be held and accepted. *My heart locked and bolted itself against that perfection.*[36]

He must press on, he must work, he must suffer. But the childhood world is still with him, present but inaccessible, or accessible only in special moments like this. Instead of feeling, as Reid did, that adult reality must be rejected because it falsified the childhood dream, Muir feels something easily mistaken for the same thing, but really opposite. He feels that his childhood experience brought him into touch with an underlying reality which is invisibly present always, for all adults as well as children. The way to recovery of it is not through denying the present and hankering after past glories, but through piercing a film of unreality. At the end in Rome he is able to do this. So there is no regression and no nostalgia. His first and last worlds are identical in the way the acorn and the oak are, which do not look alike.

(iv)   *Paradise Shared: Eleanor Farjeon*

We have seen that solitude may be purely subjective, something in the mind of one child, who might appear to a parent or onlooker to be constantly in

[35] Ibid., p.66.
[36] Ibid., p.103. My italics.

the midst of a crowd of children, or solemnly attending to the conversation of adults. Eleanor Farjeon's book[37] introduces us to the idea of a
shared solitude, in which a group of children—four in this case—create a
world separate from that of adults with its own rules, with a powerful
sense of authority, and with a strange persistence which can enable it to
last into adult life. Whereas the private paradise of the solitary child is
often fostered by a strongly ordered traditional society, like Muir's Orkneys, the Farjeon parents unwittingly helped to create a group paradise
by abdicating authority. They were good-natured, happy-go-lucky,
extravagant artistic people, connected with the stage. They were indulgent and affectionate, but careless parents. Where the solitary child may
seek to escape from a world of adult order felt to be too rigorous and
exacting, the Farjeon children found that their parents' world was not
exacting enough. They were uneasily aware of a void where parental
authority should have been; and they set out to create for themslves, in
mute reproach for parental spoiling and inattention, the satisfying structure of authority. They were disturbed by the impusive, Peter Pan-like
quality of a father who could buy enough fish for twenty or thirty families because it was 'so cheap'. Significantly, this episode, which in
another book might have been only an amusing minor item, appears in a
solemn preliminary epigraph, under the heading *A Note on My Father*.

The children felt the need to compensate for this unpredictable irres-
ponsibility by endowing the elder brother with the authority the father
would not exercise. But as, after all, they were still children this authority extended only to a world of games and dreams. The author was the
second of a family in which the first, third and fourth child were boys.
She thus becomes a kind of maternal adjutant to the authority of Harry,
the elder boy, over the younger ones. They all had an obscure intuition
that their paradise of games and secrets had to be earned by discipline and
obedience. As the parents did not make them obey, they would make
themselves obey. And unlike many Victorian parents, Harry obeyed his
own precepts and was as stern a critic of himself as of his siblings. The
paradise was hedged in with prohibitions which had a distinctly superstitious character. The children turned rules they had made themselves, or
which Harry had made for them, into idols, to offend whom would produce sensations of guilt. But the rules, which may not be broken, may be
evaded:

[37] Eleanor Farjeon, *A Nursery in the Nineties*, 1935.

Any Person making a statement doubted by any Other Person can be challenged by the Other Person to repeat the Statement, followed immediately by three taps with the Right Forefinger on the Doubter's Left Shoulder, during which process the Tapper shall say: 'One! Two! Three!' . . . Anyone employing this Formula correctly for a False Purpose will lose the Confidence of the Nursery for ever.

Nobody ever did. But the complicated procedure, which must be carried out exactly, admitted of infinite misapplications which, if committed by the Tapper and unnoted by the Tappee, provided routes of escape for a good round Lie. *If you could get away with it*, you could not be brought to justice.[38]

I once heard an eminent Oxford law don, chuckling over the Law Report in *The Times*, which told how the Court of Appeal had quashed a conviction for theft on a technicality. He kept repeating: 'Very bad justice—but [with enormous emphasis] *very good law.*' We may feel that the Farjeon children were precocious in the grasp of the ways of the world.

But, if we look at the matter with a wider view, we shall find something more interesting. The general tendency of English education before 1914 was to stress parental authority, obedience, rule and law, and to despise, distrust or altogether forget the aesthetic, the imaginative and the visual. In a certain kind of child, like Ruskin or Forrest Reid, this education set up a lifelong thirst for visual beauty and imaginative experience. This pattern, of parents laying down rules, and the children thirsting for visions, is so persistent in the autobiographies of the nineteenth century that one can easily make the mistake of supposing that it is in the nature of adults to be legalistic and of children to be shyly imaginative. What the Farjeon example shows is that children have a natural tendency to compensate for any one-sidedness in their upbringing. Human nature requires rule, restraint, authority, and also freedom, independence, beauty and fantasy. There is in every child a strong tendency to unconscious protest against an error in the proportions.

In the Farjeon family this tendency was so strong that it easily outlived the years of childhood, and resulted in an unusual degree of solidarity between the siblings as adults with separate lives and responsibilities. When only Eleanor and one brother survived, they felt that they were carying on the tradition of the childhood game for the two who were dead. And Eleanor felt the same when she alone survived. Fascinating as

---

[38] Eleanor Farjeon, op. cit, OUP ed. 1980, pp.298–9.

this is as a case-history, it is also a limiting factor for the book as auto-biography. The childhood game remained a bond and a haunting memory. But it was hardly formative, as Hudson's and Muir's childhood experience was; and we really learn very little about Eleanor as an adult. So, without being a great autobiography, the book remains a very instructive case, which helps us to see other accounts of childhood in sharper outline.

(v) *Paradise to Order: Christopher Milne*

The books discussed in this chapter have stressed the child's inner imaginative separation from parents. Even if, as for Muir, the paradisal world consists of a living adult culture of which parents are part, the child's perception of this remains secret, shyly incommunicable and unguessed by adults. Even if, as for Eleanor Farjeon, the childhood dream is a shared experience, it still depends for its essential quality on the exclusion of parents. Christopher Milne's book[39] shows us the opposite case—probably a very rare one. It shows us what may happen if the child is confronted, before the age when he is likely to invent any coherent imaginings of his own, with a regular, literary childhood dream invented by his father, and when his own childish privacies are invaded by a public curious about the family sources of his father's well-known books. The father was A.A. Milne, one of the most successful of all writers for and about children. The child endured from the dawn of memory the strain of being a public figure. No attempt was made to disguise his identity. His real name became part of the fiction. His actual nursery toys became imagined familiar friends to thousands of contemporary children. The landscapes described were those among which he lived. There was a curious interplay of paternal and filial inventiveness:

This bridge still stands and still looks much as it did when Shepard came there to draw it: it is Poohsticks Bridge.

It is difficult to be sure which came first. Did I do something and did my father than write a story around it? Or was it the other way about, and did the story come first? Certainly my father was on the look-out for ideas; but so too was I. He wanted ideas for his stories, I wanted them for my games, and each looked towards the other for

[39] Christopher Milne, *The Enchanted Places*, 1974.

inspiration. But in the end it was all the same: the stories became a part of our lives; we lived them, thought them, spoke them.[40]

The imaginative process was pre-empted. Privacy was invaded. He was an only child with few friends. The weight of the father's powerful myth was bound to be felt as oppressive.

But not quite in the way one might expect. Most readers, I imagine, open Milne's book, as I did, expecting a protest at being sentimentalized, turned into a pattern child, and arrested in time, caught forever in the transient years when nursery toys seem important. Milne perhaps partly feels this, and certainly feels that this is what we may expect. But his main complaint is different.

He quotes with some bitterness his father's *Preface to Parents*, written for an edition of his verses:

In real life very young children have an artless beauty, an innocent grace, an unstudied abandon of movement, which, taken together, make an appeal to our emotions similar in kind to that made by other young and artless creatures... Heaven... does really appear to lie about the child in its infancy... But... there is a natural lack of moral quality, which expresses itself, as Nature always insists on expressing herself, in an egotism entirely ruthless... The mother of a little boy of three has disappeared, and is never seen again. The child's reaction to the total loss of his mother is given in these lines:

James James
Morrison Morrison
(Commonly known as Jim)
Told his
Other relations
Not to go blaming *him*.

And that is all. It is the truth about a child; children are, indeed, as heartless as that.[41]

The son leaps into the attack, with the pent-up fury of one who has been basely misrepresented for fifty years:

Is it? Are they? Was I? I cannot pretend to know for sure how I felt about anything at the age of three. I can only guess that though I might

[40] Milne, op. cit., Penguin ed. 1976, p.72.
[41] Ibid., pp.40–1.

not have missed my mother had she disappeared, and would certainly not have missed my father, I would have missed Nanny—most desolately.

Then, in an interesting passage, he goes on to deny that the obsessive concern with woolly toys is wholly egotistical. He maintains, fairly enough, that the child sees in his own relation with the toy animal an image by which he can comprehend his parent's or nurse's relation to him. And he continues with this severe rebuke to his erring father:

Undoubtedly children can be selfish, but so, too, can adults. By accusing the young of heartless egotism are we perhaps subconsciously reassuring ourselves that, selfish though we may still be, there was once a time when we were worse.

Warming to his work, he takes up his father's quotation from Wordsworth's Immortality Ode. He points out that while Wordsworth means to say that the child really is near to heaven, his father means that this is how it appears to the onlooker, with the implication that the onlooker is deceived. When he read the whole poem, 'it awakened an echo in my heart'. Asked to choose between the two views of childhood, he is for Wordsworth.

It is significant that both father and son should quote Wordsworth, but should mean opposite things by quoting the same words. For behind the artificial paradise of his father's book, another seemed to be lurking, almost but not quite blotted out by the first. With a symbolic appropriateness—it is impossible to say whether this is consciously designed by the adult writer or not—he comes nearest to it when one of the nursery toys has been lost:

We went back and searched and searched, but in vain. Opposite the orchard were the fields and woods we visited on our flower picking expeditions. This wood for primroses, the ash plantations for orchids, the larger wood beyond for bluebells . . . Nanny and I would gather whole basketfulls. And it was here—more especially than anywhere else—I would find that splendour in the grass, that glory in the flower, that today I find no more.[42]

Quoting Wordsworth, he seems to have wrested him from his dead father's grasp. And it is significant that Nanny was his companion. The

---

[42] Ibid., p.74.

preference felt for Nanny over parents was a common problem of the upper and middle classes in those years. Usually, though, its causes were different. It arose from the comparative neglect of children shown by busy or pleasure-loving parents who could afford to pay others to take their place. But the Milne father was nearly always at home, and took an interest at once obsessively personal, professional and lucrative, in the child's thoughts and feelings. The preference for Nanny was not a reaction to neglect but a plea for privacy. With her he could be himself and invent a mythology of which his father would be ignorant, or just experience something too simple and intangible to be put into words. And the raw material of this was the very same landscape that served also as material for the official mythology of his father's books. One could not ask for a finer tribute to the imaginative resourcefulness of childhood or to the unlimited plasticity of simple experience.

(vi)   *Emotion Recollected in Cynicism: Lord Berners*

Every autobiographer of any merit tries in some way to detach himself from the pressure of experience in order to reflect, to form events into a pattern, to discriminate the important from the trivial, to interpret, to judge. But those considered so far in this chapter have all been convinced that their childhood provided them with a key to the understanding of their adult life; and there has often been the unspoken assumption that no adult experience could be so crucially formative as earlier ones. Berners[43] is an exception to all this. While his memories of childhood are conveyed with a vividness equal to that attained by most of the others, he does not stress continuity. He treats childhood as another country where they do things differently. He does not appear to ask himself the question, 'How did all that make me what I am now?' Indeed, he shows little interest in his present state, which we are left to infer from his literary tone, from his selection of incidents from childhood, and from his method of judging his childish self.

If we look at his sequel, an account of life at Eton,[44] which is much less interesting, we shall find him evasive about the kind of man he was becoming. In *First Childhood* he is not evasive, but he is detached and satirical. His aim, very successfully carried out on the whole, is first to

[43] Lord Berners, *First Childhood*, Constable, 1934.
[44] Lord Berners, *A Distant Prospect*, Constable, 1945.

recreate childhood experience and then to assess its significance as an intelligent adult onlooker, privileged to know the child's hidden feelings, might have judged it.

Thus, when he describes how he attempted to use a magic wand to turn his cousin Emily into a toad, he ends his account by quietly conveying his adult sense of the credulity and egoism of childhood in these words: 'This unfortunate experiment . . . convinced me that I had no real aptitude for magic.'[45]

When he was puzzled at the mysterious ways of adults, he interprets back with his adult knowledge, showing how his father gave evidence that he had married his mother for her money. Then he offers us a combination of the remembered words which provided the clue and the later knowledge of life which enabled him to understand them. Or he gives a literary gloss, derived from later reading, on the billiard room:

In the daytime, under the melancholy skylight, there was something peculiarly depressing about that empty expanse of green cloth and those green shades which seemed to annihilate even the greenest of thoughts.[46]

The use made of Marvell's garden is characteristic. To transpose a piece of profound poetry into a wry joke fits his general defensiveness, his knowingness, his unwillingness to be caught, to be carried away, to be guilty of overmuch enthusiasm. All this is seen most clearly in his account of an episode, which can only have been at the time unintelligible and perhaps disturbing as well.

He tells of the visit of Vivian Pratt, 'distantly related to a ducal family'. 'It was said of him that he had odd mannerisms, that he was effeminate, and there criticism ceased.'[47] He moved with an undulating gait and had a mincingly ingratiating voice. He used to annoy Berners' mother by calling her 'Dear Lady'.

I gathered that my father did not care very much for Mr Pratt, and certainly his behaviour, when Mr Pratt was present, and his comments after he had left, seemed to suggest that he understood him better than my mother appeared to do. I remember one day Mr Pratt saying, 'I often think that the best things in life are behind us.' My mother was

[45] Lord Berners, *First Childhood*, p.35.
[46] Ibid., p.59.
[47] Ibid., p.100.

inclined to agree with this sentiment and was a little puzzled when my father broke into a malignant guffaw of laughter, which *seemed hardly justified by the innocent nature of the remark.*[48]

There must really have been three stages, the first where the child was surprised at an 'innocent' remark receiving such a response, the second when gradually or suddenly he came to understand his father's coarse merriment, and a third when he sat down to recreate the memory when he was about fifty years of age, and wrote the passage quoted. It is highly characteristic of his method that he ignores the second stage altogether, gives us no clue to its nature, or to the age when it occurred. Was he alone or with other boys? Was he shocked, or triumphant, or merely curious? Did it affect his view of his father? There is no suspicion of an answer to these or any other questions that might be asked.

The reason for the gap is plain. *Nil admirari* is his watchword. He cultivates an Augustan sensibility, a bland acceptance of human nature as it is. He believes himself to be approaching childhood in the spirit of scientific enquiry; and naturally, he is more at home with the direct and simple childish ways of apprehending experience than with the conflicts and intensities of adolescence.

Yet in a way he seems to be deceiving himself. If he had been a real Augustan he would not have written the book at all. 'I lisped in numbers for the numbers came' writes Pope, thinking it worthwhile to tell us this because it will help us to understand his adult poetic achievement. But he tells us nothing of his childhood games or dreams (if any). To write a book entitled *First Childhood* is to place yourself firmly in a post-romantic literary milieu. The detachment is secondary, the Augustanism acquired, and, perhaps, weaker than the author would like to think. And he did really have the childhood dream which places him in this chapter, though he lost little time in feeling ashamed of it:

One morning, during an arithmetic lesson, at his first school there rose up in my mind's eye so vivid a picture of a certain hedgerow at Althrey where, about the same time last year, a golden-crested wren had built its nest, that I burst into tears. I found it impossible to explain what had really upset me, and so I complained of feeling queer in the stomach.[49]

[48] Ibid., p.102. My italics.
[49] Ibid., p.140.

With airy adult dismissiveness, he describes the dose of castor oil he was given as 'as good a cure as any other for sentimental visions of this kind.' But the wren, and the little boy weeping as he remembers it, are more vivid to the reader by far than the clubman's comment: perhaps to the writer too, or he might not have wished to write at all.

And though Berners himself does not tell us how his childhood experience formed him as an adult, he leaves us clues, perhaps without realizing that he does so. He strikes us as a man who is above all afraid of appearing naive, of failing in worldly poise; and the source of this character, in part, is to be found in his desperate attempts to conform to the premature sophistication and herd mentality of the prep school. It is entirely typical that he felt the need to conform to the schoolboy code by blaming the informer against a bully, though he himself was the chief victim of bullying. He had to conceal his dreamy character, his tender sensitiveness. More than forty years later he reveals it, but shyly, with an embarrassed upper-class good-taste, mingled with satire. But he does not succeed in concealing the fact that it is lurking there still.

V
The Child at Home

For him it was impossible to do right but in a spirit of defiance; and the first condition of his progress in learning, was the power to forget.

(Ruskin, *Modern Painters*, III, 1856. Part IV, Chap. XVIII)

(i) The Dominant Father: Victor Gollancz

Autobiography has a tendency to be impressionistic, and somewhat form-less, since a person's idea of himself lacks the clearness of outline that we tend to attribute (wrongly, no doubt) to the external world and to the characters of others. Even at the simplest level it is hard to look in the glass and obtain a clear idea of one's own appearance. Strongly analytical autobiographies are the exception. Occasionally, though, we encounter an autobiographer, like Newman or Mill, whose analytical powers are as strong as his emotions, and as clear as his memories. Gollancz is one of these. The characteristic of his work is that everything is intelligible. He defines himself at every point by reference to his parents and his upbringing.

The upbringing combined exact adherence to Mosaic law with the ordinary English patriotism of gentile homes. And, as in some such homes, perhaps actually though, a minority, the father was completely dominant over the mother. So Gollancz sees all his future life and history in terms of a conflict between law and liberty, coupled with, and partly cutting across, another conflict between reason and emotion:

> *Emotionally* my opposition to physical compulsion of any kind, from concentration camps at one end of the scale to passports and direction of labour at the other, has always been quite undiscriminating. I detest prisons and conscription (especially conscription) and party whips and drilling and saluting and ticket-collecting and barriers at railway stations and a hundred and one other things that you can supply for yourself: and I react to policemen, not as to the necessary custodians, and in the main very kindly ones, of a peaceful way of life, which is what my reason tells me that they are, but as to the impudent symbols of an alien authority.[1]

We are dealing here, not only with a highly emotional man, but with a first-rate academic mind; and we can admire the precision and the humour with which the examples are chosen both to express and to laugh at his own uncompromising confusion between legitimate administration and the extremes of tyranny. The effect is as precise as Pope's line for expressing moral confusion: 'Puffs, powders, patches, Bibles, billets-doux.' And he is just as clear about the sources of all this:

a passion for liberty in every possible meaning of the word . . . liberty

---

[1] Victor Gollancz, *My Dear Timothy*, Gollancz, 1952, p.107.

for myself every bit as much as for every other living thing and for every other living things every bit as much as for myself. This passion, clearly always latent in me, came blazing up, I think, as a reaction to two particular manifestations of the mental climate of our home: namely, my father's attitude to my sisters, and his religious orthodoxy.[2]

And he speaks of the ban on any travel on the Sabbath (except on foot) as 'one of the things that made me detest orthodox Judaism almost as soon as I was born'.[3] This must be an exaggeration, and one is aware of the academic mind, finely-tempered by the classical education and respect for evidence, smiling at the emotions which cause him so to exaggerate.

If we tend, loosely enough, to characterize people as 'intellectual' or 'emotional', the distinction is useless here. Gollancz was so intensely emotional that he can say with obvious sincerity that ever since the age of six when he saw pictures of the battle of Balaclava, the horror of war, even though on the other side of the world, has been like a horror in the same room with him. The clash of intellect and feeling sometimes seems like that of irresistible force and immovable object—unless they could be harmonized.

As we would expect, his relation to Judaism is really much more complex than the sweeping denunciations so far quoted would indicate. We can distinguish four main elements.

Firstly the legalistic aspects of his father's religious way tended to foster a self-righteous censoriousness. He describes with some heat how his father would intone ritual prayers before eating on the Sabbath, and in the same breath with the last Hebrew word, would say in English some trivial thing about the food or a lost household article. This showed, in the son's view, that his mind had been far from his words during the recited prayer:

It was wicked of me to feel so censorious about this, but I couldn't help noticing it; and I am describing my feelings as they actually were, and not as they ought to have been.[4]

In a way, he was censuring his father for not being orthodox enough, in a spirit entirely consonant with the drift of Old Testament prophecy, which so often stresses the inner disposition of the heart as against

---

[2] Ibid., p.38.
[3] Ibid., p.35.
[4] Ibid., p.95.

mindless formalism. But, on the other hand, he was in rebellion against a system where so much was purely formal, that in the son's (perhaps jaundiced) view, it became a positive invitation to hypocrisy. This theme recurs more forcefully when he recalls the synagogue ceremonies for the Day of Atonement.

The second reaction may be seen as a subtle way of justifying the first. Like many people (Dr Johnson for instance) who combine an exceptionally strong self-will with very sensitive consciences, there was in Gollancz, as he very clearly sees, a strong tendency to over-demand, to require of himself more than others required, more than was reasonable, more than his consciously-held standards could sensibly be held to entail. Writing of schooldays at St Paul's he says:

> If . . . we had a hundred lines of Virgil to prepare for homework, this job, being compulsory, possessed no reality for me at all; I did it as something meaningless, and then went on to the real thing—an 'extra' hundred. The explanation is no doubt a guilt feeling, which has always been very strong in me, coupled with a hatred of external authority and a passion for self-direction.[5]

Very clear-sighted in finding causes, he yet perhaps omits a factor we may think significant. If one is a finely-gifted classical scholar with strong literary sensibilities, may it not be a pleasure to read another hundred lines of Virgil? It is characteristic of Gollancz that it does not occur to him to mention this, or (probably) to think of it.

This over-demand led, as he clearly sees, to a subtly-concealed kind of self-righteousness:

> I believed in 'judge not, that ye be not judged'; I believed in it genuinely and passionately, and I believed that my belief involved my whole being; but if anyone had told me that he thought the injunction was folly I should have judged him most bitterly . . . If a man was condemned to death for a particularly atrocious murder, I felt for him, lived in him, asked myself whether, given his background and circumstances, I might not have myself done the same; but if my father had said 'Serve him right' I should have burst out into furious invective, and it would never have occurred to me to ask myself whether, given my father's background and circumstances, I might not myself have said the same.[6]

5 Ibid., pp.11–12.
6 Ibid., pp.150–1.

He goes on to explain that he did not believe himself to be good, was sharply aware of some of his moral failings, but was nevertheless, 'self-righteous in my attitude to other people's self-righteousness'.

He goes on:

This is not to imply that my embryo Christian morality was merely theoretical. The essence of it, on the contrary, was precisely that it was not theoretical. Morality, I believed, must engage a man's whole life; and in one sense it engaged the whole of mine. But not in the final sense, not in the only sense that ultimately matters. I had still to learn that what finally matters is not the *about* what but the *from* what . . . that all battles are shadow battles except the battle a man fights in the innermost citadel of his own being . . . and that something must happen to him, some free acceptance of an offered grace, before this battle can be won.

These quotations are rather full; but I hope they are justified by the unusual clearness and eloquence of the language and by the exceptional importance of what is being said. He understood his own strength and weakness very well; moreover, he knew that, despite the gradual growth of deeper perceptions, he was still, as he wrote, fighting the same inner battle with varying success.

His closeness to St Paul here must have occurred to him; and no doubt he refrained from mentioning it out of modesty; also because he wished to emphasize the unique newness in each generation and each person of every experience of an age-old problem. And just as St Paul, though rejecting the Mosaic Law, also speaks of it positively as a 'schoolmaster' in preparation for the Gospel, so too does Gollancz wonder whether the tight religious system of his childhood, even though he believes his rebellion against it to be justified, may not have been the source of his own religious temperament and his own quest for Christ.

It was difficult for him, especially in fiery adolescent years, and not easy even in retrospect, to distinguish between the Judaic and the merely conventional, lower-middle class elements in the ambience of his childhood. Here, the subjection of women was a crucial and difficult case. He speaks bitterly of the treatment of women in the Synagogue. But surely there must have been Jewish families at that time in which women were actually dominant. The real source of the father's neglect of his daughters' intellectual needs may have been quite other. He may have absorbed it from the ethos of the class of small traders to which he belonged, from the *Daily Telegraph*, of which he was a constant reader. He may have been influenced adversely by the suffragette campaign. If Gollancz's admirable analysis has a fault, it is that his distinctions here are not sharp enough. For he is dealing, after all, with a topic of perennial interest, which takes innumerable forms—the confusion of high and low values. The highest values have often been used to buttress the lowest, as Hitler used his generals' respect for their oath of loyalty to disarm their opposition to genocide. But even more insidious are the times when, fortuitously, the high and low values offer for the moment identical precepts. Drunkenness is discouraged by the highest religious authorities, but also by commanding officers and sporting coaches. Marital fidelity and fecundity may be enjoined in the spirit of the Gospel or in that of Mussolini and Brezhnev. Obviously, Gollancz's father was far from being as analytical as his son, and more attention might have been given to the practical difficulty of deciding on what principle a decision (such as to deny the daughters education) was really being made, and on what principles the son was opposing it.

But to return to the essential point:

> What have I to do with it, Judaism though born of the race? . . . I grow proud of that essential glory at the heart of Judaism which, for all its fossilizations and obscurations and killings of the spirit by the letter, was nevertheless destined, through Christianity, to sow good seeds in a stony world.[7]

In writing this, he brings together his own history with general history; and not in the least because he sees himself as a man of destiny, but because he humbly finds in himself a thread of a universal pattern.

But although this was a family in which the father was dominant, the mother also is a distinct presence in the book. She was, in a timid and neurotic way, a sucker for every new idea or fashionable craze, good, bad and indifferent. Mesmerism, telepathy, Herbert Spencer, Liberal Judaism, Ibsen, Wagner and the subconscious jostled together in her hospitable mind. And just as the son defined himself largely by opposition to the father, so less obtrusively, he defined himself by likeness to the mother. She was the source, not only of his life-long 'crankiness' but of his deep fear of life. He calls her 'the most terrified creature I have ever known'. The strain imposed by these conflicting influences of father and mother on a temperament naturally over-intense must have been acute. Gollancz brilliantly uses a comparatively trivial thing, his struggle over vegetarianism, as an image of it.

[7] Ibid., p.48.

He was drawn to vegetarianism by his exacting conscience and his exceptionally keen awareness of suffering, as well as by a more rarefied intuition of the oneness of all life, akin to some oriental philosophies. He was a practising vegetarian for two or three years as a schoolboy, and then gave it up:

> I cannot remember the reasons for my apostasy. It certainly didn't spring from a desire to conform, for this was never a temptation to me; nor from a dislike of making a nuisance of myself . . . for consideration of that kind was no part, I fear, of my attitude to my parents. Nor again, I think was it then, as it surely is now, the result of moral weakness . . . it was a question, rather, of fighting. . . . a hatred of flesh-eating that had become all but compulsive. Even when I was able to eat meat again I could not cut it at first with an ordinary steel knife, for this I thought cannibalistic. I divided it painfully with the sharpest silver fish-knife I could find.[8]

This is an enigmatic passage, and I am not sure that I fully understand it. But some points are clear. The word *apostasy* indicates that one part of his mind found in this a fundamental issue. But there was a contrary impulse —not a sensual one, though he is perfectly frank throughout the book about his delight in good food—which rejected vegetarianism as life-denying, as an aspect of fear, a reflection, perhaps, of his mother's fear of life. He had to reject this, however painfully. He had to return to the main stream of life. He had to check his hypersensitiveness, his intense scrupulosity, his naiveté. (And he did—he was a very astute publisher.) Finally, there is the strangest point of all, the knife. The word *cannibalistic* seems totally meaningless at first sight; and in a less exact user of words one would be inclined to dismiss it as a mere muddle. But what he seems to be feeling towards is the idea of animal sacrifice—his early years will have been steeped in accounts of it. The steel knife may have represented to him the mere animal urge to eat another animal; the silver knife a conscious moral action of which the Old Testament sacrifices of bulls and goats were a type. But by eating meat he was giving up something, as in a pagan or Judaic animal sacrifice. What was he giving up? He was giving up both his eccentricity and his pharasaical moral superiority. And yet, in part he is doing so unwillingly; and he is troubled by the fact that the sacrifice works at a low, sensual level to his advantage. Without it he could not have been the gourmet he was. The mysteriousness of all this

34 Ibid., p.53.

is all the more impressive for the contrast with the general lucidity of his tone and his distinguished command of language. Even if we are not sure we understand we feel we are near the heart of him here.

(ii)   *The Dominant 'Mother': Augustus Hare*

Augustus Hare's 'mother' was not a mother but an aunt. His real mother handed him over to his unmarried aunt, 'more perfunctorily', as Walter de la Mare put it, 'than if he had been the least promising of a litter of pedigree puppies'.[9] He always uses the word *mother* for this aunt and Italima for his mother in the flesh, and I shall use the forms that he did. His sense of rejection by Italima and his father was strong from the first. He calls himself:

> a most unwelcome addition to the population of this troublesome world, as both my father and Mrs Hare were greatly annoyed at the birth of another child, and beyond measure disgusted that it was another son.[10]

This was in 1834, and one can sense the child's bitterness in the tone of the sixty-year-old writer. So his maleness very early received a double blow from which it never recovered. He was first rejected for being a boy, and then smothered with obsessive feminine interest. He clearly understands in his own way, though he does not say, that it was to be expected that he would grow up effeminate and homosexual.

But though the mother made him the centre of her life, she was not indulgent all the time. She had a stern side; and here we have the key to Hare's extraordinary ambivalence about her. On the one hand, she was the one who saved him from being despised and unwanted. On the other, she was a stern, unyielding mother, in some ways like what Mrs Ruskin might have been if she had been widowed early and had had to bring John up alone. And behind this clear opposition is a shadowy third term, pervasive but unspoken, without which the reader can hardly make sense of the story; her suffocating love turned him into what he was, a tame spare man, treated like a convenient piece of furniture by innumerable hostesses at endless house-parties, who could always be relied upon to wind the wool or draw the curtains while ladies talked over tea, and

[9] Walter de la Mare, op. cit., p.239.
[10] Augustus Hare, *The Story of My Life*, 6 vols, 1896–1900, George Allen, I, p.42.

men were out hunting or shooting. He is ambivalent about this too. He is vain that he knew 'everybody'—he was related by blood to an incredibly large number of the sort of people who gave house-parties—he was 'dear Augustus' to innumerable dowagers, and yet he resents his status as a domestic pet, a well-bred tomcat that had been 'fixed'. And inwardly he blamed his mother for all this.

He was precocious, especially in his thoughts about religion and in his rebellion against the system imposed, again very similar to that prevailing in the Ruskin household. And, as bright children often do, he was quick to perceive the point of inconsistency in what he was taught which derived from a confusion of values between religion and respectability:

> I remember Uncle Julius going into one of his violently demonstrative furies over what he considered the folly of 'Montgomery's Poems', and his flinging the book to the other end of the room in his rage with it, and my wondering what would be done to me if I ever dared to be 'as naughty as Uncle Jule'.[II]

In this respect, despite several unusual features, his upbringing must have been typical of thousands of cases. A child would be taught that we were all sinners, but at the same time he would be given to understand something incompatible with this, that adults were always right and children, where they disagreed with adults, still more if they criticized them, always wrong. Adults were sinners in general, but never in any particular case. The eye of childhood is unerring in detecting such confusions and evasions.

The regime involved a strict timetable. The wish to be alone, to please himself, to do nothing at all, was very strongly developed, and there were punishments, often administered by the erring visitor, Uncle Julius. Sometimes, feeling and punishment to be unjust, he would determine to do 'something horrible to be whipped *for*', though his conception of the horrible was an innocent one, and meant only giving three unnecessary shrieks.

He regarded the uncle as an outsider, and a mere instrument of his mother's policy, which seems to have been true enough. His ambivalence towards his mother's tender strictness is well shown in the following:

> My dearest mother was so afraid of over-indulgence that she always went into the opposite extreme: and her constant habits of self-examination

[II] Ibid. I., p.68.

made her detect the slightest act of especial kindness into which she had been betrayed . . . Nevertheless, I loved her most passionately, and many tearful fits, for which I was severely punished as fits of naughtiness, were really caused by anguish at the thought that I had displeased her or been a trouble to her.[12]

Sternness did not inhibit the boy's love; it rather intensified it, so that he calls his parting from her when he was sent to school 'an intense agony of anguish' and can scarcely bear to think of it after fifty years. The ominous undercurrent of fierce criticism, or even hatred, which he directs at her is only partly due to her sternness, or the unpredictability which made her promise him delicious puddings, and then, when they were put on the table refuse him permission to eat them. It was a protest too, at the intolerable burden of love, not only of hers for him, but of his for her. And behind that, is the resentment of the consequent deflection of his sexual feelings on to boys. With considerable art, he places together this account of her love with the first adumbration of such feelings, which comes in contrast to his first experience of bullying at school:

Gradually I had the delight of feeling assured that Alick liked me as much as I liked him . . . Our affection made sunshine in the dreariness. My one dread was that Alick would some day like another boy better than he liked me. It happened. Then, at ten years old, life was a blank. Soon afterwards, Alick left the school, and a little later, before he was fifteen, I heard that he was dead. It was a dumb sorrow, which I could speak to no one, for no one would have understood it, not even my mother.[13]

We may be tempted to a mental substitution of the words *least of all* for *not even*.

But all this did not have the effect of making him less hungry for expressions of mother love; and he seems, like many children perhaps, to have the power of forgetting during the seemingly interminable school term, what his mother was like, so that he always had expectations that were always disappointed:

How vividly, how acutely, I recollect that—in my passionate devotion to my mother—I used, as the holidays approached, to conjure up the most

[12] Ibid., I., p.107.
[13] Ibid., I, p.172.

vivid mental pictures of my return to her, and appease my longings with the thought of how she would rush to meet me, of her ecstatic delight &c; and then how terrible was the bathos of the reality, when I drove up to the silent door . . . I often sobbed myself to sleep in a little-understood anguish—an anguish that she could not really care for me.[14]

This is especially poignant because it is plain that she did care for him very much, and what he was lamenting was a mere difference of style.

As must have been common about 1840, he turned to the older generation for a little support against the stifling negations of the one between. Grannie took in *Pickwick*, but she was careful to have her maid bolt the door before she sat down with it by the fire for fear of discovery by a shocked and accusing daughter.

When his mother died Hare was thirty-six. It would be easy to misunderstand the passage in which he tells of it:

When the sweet eyes closed and the dear face lost its shadows of colour, I kissed my own Mother for the last time and came away. The first snowflakes of winter were falling then. They do not signify now: no snow or cold can ever signify any more.

But Oh! the agony, the anguish![15]

And after a lengthy account of various details and quotation from Jeremy Taylor, he concludes: 'But yet—oh my darling! my darling!'

Comparing this with the acid portrait of the dead woman which he has been sketching for three volumes, and noting the derivative character of the prose (influenced most of all perhaps by *The Old Curiosity Shop*) we may be tempted to dismiss this as hypocrisy. This would be unfair. A crisis, especially the crisis of final loss of the beloved's presence, will often affect ambivalent feelings in this way. The positive feelings are intensified and the hostile ones for the time totally suppressed. The sense of being maimed, unmanned was uncomfortably near to the reality of the case.

Two volumes later, when the story has moved on some fifteen years, he gives us succinctly, and with a wry attempt at detachment, the consequences. He gives a brief summary of nine young men, identified only by a number to whom he 'tried to be useful'.[16]

It is a catalogue of disappointment and disillusionment on Hare's side

14 Ibid., I, p.201.
15 Ibid., III, p.404.
16 Ibid., V, p.462.

and of weakness, deception, vice and shame on the other. He ends each account with a terrible, dismissive phrase: 'No 2 was an utter collapse,' 'No 3 vanished into chaos,' 'That is the end of No 7.' Perhaps most poignant of all is No 8, who was 'excessively good-looking' and who 'openly says that, as he has gained all he can from me, he naturally prefers "those who can be more useful" to him'.

For all its immense prolixity and innumerable boring anecdotes, Hare's book remains one of the most exact in the whole history of autobiography in showing cause and effect.

(iii)   A Fluid Background: Stephen Spender

Our last two examples will have been misleading if they led anyone to suppose that rigid discipline is the cause of all troubles arising from the home. Stephen Spender was born into a family that offered him the chance to be on either side of several important boundaries. He was Jewish, but only partly:

> Having mixed blood really puts one in the position of being able to choose whether or not to think of oneself as a Jew. *One has the power, more or less, to become what one thinks.*[17]

The family was cultivated and affluent, and some members were distinguished. His father adored Lloyd George, but his uncle, the historian J.A. Spender, was an unreconstructed nineteenth-century liberal, still hankering in the 1920s, when Spender was in his teens, for the return of Asquith. His grandmother, to whom he seems to have felt the closest ties of all, used to say, 'Dear Stephen, say something quickly to shock me,'[18] but would then repeat his reply to his Asquithian uncle who 'was profoundly disturbed at his having spoken of coarse things to his grandmother'.

The grandmother seems to have been one of those dangerous people who combine a lively intelligence with a complete lack of practical sense and of understanding of human nature.

Both his parents died during his adolescence, and one of the oddest things about the book, in which he always presents himself as a budding poet of strong feeings and exquisite sensibilities, is that he is not surprised

[17] Stephen Spender, *World Within World*, Hamish Hamilton, 1951, p.14. My italics.
[18] Ibid., p.16.

at the tepidity of his response. He was on a walking tour near Dartmoor
with a friend:

> We were both traversing crises in our adolescence. We made frightful
> confessions to one another which left me shaken, as though with sob-
> bing. All this was completely absorbing, a passionate mingling of
> beauty and wickedness and nature and world, in which I plunged my
> intensified living while my father was dying. But the telegram arrived,
> and I took the train home. I was in such a calm, equable mood when I
> reached Paddington that my godfather, who met me, thought that I
> could not have understood the significance of the telegram.[19]

At this point we realize that we are not reading one of the most distinguished autobiographies. There is a strange lack of curiosity about the
sources of these unexpectedly contrasted reactions, this total loss of the
sense of the magnitude and scale of events. Spender, in effect, leaves us to
do the work for him. Some points are fairly obvious. He felt that he had
too many guides and mentors. With grandmother, uncle, other relatives
and adoring and fussy servants, he felt over-protected, especially at a time
when the shadow of Hitler was beginning to obscure many lights, and to
be a Jew (or half-Jew) living comfortably in one of the most affluent parts
of London could easily seem ignoble. Then there may have been the feeling that his father could never have understood the young man the walking tour had shown him to be. Conscious, perhaps more than he likes to
admit, of being a weak, pliable character, he may have found any reduc-
tion in the number of separate personal pressures something of a relief.
The ordinary role of father as breadwinner did not seem important in a
closely-knit and prosperous family like his.

But there is something else. There were so many influences, so many
choices, so many possibilities that he seems to have lost the power to feel
very deeply. Sometimes, he asserts that he did feel, as on the walking
tour, but leaves the nature of the feeling curiously vague. At other times
he records a conscious effort to feel more, and more precisely, than he
really did. Thus:

> 'Charm'd magic casements, opening on the foam
> Of perilous seas, in faery lands forlorn,'

conveyed no attractive picture to me. But that they were often quoted
as 'pure poetry' illuminated them nevertheless, and just as getting out

---

[19] Ibid., p.19.

of a boat at a quayside and seeing some ships, I was later one day to
cover my disappointment by saying to myself, 'This is France', bring-
ing my whole conception of France to bear on my glimpse of Calais or
Dieppe, so when I read these lines, I said to myself: 'This is poetry.'[20]

Spender was just over twenty years younger than T.S. Eliot. It would
have been very natural if, after quoting the lines of Keats, he had gone on
to speak of the decay of romanticism, of the feebleness of 'Georgian
poetry', of the boredom inflicted by old-fashioned schoolmasters retailing
forty years on their own adolescent enthusiasm for Keats or Tennyson or
Swinburne; and then gone on to discuss *Prufrock* or Wilfrid Owen and
his own early experiments in verse. But none of this is to be found.
Instead, we have only this curious repeated uncertainty about what he
felt or whether he felt at all. Perhaps he was in a state of chronic emotional over-stimulation. Just as a person with a queasy stomach cannot
feel attracted to food, but if offered a series of dainties, will be willing to
admit that they are all good for anyone who is hungry, so here. He sees
himself, above all, as a poet, but is no more confident of his real tastes in
poetry than in anything else. His father used to read him Wordsworth
(he oddly describes some of his most difficult poems as 'simple', falling
into a characteristic error of philistine fourth-formers), his grandmother
took him to see Ibsen and Strindberg and modern paintings, which his uncle
dismissed as a mere passing fashion. They were all trying to influence
someone who was so easily influenced that he was not really influenced at all.
He was like a man at an endless committee meeting, full of acrimonious
argument and passionate debate, who constantly rises to his feet and says:
'I agree with the last speaker.'

He had so little idea of the self that later, in adult years, he was constantly using the people he met as a device to cast light on his inner
obscurity. Of one he writes: 'I saw his faults as projections of my own
guilt.' He even allowed his affectations to be foisted upon him. When he
found his Oxford contemporaries cared only for 'games, drinking and
girls' (with characteristic homosexual insouciance he fails to reflect how
unsuitable those three nouns are to form a *list*) he 'took revenge on them
for disappointing me':

I became affected, wore a red tie, cultivated friends outside the college,
was unpatriotic, declared myself a pacifist and a Socialist, a genius . . .
On fine days I used to take a cushion into the quadrangle, and sitting

[20] Ibid., p.92.

down on it to read poetry . . . I aped my own exhibitionism, effeminacy, rootlessness and lack of discipline.[21]

He ends his books by quoting his mother's words the night before she died: 'Tell them I have had a very happy life.' But it does not seem to occur to him that as his mother was a very shadowy figure in the early pages of the book, and even her death was hardly felt, this ending can only have the effect of a purely literary device, and an inept one at that.

This brings me back to the phrase which I italicized in my first quotation: 'One has the power, more or less to become what one thinks.' In the light of what follows, this acquires an ironical ring not intended by the author. The real drift of the book, and the cause of the curiously vague impression it makes as a whole, despite some sharp episodes, is that he never knew what he had become. Whether among respectable burghers in Hampstead or in homosexual brothels in Berlin he was always watching himself in puzzlement, wondering who he was.

(iv)   Deprivation: Winifred Foley and Neville Cardus

These three examples, different as they are, are alike in recording the life of families wealthier and more cultivated than most. And, naturally, the bulk of the available evidence comes from such families. We may redress the balance a little by referring briefly to two different cases. Winifred Foley tells the story of a very poor family in the Forest of Dean.[22] The family was normal, affectionate and reasonably cheerful under difficulties. But we see, nevertheless, how poverty and close propinquity to parents and siblings stripped the grandeur and mystery from the parental office. ('Mam was a dab hand at cadging anything that was going.') In place of the moral training which other children received, the author gradually learnt a shared worldly-wisdom, strongly tinged with cynicism, though a little moderated by the father's utopian brand of politics. They were all too near to study each other as carefully as middle-class children do. Emotional tenderness was crowded out by hunger, coarse humour and endless contriving to obtain necessities and a few cheap luxuries. The great forest in which they lived is a presence, but more in a practical than in a numinous sense. It was a place where you might lose your way and be robbed,

---

[21] Ibid., p.33.'
[22] Winifred Foley, *A Child in the Forest*, 1974. She was born in 1914.

where you might forget the time and be punished for being late. Only when the author is old enough to leave it and go to work in London, does a shadowy sense of the forest's mysterious quality invade the prose —to be quickly passed over. The loss of a baby brother in a large hungry family is not treated as a great event. The mother had kept a few of his baby clothes, though in general the women pooled baby clothes to help each other out. (The author does not comment on this touching external proof of the mother's feeling.) And what might have been a moving or else a macabre scene when the mother dresses up the author's doll in the dead child's clothes is dismissed summarily in a few lines. It is treated as a mere attempt to check the child's crossness at finding the doll ugly and cross-eyed which led to her rebellious remark that 'Feyther Christmas could 'ave the bugger back'. All the crises of life and its most moving events are conveyed in this same, brisk, shrewd, no-nonsense style. Life is too busy and too short to grieve or regret, or ponder, but not too short to laugh. And behind it all is a deep fear of being soft, of being deceived, of being taken in, of being preached at, of forgetting for one single moment that 'things are as they are, and the consequences of them will be what they will be'.

Neville Cardus belonged to an infinitely more remote world.* He did not know who his father was; his mother and his aunt were prostitutes. He tells us: 'I lived to lie in bed and watch my mother as she prepared for the evening adventures'[23] and he says that he took a particular interest in watching her get into her corsets. Her 'reddening face and suppressed curses were my constant delight'. There is a good deal in this vein, but he does not altogether convince us that the wounds inflicted were as slight as he says. Being an avid reader at an early age, he soon begins to use literary examples as a kind of distancing affect. He compares his aunt to Beatrix Esmond, ignoring the enormous contrasts between the kinds of life the two lived. But he conveys very well the inner solitude that he created for himself, walking the streets of Manchester and living imaginatively in the lives of characters in Victorian novels that he read in the Public Library. He is rather shy of making connections, or perhaps artfully prefers to leave the reader to make them. Having been forced into contact with overt evidences of sexuality much earlier than most, he is

---

* Cardus was always apt to improve his anecdotes, and doubt has been cast on his autobiographal veracity. Yet the connection established between his childish and adult life carries conviction, *because it is so little stressed.*

[23] Neville Cardus, *Autobiography*, Collins, 1974, p.14.

much later than most in developing any curiosity about it. Surely this must have been the result of delayed shock, but he does not say so.

When he comes to describe his marriage, he allows the facts to speak for themselves, so that they acquire a curious symbolic pathos. As a cricket reporter for *The Guardian*, he went to Old Trafford as usual on his wedding day. When he returned with his wife after the ceremony:

> While I had been away from the match and had committed the most responsible and irrevocable act in mortal man's life, Lancashire had increased their total by exactly 17.[24]

He does not actually say that it was a *mariage blanche*, but perhaps he thought we would be able to infer this.* But if his upbringing prevented him having any personal interest in sex, it left him with immense zest for life in general. Perhaps he is less than explicit about cause and effect because he wishes to ensure that we do not see him as a maimed creature. But really there is no danger of that.

[24] Ibid., p.143.
* Nor does he say that he lived in the National Liberal Club and met his wife every day for tea, and he is writing before the time when he moved into her flat after her death, never having slept in it before. *Private Information.*

VI
The Dedicated Child

My religion collapsed under the weight of the morality laid upon it.
(Sheila Kaye-Smith, *Three Ways Home*, 1937, p.39)

I suddenly matured like a weed.
(Thomas Merton, *Elected Silence*, 1949, p.78)

I am not talking about what is sublime, but about what is true.
(Ruskin, *Modern Painters*, 1856 Part II, Sect. II, Chap. II, Para. 5)

(i) *Ruskin*

Ruskin was in his sixty-seventh year when on 10 May 1885, he wrote the brief preface to *Praeterita*, and described it as 'speaking of what it gives me joy to remember'. Like most of the more memorable statements in the book that follows, this one is ambivalent, combining the characteristic lucidity of the author's plainer style with the subtle disturbance often caused by the unspoken. He meant that he would not speak of his marriage and its annulment or of madness; and though he would speak of Rose La Touche, he would do so in a way that would not reveal the agony she caused him. Instead, he would write at length about his childhood.

But did it really give him joy to remember it? In some ways, no doubt, it did. For people whose power of imagination is so strong that it makes them fear for their sanity, the past is a secure citadel, where the unknown can never enter, where the light falls evenly. For Ruskin two special circumstances could reinforce this appeal. His adult sexual nature, though closely associated with some of his deepest emotions and most sacred memories, had brought him in the end nothing but grief. To revisit childhood would thus be felt as a vacation from persistent pain. And the clear evidences of budding genius in his childish precocity might be comforting to one who, for all his achievements and pervasive sense of his own rightness, was at heart uncertain of the lasting effect of what he had written and done.

Yet 'joy' would never be the first word to come to the reader's mind. From the first the account is double-edged; and it is so in two different ways, in its treatment of happiness and unhappiness, and its magisterial awards of approval and disapproval to his parents and to himself.

Right at the start, and unobtrusively at first, he sets the literalism, the respectability and the commercial probity of his parents against the power of that imagination which would be the guiding (and wandering) star of his own life. Thus he writes of the garden of his aunt's house at Perth:

> full of gooseberry-bushes, sloping down to the Tay, with a door opening to the water, which ran past it, clear-brown over the pebbles three or four feet deep; swift-eddying—an infinite thing for a child to look down into.

And in the next paragraph[1] he tells of his father paying his own father's debts when there was no legal obligation:

[1] Ruskin, *Praeterita*, ed. Hart-Davis, 1949, Chap. I, Sects. 4 & 5.

for which his best friends called him a fool, and I, without expressing
any opinion as to his wisdom, which I knew in such matters to be at
least equal to mine, have written on the granite slab over his grave that
he was 'an entirely honest merchant'.

For those readers in the 1880s who had followed Ruskin through the
1860s in his ferocious attacks on the trading ethos of the time[2] this
phrase, though true and literally meant, will have had a hollow ring.

But Ruskin was one of those rare people who could picture their parents
in youth; and he balances this with an account of his father as a 'dark-
eyed brilliantly active and sensitive youth of sixteen', constantly engaged
in 'flashingly transient amours'[3] and unobtrusively guided by the older
girl who was to become his mother. But he quickly reverts, as no doubt
the father did in fact, to a tone more reminiscent of the lapidary inscription, when he tells how his father, tiring of temporary attachments, decided to marry his trusted confidante:

> My father chose his wife with much the same kind of serenity and
> decision with which afterwards he chose his clerks.[4]

It is the privilege of a great autobiography, which this is, to give us
data for disagreeing with its conclusions. What we read of the mother's
character may well make us wonder whether it can have been quite like
that, even if Ruskin père innocently thought it was. We do not doubt
that Mrs Ruskin capably arranged it all, and that her surprise was feigned,
though her delight was not.

His mother thus enters the story before her marriage as the element of
stability, long views, and stern repression of the imagination. Later,
when the family tours Europe and the young Ruskin is exultant amid the
treasures of twenty-five centuries, we are still aware of her in this role, a
waiting presence in the carriage or the hotel, ready to calm excitement or
reprove excess, seeming at times almost as much older than the father as
she is older than the son.

When he comes to speak of himself, Ruskin is no less ambivalent.
There was always a strong provocative and combative streak in him; and
it was characteristic that he should begin an account of a Puritan upbringing with the names of Homer, the 'unchristened heart', and Walter

---

[2] In such works as *Unto this Last* (1860) and *The Crown of Wild Olive* (1866).
[3] *Praeterita*, Chap. VII, Sect. 143.
[4] Ibid., Sect. 145.

Scott who analysed the Covenanters with a lofty intellectual (though not unfeeling) comprehension. Characteristic, too, that he, the inspirer of most of what is passionately serious in English socialism, the man who had been censored by Thackeray[5] for daring to question the received economic doctrines, should proudly say: 'I am . . . a violent Tory of the old school—Walter Scott's school . . . and Homer's.'[6]

This is followed by an intensely ironical passage in which he contrasts the reading of Scott and Homer on weekdays with the Sunday fare of Defoe and Bunyan. But the irony, as so often later, is directed mainly against himself. He speaks as if the trivial selfishness of preferring hot mutton to cold had prevented him from becoming an evangelical clergy-man. This is the first light-hearted approach to two persistent themes, his own selfishness and the horrors of the Puritan Sunday. He seems deter-mined, violent against himself as against all other enemies, to present this selfishness both as his own fault, and as the natural consequence of his parents' folly. He compares himself to a 'little floppy and soppy tadpole —little more than a stomach with a tail to it,'[7] but it is a selfishness bene-ficently shielded from fear and from all the self-regarding emotions child-ish fear can arouse. He was not even frightened when seriously bitten in the face by a dog.

Ambivalence reaches its height when he speaks of that terrible Sunday which sounds like the slow tolling of a bell threatening doom through all Victorian literature:

> the horror of Sunday used even to cast its prescient gloom as far back in the week as Friday—and all the glory of Monday, with church seven days removed again was no equivalent for it.[8]

We are reminded of Clennam in *Little Dorrit*, of Mrs Proudie as well as of innumerable passages in other autobiographies. But Ruskin, though as vehement and eloquent in his denunciation as any of the others, is alone in countering the denunciation with praise. He believed in discipline as strongly as he disliked it, and he speaks of Sunday as 'useful to me as the only form of vexation which I was called on to endure'.[9] Why, one wonders, apart from his natural vehemence at all times, was Ruskin's denunciation so

---

5 As editor of *The Cornhill Magazine*.
6 *Praeterita*, I, Chap. I, Sect. 1.
7 Ibid., II, Chap. III, Sect. 42.
8 Ibid., I, Chap I, Sect. 21.
9 Ibid., I, Chap. VII, Sect. 148.

severe? Why was it so terrible for children to have to give up amusements for one day a week, and listen to a sermon which they found dull?
Especially, in the case of children whose parents' general inclination was
to spoil them, children who had servants to run after them and adore
them, and plenty of amusements on six days of the week?

One may answer that time is long in childhood, and the sense of fairness very strong, so that an irrational ban on innocent amusement may
take on the appearance of cruelty. But no one who has entered imaginatively into the emotions of horror and rebellion which the Protestant
Sunday aroused will be entirely satisfied with this answer. The truth is
rather that the Protestant Sunday became for Ruskin and for many others
a symbol of something they hated more deeply than perhaps they
knew,— something they could not fully understand in childhood, or
analyse in maturity. Ruskin came to the heart of it when he said simply
'I had nothing to love.'[10]

He goes on:

> My parents were—in a sort— visible powers of nature to me, no more
> loved than the sun and the moon: only I should have been annoyed and
> puzzled if either of them have gone out . . . still less did I love God; not
> that I had any quarrel with Him, or fear of Him; but simply found
> what people told me was His service, disagreeable; and what people
> told me was His book, not entertaining.

We are dealing here with something very different from the religion of
the Clapham Sect, and still more different from the Puritanism of the
seventeenth century. But there can be little doubt, for those who have
read extensively in the memoirs and novels of the period, that the variety
of Protestantism '(unknown to Bossuet!)' of which Ruskin's is the classic
account became dominant in the English commercial classes before 1840.
Its essential feature was to turn religion into law, to reverse the process of
which St Paul speaks, where grace overcomes law, and love takes the
place of obedience. It was an intense form of Judaizing. The Incarnation
was forgotten or reduced to an unfelt formula, sacraments devalued, the
material world became dead, unpenetrated by the Divine, and therefore
only suitable for manipulation for profit. Sunday was absurdly equated
with the Jewish Sabbath, which also had the useful effect of concealing
its real origin in Resurrection and perpetuation in the Eucharist. Religion became an acceptance more or less willing of superior power, and

---

[10] Ibid., I, Chap. II, Sect. 50.

all real energies were released for making money. We cannot really wonder at the bitterness with which the system was hated.

It would be over-dramatic to say that Ruskin's father undermined fatally all the patient work his wife had put into inculcating this system when he agreed to a family foreign tour, since a boy of Ruskin's sensibilities would before long have encountered art somewhere for himself. As it was, the felt contrast with the Catholic tradition was early and starkly immediate:

> At Abbeville I saw that art (of its local kind), religion, and present human life, were yet in perfect harmony. There were no dead six days and dismal seventh in those sculptured churches: there was no beadle to lock me out of them, or pew-shutter to shut me in.[11]

That last image, essentially a prison image, represents perfectly the religious experience of his childhood, exactly what St Paul calls 'bondage to the Law'. From one point of view the whole of Ruskin's later life can be seen as a struggle between this bondage (which, it should also be emphasized, he in some ways approved, though he could never love it) and the sacramental spirit of Catholicism, mediated to him through art. His rebellion against childhood was never complete; and he sounds almost like Dickens, whose ignorance of art was as total as Ruskin's knowledge was great, when he writes: 'all the Catholic Cantons of Switzerland . . . are idle and dirty, and all Protestant ones busy and clean'.[12] And we shall find him much later vainly trying to discover a Protestant element in some of his best-loved architectural features of mediaeval Venice.

All this should not surprise us. Ruskin was in every way a divided man, a rigid moralist and one of the most gifted of all aesthetes, a passionate lover whose marriage was annulled on the score of impotence, a writer remarkable both for his lucidity and his torrents of ornate eloquence, the 'most analytic mind in Europe' who became a raving maniac, and in lucid intervals wrote with touching simplicity and directness of his memories of that condition. The greatness of his autobiography has (in large part) the same source as the greatness of his life and achievement. He could never submit to his parents, nor altogether escape them. He could never believe their teaching and he could never reject it.

Another important feature of this version of the Protestant ethos was that all authority was concentrated in the parents. Like Islam, which in

---

[11] Ibid., I, Chap. IX, Sect. 181.
[12] Ibid., II, Chap. I, Sect. 8.

some ways it resembled, the ethos abolished the distinction between
religious and secular authority. This was convenient because it meant
that religious duty could be so closely amalgamated with secular ambitions that the two would become indistinguishable. Ruskin conveys this
impossible identity of opposites, become like so many contradictions in
England a perfectly plain and prosaic fact, in two eloquent, bitter and
unforgettable passages:

> My mother had, as she afterwards told me, solemnly 'devoted me to
> God' before I was born; in imitation of Hannah.
>   Very good women are remarkably apt to make away with their
> children prematurely, in this manner: the real meaning of the pious act
> being, that, as the sons of Zebedee are not (or at least they hope not),
> to sit on the right and left of Christ, in His kingdom, their own sons
> may perhaps, they think, in time be advanced to that respectable posi-
> tion in eternal life[13]

The word 'respectable' here is as much packed with meaning as any
single word known to me in any literary context. It contains within itself
Ruskin's definitive judgment of the whole ethos which my last few
pages have been attempting to analyse.

The second passage is more amusing and in a way sadder because it
seems to universalize the inconsistencies of his father as part of the ever-
lasting contradictions of human nature:

> His ideal of my future—now entirely formed in conviction of my
> genius—was that I should enter at college into the best society, take all
> the prizes every year, and a double first to finish with; marry Lady
> Clara Vere de Vere; write poetry as good as Byron's, only pious; preach
> sermons as good as Bossuet's, only Protestant; be made, at forty,
> Bishop of Winchester, and at fifty, Primate of England.[14]

What Mr Ruskin meant by the 'best' society, can be surmised from his
decision to make John a gentleman commoner at Christ Church—a characteristic nineteenth-century incursion of the merchant class into an aristocratic preserve.[15]

It is a tribute in a way to the parents that, when the son was able to

---

[13] Ibid., I, Chap. II, Sect. 19.
[14] Ibid., I, Chap. X, Sect. 212.
[15] Ruskin supposes that the tutor must have said 'that it would be good for the college
to have a reading man among the gentlemen commoners'.

understand them and their hypocritical confusion between sacred and secular with such perfect precision, he yet felt their influence with unusual power long after they were dead. Indeed, he experienced a partial reversion to their ethos, reflected in his change from finding the 119th psalm 'chiefly repulsive' to finding it in his later years 'precious . . . in its overflowing and glorious passion of love for the Law of God'.[16] This, the longest in the psalter, is concerned with minute observance of the Mosaic law.

Ruskin has a way of signalling a deep inner change by a changed attitude to a literary text; and another very significant one is *Don Quixote*, where the change is perhaps unexpected. He says that in childhood when his father read it aloud he could 'laugh for ecstasy'; but that now 'it is one of the saddest, and, in some things, the most offensive of books to me'.[17]

In that change of feeling he encapsulates, with the brevity and precision of a great writer, much of the history of his own life. In his childhood, paradoxically at the same time over-cossetted and over-disciplined totally secure but a little bored in a tiny universe of which he was the acknowledged centre, the sophisticated amusement provided by Cervantes was received with rapture. In his late years, acknowledged to be a great prophet, but neglected and ridiculed for being so by a public that thought he had wasted incomparable powers in tilting at windmills, the earthy realism that encompasses and usually stifles every Quixotic figure could only afflict him with intolerable regret. The great British public, that was in so many ways so like his parents, in its commercial values, its naive philistinism (compatible with a keen technical interest in art and a desire to possess old masters), its illusions, its dullness, its superhuman effectiveness in competition with the world—the great British public had conquered him; or so, in dismal moments he must have felt, and Quixote became the emblem of that defeat.

Yet *Praeterita* was certainly meant to be, and perhaps is, Ruskin's calmest, and most balanced book. If he found it difficult, or sometimes impossible, to be mild, he could at least redress one extreme with another. He turns from satire against his parents to savage blame of himself, especially his idleness (rather an odd judgment, this) and his 'venomous' conceit, which grew at Oxford as he 'began to perceive the weaknesses of his masters'. And he balances his criticism of his parents by speaking of 'the

---

[16] Ibid., II, Chap. II, Sect. 46.
[17] Ibid., I, Chap. III, Sect. 68.

sick thrill of pleasure through all the brain and heart with which ... I used to catch the first sight of the ridge of Herne Hill, and watch for every turn of the well-known road'.[18] He does not say whether it was the place or the inhabitants that had the stronger appeal; we may surmise that it was the place.

But the time comes when this view back from the world to the kingdom of childhood is opposed by another, felt yet more passionately, a view of longing for what was outside the citadel. When he fell in love with Adèle Domecq, 'who of course reduced me to a mere heap of white ashes in four days', he would look out over Shooter's Hill, 'where I could see the last turn of the road to Paris', where Adèle was.[19]

Here one can only register admiration for the plainness, the economy and the depth of Ruskin's art. By giving us the two views of the road, the road home and the road away, he brings together in intelligible symbolic form the lifelong pull back to childhood where he was a kind of disciplined infant king under strict tutors, and the glamour of the world with all the dangers of adolescence. These dangers were experienced in a very pure form. There was no temptation to dissipated habits. But (he implies) the purity increased the intensity, and therefore, in a way, the danger.

Particularly important in the quotation above are the words 'of course'. We are bound to link them with the previous statement that he had nothing to love, and with the assumption made throughout, too deep to need stating, that his nature was capable of the heights of passionate feeling. He explicitly blames his parents for allowing him to come so completely unprepared to his first contest with passion. (I do not remember another case of an autobiographer blaming his parents for the onset of first love.) Yet even those who are taught to love God, and who are also able to love their parents, are not always immune to adolescent passions. Does he mean that love within the home would have been a prophylactic against Adèle's influence? Or does he mean that he ought to have been shielded until he was older from the impact of feminine charm? Either way, we may think that in this instance at least, the parents are being treated a little unfairly. Indeed, there may be an unconscious reversion to childish dependence, as if the process of parental shielding could go on for ever. We may find much fault with the Ruskin parents without being able to see clearly how they could have prevented this disaster. And,

[18] Ibid., I, Chap. VII, Sect. 155.
[19] Ibid., I, Chap. X, Sects. 206 & 209.

inadvertently perhaps, he bears witness to this himself, when he tells of a later time when a girl 'was the light and solace of all the Roman winter' although he never managed to get within fifty yards of her.[20] Would any system of upbringing have sufficed to tame such a spirit?

Here again, as always, Ruskin is ambivalent. Having blamed his parents for letting him encounter too soon the dangerous attraction of women, he reverts to his acid criticism of his mother's endless coddling, her treating him as a child when he was really a man, which led her to leave his father to come and live with him in Oxford when he was an undergraduate. If the parents had been able to read his book they might have felt that he was very hard to please. Accidental unfairnesses though—for Ruskin was always fair in intention—in no way detract from the wonderfully exact sense of inevitable, long-drawn-out consequences, the marvellous combination of vivid impressions with mature judgment. Even the unfairness springs in part from a determination to present inconsistent emotions as they were felt at the time. *Praeterita* is surely one of the greatest of autobiographies, and especially because of its power of linking the experiences of childhood with the formation of character, and the development of genius. And the deep irony of the whole story is that the consecrated child, nurtured to be a genius, really was a great genius, but yet the nurturing of him to be a genius maimed and disabled him. This is the central idea of the whole work, breathing unspoken in every line. It has a tragic grandeur.

(ii)   *Edmund Gosse*

Gosse was some thirty years younger than Ruskin, and *Father and Son* (1907) came a little more than twenty years after *Praeterita*. Philip Gosse, the father, was clearly a much abler man than Ruskin's father; and probably his mother was abler than Ruskin's mother. Yet the sensation of narrowness, strong enough in Ruskin's childhood world, is much stronger still here. To balance this, we find Gosse's parents perfectly sincere, after the dubious Ruskinian worldly shufflings. The Ruskin family was typical of many, and unusual only in that the son and heir was a great genius. The Gosse household was in every way exceptional; and has often been misinterpreted by being supposed much more typical than it was. It was exceptional especially because what in the surrounding Protestant society

---

[20] Ibid., II, Chap. II, Sect. 39.

were prejudices, impressions and tendencies became here clear, intelli-
gently-held principles. In the world of the Dickensian Christmas, we
have here a man consistent enough to regard a Christmas pudding as a
work of Satan. Gosse expresses this with eloquent words which strike us
at once by their unlikeness to Ruskin's humorous or bitter ambivalence:

> Here was perfect purity, perfect intrepidity, perfect abnegation; yet
> here was also narrowness, isolation, an absence of perspective, let it be
> boldly admitted, an absence of humanity. And there was a curious
> mixture of humbleness and arrogance; entire resignation to the will of
> God and not less entire disdain of the judgment and opinion of man
> ... They [the parents] lived in an intellectual cell, bounded at its sides
> by the walls of their own house, but open above to the very heart of
> the uttermost heavens.[21]

Nothing about writing like Byron or about Lady Clara Vere de Vere
here.

The interest of Gosse's book is that it records a rare, almost a unique
case, and thus, while almost useless for general intellectual history, is all
the more valuable as autobiography. Philip Gosse, a fairly distinguished
scientist of the second rank, really was unaware that there are many
different styles of writing (several of which are to be found in the Bible),
and he really did read the Bible in the same way as he read a scientific
paper, with the vital difference that the second was written by a fallible
man, and the first by God himself. And we find here a great intensification of that tendency, noted above in the Ruskin family, to the coales-
cence of religious and secular authority. Philip Gosse was always the head
of his own sect, preacher, interpreter, administrator all in one; and for
the young Edmund, girt with paternal authority as well. It is some relief
to us, though not much perhaps to the son, in contemplating this oppressive
burden of universal authority, that he was a much more lovable man than
Ruskin's father; and the book's art is such that by the end our sympathy
may be equally divided between father and son, or even inclined more to
the father. After the mother's death, the father and the precocious son
are the only educated and intellectual members of a small rustic congregation. This naturally led to a strong development of conceit in the son.
The author makes skilful use of an incident that occurred when he was
four. A lady showed him a print of a human skeleton, asking if he knew
what it was, to which he replied, 'Isn't it a man with the meat off?' This

[21] Edmund Gosse, *Father and Son*, Heinemann Popular ed., 1909, pp.14-15.

precocity was interpreted as a sign of budding genius, which Gosse's later career did little to support.

But he gives us also the deeper significance of this anecdote. It shows the absence of mystery, even of piety, in the education, albeit a desperately serious and intense one, that he received. Philip Gosse has often been blamed for allowing *Genesis* to influence his scientific vision; and this criticism of works like *Omphalos* must be allowed to be fair. But a much deeper criticism is implicitly made here by the son. He allowed his scientific detachment, and the terrible accumulation of facts, to overwhelm both his religious speculations and his family life. It is at this point, perhaps, that he is most untypical of his middle-class contemporaries. They were, as a rule, hedged about with pieties, sentiments and pruderies. they were often sentimental, seldom ruthlessly realistic. The Bible, the Royal Family, polite manners, class feeling, snobberies and decorous ambitions, were compounded into a spirit of subtle worldliness. Of all this the Ruskin family is a prime example. But it was not so here. At the age of four the unfortunate child had acquired the ethos of the laboratory, even of the dissecting-room. Gosse saw this clearly and expressed it well:

> the system on which I was educated deprived all things, human life among the rest, of their mystery. The 'bare-grinning skeleton of death' was to me merely a prepared specimen of that featherless plantigrade vertebrate *homo sapiens*.[22]

A religion deprived of all mystery is usually a religion held in Laodicean spirit; but not in this case. It was a religion reduced to the level of a scientific theory, and then held with passioante devotion and sincerity. This in a situation in every way exceptional was the most exceptional feature.

But emotion is part of human nature; and even those who vainly try to turn themselves into machines will be foiled by the hidden emotional drive behind that very attempt. Naturally, the unsuspected reservoir of emotion overflowed in the direction of the only child; and naturally, too, it led to viewing him as far more gifted than he really was, and as destined to be the Charles Wesley or George Whitefield of his age. 'I cannot,' says Edmund, 'remember the time when I did not understand that I was going to be a minister of the Gospel'.[23]

The same unacknowledged emotional pull led his father, the undisputed

[22] Ibid., p.26.
[23] Ibid., p.186.

leader of the tiny sect, to decide that Edmund was the solitary exception
to the rule that only adults could be baptised and enter into full communion with the saints. In all other cases a full personal conversion was held
to be indispensable. The father, honest as always, admitted to the congregation that no apparent conversion had taken place in the boy, but main-
tained that a hidden conversion had occurred in infancy. He waived his
usual right to examine candidates and decide alone whether they were fit.
Edmund was handed over to two worthy and overawed members of the
congregation, with his father playing stage manager. They were much
more nervous than the boy, and were so long in coming to the point that
he had to lead them to it himself.

> Neither had ever been into our drawing-room since it was furnished,
> and I thought that each of them noticed how smart the wall-paper
> was. Indeed, I believe I drew their attention to it.[24]

(This worldly touch is one of which the father would have been incapable at such a solemn moment.) Later, 'each examiner strove to exceed
the other in the tributes they paid to my piety': The ceremony of baptism,
partly, no doubt, because of the father's injudicious and largely unconscious favouritism, was interpreted by the son as 'an initiation to every
kind of publicity and glory'.

His father did give him a gentle warning about spiritual pride:

> This was certainly required, for I was puffed out with a sense of my own
> holiness. I was religiously confidential with my Father . . . haughty with
> the servants, and insufferably patronizing with those young companions
> of my own age with whom I was beginning to associate . . . the other
> little boys presently complained . . . that I put out my tongue in mock-
> ery, during the service in the Room, to remind them that I now broke
> bread as one of the Saints and that they did not.[25]

But the obverse of this precocious sense of superiority was loneliness.
Naturally, its burden became heavier when his mother was stricken with
mortal illness and then died. As she was dying she begged her husband to
place the boy's hand in hers:

> Thus was my dedication, that had begun in my cradle, sealed with the
> most solemn, the most poignant and irresistible insistence, at the

[24] Ibid., p.186.
[25] Ibid., pp.94–5.

death-bed of the holiest and purest of women. But what a weight, intolerable as the burden of Atlas, to lay on the shoulders of a little fragile child.[26]

Afterwards, still only in his eighth year, he felt that 'time had ceased to move'. Even his dreams were interminable, and 'hung stationary from the nightly sky'.

Naturally, there were moments of relief in this generally sombre existence. The boy developed genuine scientific interests of his own, and a certain precocious talent. Seeking rare sea-creatures by the seashore, he could forget his father's sadness and his own melancholy for a time. At other times, 'the street was his theatre', and he waited happily for the reappearance of the Jersey onion-man with his song:

> Here's your rope . . .
> To hang the Pope . . .
> And a penn'orth of cheese to choke him.

('My father did not eat onions, but he encouraged this terrible fellow, with his wild eyes and long strips of hair, because of his "godly attitude to the Papacy".')[27]

Above all, as might be expected of a lonely child with an intellectual father, too sad in his bereavement to offer the boy companionship, he read avidly, and here too he was precocious, and laid the foundations of his future life of literary scholarship.

All this led to a strange kind of syncretism:

> I was at one moment devoutly pious, at the next haunted by visions of material beauty and longing for sensuous impressions. In my hot and silly brain, Jesus and Pan held sway together, as in a wayside chapel discordantly and impishly consecrated to Pagan and Christian rites.[28]

Perhaps this is not a very uncommon state in adolescence. But it must have been encouraged and intensified by the extreme literalness of the training he had received. The parents had combined cultivated intelligence and seriousness of purpose with a complete lack of imagination.

Their way of reading Scripture was but one instance of something general. This had two opposite effects on the child, both of them

[26] Ibid., pp.72–3.
[27] Ibid., p.80.
[28] Ibid., pp.306–7.

unfortunate. On the one hand his private dreams, and his early experiences, innocent enough in themselves, of secular literature, acquired for
him a lonely flavour of guilt. On the other, he might be inclined to avoid
this sensation of guilt by persuading himself that his dreams were really
true, and figures of pagan mythology actual. Obviously, though, this
equilibrium would be temporary, and followed by certain disillusionment.

The other notable effect of his upbringing, and of the awed respect in
which he was held by the few adults he knew, was to endow him with a
premature authority. When the lonely father wished to marry again, he
was subjected to a searching catechism about the religious position of his
future bride:

> Our positions were now curiously changed. It seemed as if it were I
> who was the jealous monitor, and my Father the deprecating penitent.
> I sat up . . . and I shook a finger at him. 'Papa,' I said, 'don't tell me
> she's a paedobaptist.' . . . It affected my father painfully . . . he said we
> must judge not, lest we ourselves be judged. I had just enough tact to
> let that pass, but I was quite aware that our whole system was one of
> judging, and that we had no intention whatever of being judged our-
> selves.[29]

In its way this passage is the climax of the whole book. We can admire
the deft economy with which the author has woven together the comic
and serious elements in it. Especially notable is the detachment from his
past self that he achieves. In a certain superficial sense we may be tempted
to say that the father had 'asked for it'. But the passage also excites a
deeper response. No child is simply the product of his education. The
phrases might be borrowed from the father, but the personality was the
son's own, perhaps a harder one than the father's. The father possessed
an element of tenderness in his being which he lacked the means to
express to the son. The son had acquired at an unusually early age an
independent existence that was hardly touched by his continued dependence in ordinary social and economic ways. Loneliness, self-reliance, conceit and precocity had been at least as powerful formative influences as
the principles he had been taught. Here again, we have a sharp contrast
with Ruskin, who seems to be still dominated by feeling for his parents,
when adult, and already becoming a famous art critic. Together they

29
    Ibid., p.225–6.

make a warning against easy generalizations about devout Protestant upbringings, and remind us once again of the play of the unforeseen.

(iii)   *Daugher of Bertrand Russell*

Katharine Tait's book[30] has no claim to be considered a great autobiography. The author's literary talents are modest, and her power to understand herself limited. Its strong interest centres on a single point. It shows by means of vivid memories what may happen when the concept of the dedicated child is transposed into an entirely secular context. As Keynes explained, Russell was one of those who thought that the world was run unreasonably, and that the thing to do was to run it reasonably. Unfortunately, his contemporaries were unwilling to allow him unfettered control of the world, so it was not surprising that it tended to get into a mess. He was forced to restrict the practical working of his utopian vision to that circle of his own home where his authority was absolute. But it would be a mistake to think of his scheme for their education as merely that. His programme for training his children was essentially a microcosm; it was a practical illustration, even a sort of secular sacrament of the proper way to run the world. And at the start, at least, the mother was in perfect accord with the plan, and it was she, speaking for both parents, who expressed it thus:

> this is what we want to produce: a creature that understands the texture and habits of its world so completely, that when exact science is added it will manipulate that world with the sureness and grace of the artist or the dancer who performs with easy abandon the most difficult of movements.[31]

This statement is perhaps more notable for what it omits than for what it contains. There is no sense of personal relationships. The parent is seen in the role of the master-craftsman training the young apprentice. And, if this role is performed efficiently, it is not required that there should be any particular emotional attachment. The young painter wants to find a Bellini or a Tintoretto to learn from. If the master goes away for a time, or is preoccupied with other things, or has no particular affection for

---

[30] Katharine Tait, *My Father Bertrand Russell*, Harcourt, Brace Jovanovich, 1975.
[31] Ibid., p.10.

him, the pupil will not on that account be less grateful or less apt to learn. So we are not surprised to read:

> someone always had charge of us besides our parents, someone super-vised bath and bed and morning lessons and nursery meals, and per-formed many of those arduous and trifling activities that tend to lose their delicious excitement with endless repetition.[32]

The parents could go off to America, 'leaving us to wait out the deso-late weeks of absence in the care of a governess'.

'This,' Katharine Tait continues, with a bitter edge, 'was of course the English upper-class pattern.' Here was the first crisis in the history of the utopian upbringing; and it is clear that both parents were oblivious of it. Already the child is aware of the clash of two cultures, which were theoretically incompatible, but were so mysteriously fused in the parents that they were aware of no conflict at all. The theory was universal; and in order to live by it it was necessary to renounce all special loyalties and local ties. One should not belong to England, but to the world; not to the upper-class or any other class but to a classless society. But children never listen to what people say; they only hear what they mean. And what Russell meant, and what the young Katharine very early discerned that he meant, was that the position of the last great Whig aristocrat, from one of the 'families of 1688', buttressed by the possession of rare intellectual gifts, gave a certain opportune dignity and repose to egalitar-ian theory.

A further difficulty arose over the relative position of father and mother. The time would come when Katharine would be offered a bewil-dering series of stepmothers. But before that time arrived she already felt that her mother remained 'little more than one among a number of shad-ows in the bright light cast by my father'.[33] Again, the theory, which decreed that differences between the sexes were trivially biological, was of no account.

For a time, however, these strains and contradictions did little to dim the attractiveness of the ideal for the children:

> we amused ourselves with . . . planning to kill off the government. Both our parents . . . were born rebels, passionately convinced that

---

[32] Ibid., p.15. Perhaps the most delicate reference to excretory functions in our literature.

[33] Ibid., p.15.

everything the government was doing was completely misguided, if not deliberately wicked . . . we were certain that the government must be perfectly wrong and should be removed, to make way for intelligent people like our parents, who would run the country properly.[34]

Respectability was felt as a terrible ogre; the local rectory became an emblem of 'reactionary power and smug cruelty', yet at the same time it had awful fascination. In one of her few imaginative passages, Katharine Tait immediately goes on to record her return as a married woman to this dreaded rectory, which as a child she had never entered. She found it poverty-striken and desolate. Where was the comfortable security she had so envied? By now she was a Christian herself, and 'I felt I had chosen the wrong side again and was still, as always, a loser.'[35] Here, poignantly and uncomprehendingly, the author achieves a symbolic expression of the inner logic of aristocratic revolt. The people whom Russell attacked as privileged were, as a rule, less well-born, less able, less successful and less rich than himself. She has stumbled on a classic paradox of political radicalism, and expressed it as a small personal experience.

The universality of the utopian idea meant that feelings had to give way to rules. Katharine Tait is driven to compare her own upbringing to her father's, much to the advantage of the latter:

> When my father was three days old, his old-fashioned, sentimental mother wrote of him: 'I have lots of milk now, but if he does not get it at once . . . he gets into such a rage and screams and kicks and trembles till he is soothed off.' I wish he could have written about us in the same way. I do not like to think of myself as being treated with such austere benevolence, *as raw material to be shaped rather than a person to be enjoyed.*[36]

For the next generation the verdict was: 'If a child cries, it must be left to cry.' Perhaps this fairly trivial point bulks large in the memory of the sufferer because it assumes a symbolic force. The absence of emotion was frightening because again it involved a deep, unperceived, inconsistency. Bertrand Russell was, in fact, a man of uncontrollably strong emotions, as both his sexual and his political history abundantly prove. If, in this

34 Ibid., pp.19–20.
35 Ibid., p.33.
36 Ibid., p.60. My italics.

one case, he was able to follow his own 'rational' precepts, which were habitually forgotten or twisted in every other field, the child would instinctively know that she was not loved; that theory conquered feeling only because there was little feeling to conquer. But then, according to the theory, that didn't matter, any more than it matters whether a bureaucrat has an emotional interest in his book of rules. What matters is that the rules should be good in themselves, and that he should administer them fairly. The parents would have been satisfied with this analogy. The children would not.

But there was a deeper conflict than that just described—between the optimism which the system inculcated and the children's growing awareness of life. As the author says with an unwonted touch of eloquence:

> I used to think only his sunny reality was true; the darkness of rain and storm and fury existed only in my own mind. I know now that both were real.[37]

Ironically, the refutation of the father's optimism began in observation of his character. Katharine soon realized that her mother was in perpetual terror that he would desert her, as eventually he did.

> He spent much of his time sitting in an armchair reading, spectacles on his nose. Then, in the course of nature, he would get up to go to the bathroom... She would look up in alarm and ask: 'Where are you going?'
> 'To the bathroom.'
> 'Oh, all right.'[38]

It is sad to think of the many thousand false alarms the mother had to experience before her fears came true.

Similarly, the freedom of expression and of physical display inculcated in the parents' school concealed an underworld of forbidden subjects, not known to be forbidden, because their existence was not recognized:

> we were free to say anything we liked about sex, to ask any question and to compare ourselves with members of the opposite sex without concealment... The boys were terribly proud of their urinating accuracy, which we girls greatly envied, but we always retaliated by saying, 'Anyway, *you* can't make babies!' and that squelched them.[39]

---

[37] Ibid., p.68.
[38] Ibid., p.44.
[39] Ibid., p.95.

But she goes on, in a passage of particular interest:

we were allowed to say anything that we *could* say. But the fears we
were ashamed to acknowledge and the anxieties we could not put into
words had no outlet. For night terrors and loneliness, for homesick-
ness and fear of bigger children, there was little that could be done.

But things for which there is no name do not therefore cease to exist.
The assumption that the sexes differed only in the ways suggested by
the last quotation but one was also resented.

Deep underground in my soul, I wanted to say: 'Look at me. I'm a
girl. I like to dress up and be pretty. I want to grow up to be a mother.
Admire me, like me, enjoy as I am.'[40]

And all the time, the forbidden theory that the sexes were different was
being painfully dramatized before their eyes, the father, in his lofty detachment, his masculine, unconscious selfishness, and his inconstancy, a kind of
humorous parody of the Platonic idea of the traditional male; the mother in
her obsessive possessiveness, her fear of desertion, her animal tenacity, a
realization of the eternal feminine à la Thurber. And the exhibition was all
the more riveting for being officially concealed. ('I cannot even remember
where my parents slept, and of course I never knew with whom.')
    The children who had been the 'field of their joint endeavours at human
reform, became the battleground'.[41] The word 'field' is aptly chosen, and
the stress on the general character of the experiment in the word 'human'
is well-justified.
    So it was, that the abandonment of the long, strenuous and impossible
task of pleasing her father came to seem a liberation. At the same time
she came to regard progress as 'like Santa Claus and the Easter bunny',
she adopted with a deep sense of relief and liberation a belief in Original
Sin, and then there followed a belief in Divine forgiveness and grace. It is
comforting to see that she feels able to forgive her father, which, we are
inclined to guess, Ruskin never did.
    She sums up the whole history of conversion in brief words.

My earthly father loved me only when I was good . . . I was not good;
therefore he did not love me. But God did and does and always will.[42]

---

[40] Ibid., p.132.
[41] Ibid., p.124.
[42] Ibid., p.188.

VIII
Defined by the World

So convenient a thing it is to be a *reasonable* creature, since it enables one to find or make a reason for everything one has a mind to do.

(Benjamin Franklin, *Autobiography*, ed. Max Farrand, 1949, p.44)

Few Victorian autobiographers shared Augustine's recognition of the innate difficulties in telling the truth about one's life . . . In general they lack self-consciousness.

(Howard Helsinger, in *Approaches to Victorian Autobiography*, ed. by George P. Landow, 1979, p.40)

THIS CHAPTER HEADING DOES NOT IMPLY WORLDLINESS. None of the three examples chosen was in the least sycophantic, and all three were notably truthful. It implies rather that each found in a public role the chief purpose of life; and thus they came to understand themselves mainly through the reflection of themselves that they saw in the reactions of others. When people disagreed with them, criticized them, urged opposite opinions upon them, their own attitudes crystallized. Not deeply introspective, their sense of their own inner being was comparatively weak until, usually by disagreement with accepted opinions, they found themselves engaged in public arguments, in causes, in rhetorical outbursts, which led them gradually to a deeper and more exact sense of what they really were. Sometimes they surprised themselves; they learnt from their own inconsistencies. They might have nodded wryly at the little girl who said: 'How can I know what I think until I see what I say?' They all wandered very far from the life which their birth and background seemed to mark out for them; and this was not simply because they were gifted with many talents. It was rather that their talents directed them away from the line of least resistance. Beatrice Webb might have become a great political hostess, Wells might have been a self-made business millionaire, Russell might have been Prime Minister like his grandfather. In each case the ability for the role which their relatives may have expected was emphatically present; but something lying deeper in the personality deflected them from the obvious path. They did not clearly know what had deflected them; and they wrote their autobiographies partly to discover what it was.

(i) *Beatrice Webb*

In her very brief introduction to *My Apprenticeship* (1926) Beatrice Webb immediately makes the link between the self and the public world. She speaks of a 'continuous debate between an Ego that affirms and an Ego that denies' and at once goes on to ask:

> Can there be a science of social organization in the sense in which we have a science of mechanics or a science of chemistry, enabling us to forecast what will happen ... ? assuming that there be, or will be, such a science of society ... do we need religion as well as science ... ?

Probably she was unaware, in writing this, how much it shows the traces of a utilitarian background. The religious possibility is invoked less for its own sake than for its possible usefulness as a means to a desired end, which has been perceived instinctively as desirable. And so, for all the space given to religion in her two autobiographical books, and for all the genuineness of her religious feeling at times, her search is not primarily a religious one. Her sense of humour, strong in patches, failed at this point; and she did not see that it was funny to invoke the ultimate as a possible necessary factor in a limited aim.

The Potters were members of the hereditary business élite, which in the preceding twenty years had established their claim to a share in social and political power, almost if not quite on equal terms with a still influential aristocracy. Their success (symbolized by the attainment of Corn Law Repeal in the previous decade) made them eager imitators of aristocratic manners, and their wealth gave them leisure to cultivate intellectual pursuits and to patronize the arts. Mrs Gaskell knew what she was about when she made Thornton, the Lancashire businessman in *North and South*, so eager to learn Greek.

The large family led a cheerful, active, cultivated and mainly carefree life. Beatrice the eighth of nine daughters (the only son died young) watched the tide of her sisters' suitors come and go, leaving a residue of brothers-in-law. It was one of the most confident times in all English history, what W.L. Burn so aptly named the Age of Equipoise. And yet, for a quick-witted and enquiring young girl, there were puzzles and contradictions. The mother spent hours studying the Greek Testament and the Fathers of the Church; but she was also a disciple of 'the strictest sect of Utilitarian economists'. And so:

> it was the bounden duty of every citizen to better his social status; to ignore those beneath him, and to aim steadily at the top rung of the social ladder. Only by this persistent pursuit by each individual of his own and his family's interest would the highest general level of civilization be attained. It was on this issue that she and Herbert Spencer found themselves in happy accord... 'The man who sells his cow too cheap goes to Hell'.[1]

In fact her mother believed strongly in incompatible things. Her father, too, in a laxer and less reflective way, was inconsistent:

> His conception of right conduct was a spacious one, of loose texture,

[1] Beatrice Webb, *My Apprenticeship*, 1st ed. 1926, 2nd ed. Longmans Green, p.13.

easily penetrated by the surrounding moral atmosphere. What he did in the United States he would not do in the United Kingdom.[2]

The death of the son was the great grief of the mother's life, she being one of those women who find it hard to feel a deep affection for a daughter. But her father delighted in feminine society, and believed that women were superior to men. Beatrice was the favourite daughter, who married later than the others, and became the mistress of the house after her mother's death. Very revealing is the story of her asking her father for a book considered indecent, and his injunction to buy it because, though he would not allow a boy to read such a book, a nice-minded girl may read anything. Possessed of a rare combination of affection, security and personal independence, she was left to ponder why it was that they were a family who gave orders but did not obey them, and to wonder how intelligent people could swallow so many contradictions. She had an unusual appetite for facts, and an adventurous spirit. She read Herbert Spencer (a close family friend) and soon saw through the ditchwater sophistries that remain only as a monument to the credulity of many of his contemporaries. It dawned on her, as it had on Mill, that utilitarianism might logically take a collectivist quite as well as an individualist direction.

> When, in search of facts, I found myself working as trouser hand in a low-grade Jewish shop, I overheard the wife of the sub-contractor, as she examined my bungled buttonholes, remark to her husband, 'She's no good at the sewing: if I keep her I will put her to look after the outworkers—she's got the voice and manner to deal with that bloody lot.' Alas! to be recognzied—not as as scholar, not even as a 'r-e-e-l lidee' unaccustomed to earning her livelihood—but as a person particularly fitted by nature or nurture 'to give work out' and to 'take work in' in such a manner and in such a voice as to make the biggest profit, for (I say it as a justifiable retort) that bloody sweater.[3]

This is a fascinating moment in social history, when the daughter of the high capitalism, with its traditional dignities, its courtesy to inferiors, its intellectual cultivation meets the low with its fierce grasping contempt for others. The question was, was the underlying ethos really the same? Did the East End sweater reveal the concealed drives of the Potters, or was he a mere travesty? Beatrice Webb was not hasty at jumping

[2] Ibid., p.6.
[3] Ibid., pp.38–9.

to conclusions; she was very patient in amassing facts. But the facts as she saw them inclined her gradually to the view that the high and low capitalism really were versions of the same thing.

And yet they were, visibly, so different. There was an open-mindedness, a disinterested curiosity about the Potters. Was anyone else beside her father an intimate friend at the same time of Cardinal Manning and Herbert Spencer? Other associates included Galton, Huxley and George Eliot. Ideas were fun; and there often seemed no need to make a final decision between them. On Sunday mornings in London they listened with equal zest to Monsignor Capel or Canon Liddon, Spurgeon or James Martineau or Frederick Harrison, running the gamut from Catholicism to Comte via high Anglicanism and Unitarianism. But there appeared to be no call to make a decision between all these. The judgment made on them, if any, would be an aesthetic one, a mere preference. The preachers and their doctrines were like one's favourite books; one may have an order of preference, but it may change at any time, and one certainly does not discard one book because one considers that another is even better.

But this cultivated agnosticism did not penetrate everywhere. There were certainties, but all of them were secular. England, Manchester School economics, the right of the wealthy classes to be pampered by many servants, the values of London society—these were not to be questioned. No doubt her father would have shared his daughter's distaste for the sweating tailor; but he would have denied any likeness between the tailor's ethos and his own. And perhaps Beatrice's own sense of this likeness was only intermittent. She was very affectionate, very anxious to please, a little vain perhaps of her own charm and beauty. Above all, she had an enormously strong sense of facts; and were not the refinement, the liveliness, the exciting variety of the Potter family life facts? How could she deny them their own validity?

But with the strong sense of fact went an equally strong tendency to generalize. 'To me,' she says in a revealing passage, 'a million sick have always seemed more worthy of self-sacrificing devotion than the 'child sick in fever'.[4] And when her mother died, she struggled to generalize that most intimate and painful experience also.

The death of one dear and near to me did not strike me as sadder than the death of the thousands who vanish unknown around us. Either 'the all' is so inexpressibly sad that there is no increase of sadness

---

4 Ibid., p.221.

through personal affliction; or else there is a mysterious meaning which, if we could divine and accept it, would hallow all things, and give even to death and misery a holiness which would be akin to happiness.[45]

Here we have, though only advanced as a possibility, the real religious question whch her father's sermon-tasting evaded. Her deep-rooted empiricism extended to religion also. Emotions and needs were facts too. She did not know what she believed but she did know what she felt. And so, in a world where many respectable people were pretending in public to more religion than they had, she was in the opposite position. Thus she can write in her diary for 12 February, 1888:

now I enjoy my life. I have fair health, faith in my own capacity to do the work I believe in, and I have regained my old religious feeling, without which life is not worth living to one of my nature.[6]

But later, apparently without any real change in conviction she can describe herself as 'an avowed agnostic', and oppose prayers to open the proceedings of a Ladies' Committee for social work.

The phrase 'religious-minded agnostic' which she sometimes used to describe herself was a rare case of a phrase, used vaguely and loosely by a hundred journalists, being exactly applicable. She is always sympathetic in her judgment of real believers and stern against scoffers and materialists:

Where I think G.B.S., Granville-Barker, H.G. Wells and many other of the most modern authors go wrong, from the standpoint of realism in its best sense, is their complete ignoring of religion . . . The abler of these puppets of their thoughts deny it; the stupider are oblivious of it —a few are blantant hypocrites. And, that being so, there is nothing left for them to be but intellects or brutes—and for the most part they are both.[7]

She was so convinced that effective social work required a religious motive that she was driven to ascribe some hidden religious impulse to her husband, a judgment which may be thought to reveal more about the depth of her affection for him than it does of her shrewdness (equally real) in the understanding of motives.

[5] Ibid., p.89.
[6] Ibid., p.272.
[7] B. Webb, *Our Partnership*, Longmans Green, 1948, pp.448–9.

Her judgment of her own talents was unusually just; here, too, where most people are subject to fantasies or fears, her admirable sense of fact prevailed:

> Unlike one or two of my sisters, I was born without artistic faculty ... The talents entrusted to my care were a tireless intellectual curiosity together with a double dose of will-power—all the more effective because it was largely subconscious, instinctively avoiding expression if insistence threatened to prevent fulfilment. It was the 'overcoming by yielding' type of will, inherited from my father.[8]

She saw herself, as she was, as above all a professional, a professional researcher, and a professional politician and diplomat. She was appalled by the high amateurism of the English élite. She complained that while the standard of natural ability in political life was remarkably high, the standard of acquirements was ludicrously low. 'Who,' she asks, 'would trust the building of a bridge to a man who started with such an infinitesimal knowledge of engineering as Balfour or Gorst have of national education ...?'[9]

The way this begs some very interesting political questions is thoroughly characteristic. The distinction between politics and administration, though she no doubt acknowledged it in theory, was not vivid to her. Her constant cry is, find the facts, decide what actions will best ameliorate them, then carry out the policy. But this tendency to oversimplify the political process did not by any means make her inflexible. She was a diplomatic professional. Clearly, she thought hard about her status as a woman in a world of men, and a woman who had not in the least been defeminized by hard political work. Sometimes she catches herself playing the feminine, personal note, like an actor, and rebukes herself for it. At others, she worries about differing with colleagues because it is so unpleasant for a woman to be disagreeable. She has a hard, realistic judgment of the complex male attitude to such an unexpected woman as herself, a compound of chivalry, attraction, wariness and uneasy respect. Sometimes she ticks herself off for having all a normal woman's interest in clothes, but perhaps there is a lingering, unspoken thought that she is proving to herself that she is not a battleaxe, a feminist, or a discontented spinster, but one whose little differences in her extremely harmonious married life always ended in a 'shower of kisses'. On the whole, her femininity was a

[8] B. Webb, *My Aprenticeship*, p.53.
[9] B. Webb, *Our Partnership*, pp.133–4.

practical advantage which she was prepared to use, just as her class and money were; and she used all three for what she perceived to be the public good.

A sense of facts is useless without a sense of proportion; and this, too, she had. It enabled her to keep her inner conflicts within bounds. Two of these were more important than others. Marrying comparatively late, she had had time to brood on the value of the sacrifice of love which in the end she was not called upon to make. Were her abilities strong enough to warrant the view that she was called to a special work that no one else could do? In a revealing note of 1887, she explains her decision to keep two separate diaries, one for her work, and one for a record of her inner growth. Otherwise the remorseless proliferation of facts would crowd out feeling; indeed, she cultivated her feelings with care, as if afraid that they were not robust enough to withstand the hard slog of her work.

Perhaps the other, more lasting, conflict was the real source of the last anxiety, which the reader is likely to feel strange in view of the warmth and humour of the personality revealed. Her wish to benefit the poor, her sense of justice did not produce any liking for them. She felt herself to be far-sighted where they were improvident, neat where they were clumsy, rational where they were passionate and sentimental. To turn from contemplating London in the pages of Dickens to her account a generation later is not, primarily, an experience of historical change. It is a change in the sense of life. The warm, incoherent, pulsing, swarming life of Dickens's streets alarmed and distressed her. Certainly, she saw in it real evils that he preferred to ignore. When she worked as a 'plain trouser hand' in 1888, she found that the girls with whom she worked used to chaff each other about having babies by their fathers and brothers, and she learnt too that the violation of children was common. It was natural that such evils should darken her general imaginative sense of the life around her. Yet there is something else; when she writes:

Even their careless, sensual laugh, coarse jokes, and unloving words depress one as one presses through the crowd, and almost shudders to touch them. It is not so much the actual vice, it is the low level of monotonous and yet excited life; the regular recurrence to street sensations, quarrels and fights; the greedy street-bargaining, and the petty theft and gambling . . . Social intercourse brings out, and springs from, the worst qualities in East London. . . . The meeting-places, there is something grotesquely coarse in this, are the water-closets! Boys and girls crowd on these landings—they are the only lighted places in the buildings—to gamble and flirt.[10]

Her fastidiousness, like everything else about her, is honest and sensible. But the strain of the felt contrast between ideal and reality, between what the poor ought to want and what they do want, is obvious. Was it really reasonable to expect the East Enders to be what she would have been, if, with mind and sensibility unchanged, she had been reduced to their economic level? Could she not recognize that this fierce instinct of life, however wasteful and mindless, may have kept many from brooding despair? It is a pity she did not omit one or two blue-books to read Dr Johnson's answers to similar complaints among his own contemporaries; especially as she was one of the few who, like him, had the advantage of knowing the indigent and the prosperous classes equally well. It is notable, though, that while he was often irritated by the stupidity of guests at dinner parties, he never reacted in the same way to the vagaries of the uneducated. Beatrice Webb was annoyed by both, and she is at least as scathing about the stupidity of Lord Granville, when she tried 'out of politeness' to bring him into the conversation as she was with the failure of street hucksters to be interested in the social and economic consequences of their trade. And at least the street hucksters did not represent their love of gain as a sacred and solemn duty, which was what the aged Herbert Spencer was doing in 1900, living a solitary existence, surrounded by nine servants, including a secretary who had not had a holiday for ten years, and mouthing the slogans of the old political economy: 'If you are to get your rights you must be perpetually distrusting every one. And it is your duty to exact your rights.'[11]

Behind all this activity, and all these contrasts, there is always a probing, questioning mind at work. If she needs to pray, what does it mean? If she has a 'mission', who sent her? If the aim is to make people happier, what is happiness? She could not define it, but she could see well enough how inadequate was the Benthamite definition that seemed to satisfy the ever-practical Sidney:

Where the Benthamites went wrong, and most perniciously wrong, was in never attempting to verify and correct their hypothesis. . . . Hence, they omitted from their calculation some of the most powerful impulses of human nature: reverence for mystery, admiration for moral

[10] B. Webb, *My Apprenticeship*, pp.237–8.
[11] B. Webb, *Our Partnership*, p.197.

beauty, longing for the satisfaction of an established expectation, custom and habit, tradition, sense of humour, sense of honour, passionate
longing for truth, loyalty—besides a host of mean vanities and impulses none of which produce happiness or aim at producing it, but are
just blind impulses.[12]

We may suppose that such speculations, which are prominent in her
diaries, actually occupied only the interstices of a busy life. The vague,
wandering nature of her religious and psychological speculations is not
due to lack of real interest, still less to lack of intelligence. It is due rather
to the play of moods; and perhaps because her outward life was so well-
disciplined and her practical sense so strong, she may have found relief in
this abdication from her ordinary mental rigour. It is not surprising that
neither she nor her friends knew quite what she really thought, or rather,
which of the various opposite thoughts lay deepest. H.G. Wells, in conversation with Virginia Woolf, called her a Quaker,[13] perhaps meaning
merely that she found some general spiritual tendency at work in the universe. Bertrand Russell, a shrewder, but also a more astringent observer,
said: 'She was deeply religious without belonging to any recognized
brand of orthodoxy, though as a socialist she preferred the Church of
England because it was a State institution.' She felt the appeal of Catholicism, because of its light and colour, and because of its openness to the
poor; but its intellectual side meant little to her. Her own final verdict
was that if she had to live again she would remain a conforming member
of the established church, and the characteristic phrasing of this tends to
confirm Bertrand Russell's diagnosis. She would have been a 'conforming' but not a fully believing member.

The fascination of her autobiographical books lies in this: they give a
most valuable study of the complex relation between inner and outer.
While her inner life fuelled her public effectiveness, it remained vague to
her; her public life was clear, strong, effective, but, to her deepest appre-
hensions, secondary and shadowy. And they show a woman who was at
home everywhere, who knew England and all classes as few did, who
could live with the humble and influence the mighty, who was consulted
by everyone as supremely competent, and who yet was an outsider,
alone, separated in thought from her devoted husband, a spiritual stran-
ger, just as her father had been when she went with him to taste Sunday

---

[12] Ibid., p.211.
[13] Diary of Virginia Woolf, ed. A.O. Bell, Hogarth Press, 1977, pp.91–2.

sermons. But not like him, because she was no detached dilettante. For her, it hurt.

(ii) H.G. Wells

The relation between history and literary studies is endlessly perplexing both to historians and critics; and mainly for one reason. The study of literature, or any major art, is the study of talent, greatness, genius. The study of history is the study of the ordinary. Very occasionally we are privileged to square the circle by finding a writer of eminence, and some talent, who was no wiser, no subtler, no more logical than most people are. Wells was the average sensual man writ large. But perhaps this is a libel on the average sensual man, who often has loyalties, fidelity to wife and children, and a stubborn sense of fact. Wells was wafted effortlessly to fame and affluence by the first generation of general literacy and organized popular journalism. His grasp of facts, such as it was, was limited to those hard separable units that resemble the imaginary billiard balls of the physicists of his youth, who did not dream of Einstein and Max Planck. His own personal fantasies were unchecked; in the later part of his autobiography,[14] we may have the feeling that this man who is approaching seventy is still in a world of adolescent dreams. He wants to be Buddha and found a new world religion (composed entirely of platitudes); he wants to be Napoleon and found a world state; and he experiences deep satisfaction as he remembers that he has fulfilled in the main pretty well his early dreams of being Casanova.

His inexpugnable conceit is breathtaking in its comicality. Stalin thought it worthwhile to take half an hour's rest from arranging the murder of his old friends to hoodwink Wells, who reports the occasion thus:

> His harmless, orderly, private life is kept rather more private than his immense importance warrants, and when, a year or so ago, his wife died suddenly of some brain lesion, the imaginative spun a legend of suicide . . . All such shadowy undertow, all suspicion of hidden emotional tensions, ceased for ever, after I had talked to him for a few minutes.[15]

and even more splendidly: 'We were both keenly interested in each other's point of view.'

[14] H.G. Wells, *Experiment in Autobiography*, 1934. Quotations from Jonathan Cape ed. 1969.
[15] Ibid., p.804.

Obviously, in such a book, we have to look not at what he says, or even at what he means, but at what he reveals unconsciously. And here the book is unexpectedly rich. He projects himself onto a vast imaginary screen, so that the more obviously absurd his statements are when taken literally the more interesting they often are as indications of that turbulent material of the inner life, which very few autobiographers have presented in such raw, undisciplined form. We catch a vivid glimpse of his ambitious excitement when he says: 'we originative intellectual workers are reconditioning human life'. Or when, with a characteristic Darwinian metaphor (he always tends to mistake his own metaphors for descriptions of facts), he writes:

We are like early amphibians, so to speak, struggling out of the waters that have hitherto covered our kind, into the air, seeking to breathe in a new fashion and emancipate ourselves from long accepted and long unquestioned necessities. At last it becomes for us a case of air or nothing. But the new land has not yet definitely emerged from the waters and we swim distressfully in an element we wish to abandon.[16]

This sense of a world about to change completely, of the very unchanging conditions of life disappearing, does not represent anything really to be seen. Rather it is an 'objective correlative' of the sturdy, expansive life-force in an ambitious young man who knows that the world is his oyster, who desires very ordinary things, money, fame, good food, women's bodies, and knows he is going to get them. Here his depressed lower middle-class background is important. He came from parents who had never been able to get what they wanted. He would be the one to break through, to 'struggle out of the waters'; and he did. The lower-middle-class background was important in another way too. His mother's world —in his eyes at least, for he may well have been unfair to her—was a world of pretences. Life did not bear much looking into; the body was shameful; the condemnation of the neighbours was the ultimate fear; their curiosity a constant threat. He was influenced much more than he knew by these attitudes. To a large extent he simply turned them upside down. His mother almost thought that respectability was a god; Wells, with characteristic emotional illogicality, decided that God was only a respectable pretence. Indeed, all deep, mysterious and difficult things become simple and obvious in Wells's mind. He mistook the invigorating and at times amusing process of stripping off the hypocrisies of

[16] Ibid., pp.17–18.

conventional late Victorian Bromley for a profound inquiry into the
nature of the universe. There is something engaging and attractive about
his over-confidence; a certain shrewdness even in his megalomania. He is
a perfect illustration of the truth of the insight which Conrad put into
the mouth of Decoud in *Nostromo* : 'These English live by illusions that
enable them to get a firm grasp of the substance.' Of if that judgment
seems too breathless and monumental to fit the case, we can see him as a
late Victorian Sam Weller, drawing on a wide experience and an unlimited power of aphorism and humorous comparison to minister to his
unbounded appetite for life. Just as his prim lower-middle-class background suited him exactly because he could invert it, so did the hard,
unreal certainties of late Victorian popular science, and the colourful sim-
plifications of late Victorian popular journalism. It was perhaps the only
period known to history when life and its aims and meanings appeared to
be simple and palpable. All that seemed to be wanted was more of the
same.

But like so many materialists, he was also a romantic dreamer. He
writes of his earliest sexual experiments with a boyish wonder and a trace
of embarrassment, that is even touching. And when a more tender feeling came to be added, a musing, nostalgic glow suffuses the old man's
prose:

> Mary had gone. I never saw her again and I could not find her name
> nor where she had gone. But I can feel her heart beat against mine
> now, I can recall the lithe body in her flimsy yellow dress, and for all I
> know I have driven my automobile past Mary—an alert old lady I am
> certain—on some Hampshire road within the last few weeks.[17]

But how very characteristic to mention, in such a context, that emblem
of success for the lower-middle-class of the 1930s, the motor car. And,
when he is in more analytical mood, he is prepared to justify his lower-
middle-class values:

> my conception of a scientifically organized class-less society is essentially
> of an expanded middle-class which has incorporated both the aristocratic
> and plutocrat above and the present, proletarian and pauper below.[18]

And despite his admiration for Stalin, he calls Marxism 'an enfeebling
mental epidemic of spite'.

[17] Ibid., pp.183–4.
[18] Ibid., p.94.

He is amusing about his schoolboy dreams, not realizing how like the veteran writer was to the remembered schoolboy:

And I entered, conquered or rescued, towns riding at the head of my troops, with my cousins and my schoolfellows recognizing me with surprise from the windows. And kings and presidents, and the great of the earth, came to salute my saving wisdom. I was simple even in victory. I made wise and firm decisions, about morals and customs and particularly about those Civil Service Stores which had done so much to bankrupt my father. With inveterate enemies, monarchists, Roman Catholics, non-Aryans and the like I was grimly just. Stern work—but my duty[19]

It is fascinating to see how the traditional insular prejudices of his parents' class against Catholics and Jews merge into the dream of the socialist Utopia. And the confidence in science was so great that the highest praise he can offer Henry George's theory of land is to say that it 'came like a laboratory demonstration'.

A little later he found himself working long, tedious hours in a draper's shop. He makes us feel the intoxication of his escape from this prison, as, alone in a railway compartment, he hopped from one window to the other, humming a rhyme he had just invented. It is at moments like this that we feel the charm to which his contemporaries responded, but which is glimpsed only occasionally in the book. And the passage has a historical interest too; it is redolent of that Victorian sense of adventure, of infinite possibility, of a world really open to talents, that was never felt so strongly again after 1914. As a novelist, no doubt, Wells was an extremely feeble imitator of Dickens. But here he is not imitating Dickens but unconsciously recreating the life that Dickens describes, the world of the Cockney lower-middle-class on the spree, puns and marrow-pies, oysters and brandy-and-water. He has all their self-confidence, their high spirits, their earthy enjoyment of the surface of life; what he lacks, perhaps, is their shrewdness. Mr Jobling would not have been taken in quite so easily by Stalin.

In his own way he is aware of this aspect of himself:

My very obstinate self-conceit was also an important factor in my survival. I shall die, as I have lived, the responsible centre of my world. Occasionally I make inelegant gestures of self-effacement but they

19 Ibid., p.101.

deceive nobody, and they do not suit me. I am a typical Cockney without either reverence or a sincere conviction of inferiority to any fellow creature . . . I went on writing, indeed, as a toy-dog goes on barking. I yapped manuscript, threateningly, in an inattentive world.[20]

It was not to remain inattentive long.

Soon, as we should expect, his early shy fantasies of sex gave way to a tougher, more grasping spirit:

> I had an angry insurgence of sexual desire. I began to accumulate a curious resentment against my cousin Isabel because she had had no passion for me. I wanted to go out and pursue strange women. I reproached myself with my discretion about the street walkers of London during my student days. I make no apology for these moods; that is how the thought of enfeeblement and death stirred my imagination. This resentment at being cheated out of a tremendous crowning experience was to survive into my later sexual life, long after the obsession with death, from which it had arisen, had lifted. My imagination exaggerated the joy of embracing a woman until it became maddeningly desirable.[21]

And he goes on later to describe how he regarded his marriage, following a period of chastity, as a signal for as many extra-marital affairs he could manage.

Without being quite so keenly aware of it, he was just as individualistic in political vision, even though this had a collectivist cast:

> I set the highest value on people of my own temperament, which is I suppose a natural and necessary thing to do, and I believe in the long run our sort will do better than their sort, as men do better than rats. We shall build and what we build will stand at last.[22]

We are a little startled, after getting to know the author so well, that the other kind, who are dismissed as rats, are the 'smarties' and the 'pushers', uncomfortably like the impression of himself that he is intent on giving. But that is a detail. More significant, altogether, is the fact that he is talking socialism, precisely in the langauge of 'cut-throat competition' and that harsh early Victorian liberalism, which Beatrice Webb, his senior by eight years, was already seeing as inadequate to the demands of the age.

[20] Ibid., p.291.
[21] Ibid., p.300.
[22] Ibid., p.196.

All this is being written by a man well on in his sixties; and his narrative is in striking contrast to most written by men of that age. Much of it could have been written thirty years nearer the events it describes. It has the immediacy of felt experience; and for the most part it lacks the patina of time and reflection, the mournful or illuminating sense of difference between past and present. It is doubtful whether Wells developed inwardly much after his twenty-fifth year. And perhaps partly because he was at heart a journalist he did not really take in the developments of the twentieth century, in which more than half his life was lived. He wrote a lot about the war, but the war did not really affect him or alter his late-Victorian certainties. Similarly with science; he was always eager to read and comment on the latest scientific theory, and he had a flair for inspired guesses about technical developments of the future. But his philosophy of science remained in its earliest late-Victorian phase. Indeed, in this respect, he has a distinctly old-fashioned look when compared with T.H. Huxley, one of his heroes, who was some forty years his senior. If he had read and pondered Huxley's essay on *Evolution and Ethics* (1893), he might have been driven to reflect that his own loose analogies between physical process and moral reality were without foundation. No one could have believed more strongly than Huxley did in biological evolution; and no one could have seen more clearly that to argue from it to moral categories was intellectually illegitimate and practically most dangerous.

But as we read, we see that to take this warning to heart would really have been contrary to his nature. Everything conspired to make him a reckless, visionary thinker, with a strong sense of analogies and likenesses, and a weak sense of distinction, definition, limit. He was largely self-educated, and he was characteristic of the type in having a vigorous appetite for books, ideas, thoughts and imaginative sensations without a corresponding critical sense. His Cockney self-assurance, his easy success, his role as the popular sage, his extreme literary versatility, his sheer cheek, made him fond of the 'brilliant' generalization. And, in any case, his public would forget what he had said yesterday in their curiosity about what he would say to-day.

Occasionally, though, a hard moment of insight, a bitter touch of self-knowledge invades his self-satisfaction, and makes us read with greater sympathy and a much stronger sense of a penetrating mind in the author. So it is when he expresses sincere and lasting regret for replying 'like a Cockney Voltaire' to a well-meant letter of religious exhortation. Most interesting of all is his study of his own jealousy, when his long abandoned wife married again. He destroyed every relic of her that he possessed; he

burnt her photographs. This could have led him to an interesting study
of the difference between his passions and his theories. But the moment
of truth is a moment only. His content is always superior to his power of
analysis. The fascination of reading this book is that we are left to do the
most difficult and fundamental work of the autobiographer for ourselves.

(iii)   *Bertrand Russell*

Bertrand Russell's autobiography is one of the finest and most satisfying
of this century. It is one of the few which, while following the wandering, unpredictable course of experience, does justice to a grand and
simple idea. By showing an irreconcilable conflict between the thoughts
and the feelings of a highly intellectual and extremely emotional man, it
shows life, in the way a great epic poem may do, in a grand symbolic
attitude.

The kind of thinking at which Russell excelled was abstract, mathematics
and symbolic logic; his engagement in love, politics, education was passionate, inconstant, fierce, unpredictable and frequently self-righteous and egotistical. We hardly ever, in reading Russell, have the sense of a whole
human being. Wisdom was the least of his qualities. And round the central opposition of mind and heart are grouped other scarcely less intractable oppositions, the aristocrat and the radical, the romantic theorizer
and the Augustan wit, the passionate simplifier, and the shrewd man of
the world, the enraptured lover, who thinks the world well lost, and the
dangerous Don Juan.

Particularly satisfying to the reader is the way this general scheme,
which is conscious and literary, is echoed in other ways that are not conscious. The prose style can veer suddenly from reminding us of Shelley or
Walt Whitman to recalling Jane Austen or Cobbett. The brief preface,
'What I have lived for', speaks of three passions, 'simple but overwhelm-
ingly strong' . . . 'The longing for love, the search for knowledge and
unbearable pity for the suffering of mankind.'[23] His idea of love is so
exalted as to make previous romantic celebrators seem timid and conventional:

I have sought love, first, because it brings ecstacy—ecstasy so great
that I would often have sacrificed all the rest of life for a few hours of

this joy. I have sought it, next, because it relieves loneliness—that terrible loneliness in which one shivering consciousness looks over the world into the cold unfathomable lifeless abyss.

Very soon we find we are in a very different world, of family gossip, acid reminiscences and persistently uncharitable judgments, as: 'I never knew my maternal grandfather, but I heard it said that he used to browbeat my grandmother, and felt that, if so, he must have been a very remarkable man' or 'Algernon was witty, fat, and greedy.'[24]
But the political passion is just as strong as the amorous:

In 1876 my parents went to America . . . They would not foresee that the men and women whose democratic ardour they applauded and whose triumphant opposition to slavery they admired were the grandfathers and grandmothers of those who murdered Sacco and Vanzetti.[25]

Of course he does not mean that he has researched the genealogy of judge and jury in this miscarriage of justice. He means that because Sacco and Vanzetti were, in his opinion, innocent, and were found guilty, all Americans are implicitly guilty of murder; a proposition which his thinking mind would hold to be absurd. So almost on the first page of his book, in speaking of events when he was four years old, he prepares us for the political extravagances of his old age.

Clearly as he discerns, and beautifully as he conveys the opposition of thought and feeling, there is one aspect of it that seems to escape him, and which is communicated to us unconsciously. This is his extreme counter-suggestibility. This history of his opinions of Soviet Russia is a good example. He acquired first-hand knowledge of it early, on a long visit in 1920. His verdict was uncompromising:

I felt that everything that I valued in human life was being destroyed in the interests of a glib and narrow philosophy, and that in the process untold misery was being inflicted upon many millions of people.[26]

This was at a time when 'progressive' opinion in the West, of which Russell certainly conceived himself to be an adherent, was still largely favourable to the Soviets. When the war alliance muted criticism of them, he became much more bitterly opposed. In the Cold War era he veered part of the way back again. There is something in all this which

[24] Ibid., p.34.
[25] Ibid., p.16.

puzzles him more than it does the reader. We sense a puckish extrava-
gance in all his public utterances, a childish desire to shock, and perhaps
something subtler than these. Born into one of the most powerful of all
the great Whig families, grandson of a Prime Minister, and heir, before
he left the nursery, to an earldom, he felt his aristocratic privileges alter-
nately as a privilege and a burden. But mainly as a burden; he was intent
on distancing himself decisively from the Whig tradition of subtle and
cynical statecraft. There were, perhaps, two opposite elements in his
rejection, a diffused sense of guilt at being so much more fortunate than
others, and a desire, born of his sense of possessing extraordinary talents,
not to be typed as an aristocrat, who does not need very much talent to
achieve worldly success.

There are, certainly, just a few mellow passages where a temporary
harmony is achieved between the bleak abstractions of his intellect and
the restlessness of the heart:

> It is a most wholesome thing, when one's sorrow grows acute, to
> view it as having all happened long, long ago: to join in imagination,
> the mournful company of dim souls whose lives were sacrificed to the
> great machine that still grinds on. I see the past, like a sunny land-
> scape, where the world's mourners mourn no longer. On the banks of
> the river of Time, the sad procession of human generations is marching
> slowly to the grave; but in the quiet country of the past, the tired
> wanderers rest, and all their weeping is hushed.[27]

But it is significant that this passage is quoted from a letter of comfort to
a friend, and we are all, however genuine our sympathy, inclined to take
a more philosophic view of the troubles of others than of our own.

His position as a member of a great Whig family is handled with address,
and even cunning. He begins by making fun of the social assumptions that
came naturally in early years to a member of such a family. He tells how
he heard that an uncle was only a Rear Admiral, while there was a grander
rank of Admiral of the Fleet. 'This rather pained me and I felt he should
have done something about it.' He was conscious of a 'pleasurable broad-
mindedness' in talking to a woman who was not what his grandmother
would have called a lady. And he quotes a letter of 1904 (when he was
over thirty) where he speaks of members of the Amalgamated Society of
Engineers as 'excellent people, *very* respectable—indeed I shouldn't have
guessed they were working people'. We are meant, perhaps, to think,

[27] Ibid., p.169.

'See what I have escaped from.' But he wishes us to take his patriotism very seriously, and when in 1950, having repeatedly trampled on the tenderest corns of respectability, he was awarded the Order of Merit, he writes with a simplicity which is meant to startle us:

> This made me very happy for, though I daresay it would surprise many Englishmen and most of the English Establishment to hear it, I am passionately English, and I treasure an honour bestowed on me by the Head of my country.[28]

By this time we are in the third volume, and we know, almost for certain, before reading on, that he is not going to let the King off quite as lightly as that. When the King, remembering that he had been in prison as a conscientious objector in the First War, remarked 'You have sometimes behaved in a way which would not do if generally adopted', he carefully refrained from replying, 'Like your brother'. He says he has been glad ever since of his restraint; and we are left wondering whether he was rejoicing at his forbearance to a man who might have been wounded, or at being a better gentleman than his monarch. When the King told him that Lord Portal was the only man who had both the KG and the OM, 'I did not mention that he was my cousin.' Here, the old man, quite deliberately, and, as it were, with a cunning glance at the reader to see how he is taking it, is thrusting us back seventy years to his childhood conviction that he was related to everyone of importance, and that really kings ought to be better informed about this. His generally humorous approach to questions of class and family and class (there are some witty and incisive portraits of relations) serves as comic relief in a book at times portentous in its seriousness, and may conceal a persistent uneasiness about his own attitude to other classes.

Similar is his bland statement that he first met the head of his family, the Duke of Bedford, on his own ninetieth birthday. He tells us, almost in the style of an obituary in *The Times* what an excellent man he was, how splendidly unconventional, how admirable in his determination to keep Woburn as a private estate in the face of the bleak, collectivist twentieth century. He almost parodies, with a perfectly straight face, and apparently wishing to be taken literally, high Whig attitudes of a century before. But he does not say, and with a glint of unspoken humour leaves the reader to guess, why the head of his family had not bothered to make the acquaintance of his most distinguished relative until long after most

---

[28] Ibid., p.26.

people are dead. All these touches add to the self-portrait; and especially contribute to its great theme of contrast between the surface and the depths of his own nature. He is offering us, as it were, the heart of Shelley, the brain of Newton and the irony of Gibbon; and he will go on ringing the changes so that we are never able to mistake one aspect for the whole.

Passionate egoists are seldom aware of being so; their most extravagant desires tend to leave them astonished at their own moderation. And this in turn will make them, as a rule, unsatisfactory as autobiographers. Here Russell is a great exception. Right from the start he points unerringly at the unreasonableness of his own egoism, in speaking of his childish dealings with a brother seven years older:

> There was also a certain small bell which I believed to be mine, but which he at each return asserted to be his and took from me, although he was himself too old to derive any pleasure from it. He still had it when he was grown-up, and I never saw it without angry feelings.[29]

In general, his use of childhood memories is very different from the practice of the authors discussed earlier. His does not use them for their vividness, their imaginative power, their remembered glory, but much more as an objective biographer might do, as sources of insight about his character, as precious signposts to the future. Literalness, for instance, is a common feature of childhood; but Russell can make use of it to show something permanent in his nature, a passionate, untameable regret at the gulf between the ideal and the real, a real youthfulness which lasted into his nineties and even grew stronger then:

> I heard one of the grown-ups saying to another, 'When is the young Lyon coming?' I pricked up my ears and said, 'Is there a lion coming?' 'Yes,' they said, 'he's coming on Sunday. He'll be quite tame and you shall see him in the drawing room.' I counted the days till Sunday and the hours through Sunday morning. At last I was told the young lion was in the drawing room and I could come and see him. I came. And he was an ordinary young man named Lyon. I was utterly overwhelmed by the disenchantment and still remember with the anguish the depths of my despair.[30]

Like most adolescents he had learnt a few years later to conceal his

---

[29] Ibid., I, p.26.
[30] Ibid., I, p.23.

feelings better, but they were no less strong; and he indicates this by occasional sharp touches such as his need to lean against the wall to steady himself when he first heard someone reciting Blake's 'Tyger, Tyger'. And this passionate responsiveness was just as strong in philosophical as in literary or personal matters.

At Cambridge:

> For two or three years ... I was a Hegelian. I remember the exact moment during my fourth year when I became one. I had gone out to buy a tin of tobacco, and was going back with it along Trinity Lane, when suddenly I threw it up in the air and exclaimed: 'Great God in boots!—the ontological argument is sound!' [31]

And later he describes his emergence from a period when he was driven, on philosophical grounds, to disbelieve in the sensible world as an 'intense excitement', because once again he could accept that there really were tables and chairs. But there is a cunning mixture of themes here, since he sets against the freshness of this naivety his gradual sad introduction to worldly wisdom. He records sadly how McTaggart, under whose influence he became a Hegelian, eventually asked him not to come and see him because he could not bear his opinions, and then took a leading part in having him deprived of his lectureship. This was more than twenty years later, but follows immediately in Russell's narrative, so that we are able to feel the ironies of time, and the balance of opposite aspects of his own character. He does not envy the prudent of this world among whom his early years were spent. G.M. Trevelyan, a member of another great Whig family, and great-nephew of Macaulay, neatly epitomizes all these rejected influences:

> On August 4, 1914, he and I walked down the Strand quarrelling. Since then I saw him only once, until I returned to Trinity in 1944, after he had become Master. When he was still an undergraduate he explained to me once that the Trevelyans never make matrimonial mistakes. 'They wait,' he said 'until they are thirty, and then marry a girl who has both sense and money.'

The argument of 1914, naturally, was about the moral aspects of war; and in his treatment of this subject, we are conscious once again of the reflecting mind undercutting the passionate memory. He tells us that he was so convinced a pacifist that he would certainly have murdered

[31] Ibid., I, p.63.

Asquith or Grey if he had met them, as a punishment for taking Britain into the war.

His political convictions were just as liable as his philosophical ones to unforeseen leaps into change. Having been an Imperialist, he became a pro-Boer and a pacifist in five minutes; and it was characteristic that the cause of this change was not political at all, but was the emotion excited by seeing Mrs Whitehead in a state of severe physical pain:

> Within five minutes I went through some such reflections as the following: the loneliness of the human soul is unendurable; nothing can penetrate it except the highest intensity of the sort of love that religious teachers have preached; whatever does not spring from this motive is harmful, or at best useless; it follows that war is wrong, that a public school education is abominable.[32]

Once again a skilful collocation reveals his understanding of his own inconsistencies. Much of the unhappiness which he inflicted on the women he loved and on himself was due to confusing the love 'that religious teachers have preached' with love as sexual desire. For him, perhaps, the suddenness and waywardness which the world in general perceives in the second kind was felt also in the first; and so the distinction between them, which is so obvious to common sense and experience, was blurred. So, on the very next page he writes:

> I went out bicycling one afternoon, and suddenly, as I was riding along a country road, I realised that I no longer loved Alys. I had had no idea until this moment that my love for her was even lessening.

The intensity of his romanticism is well seen in the sequel. For nine years they lived together in the same house, and there was no extramarital sexual interest or activity for either. 'About twice a year I would attempt sex relations with her, in the hope of alleviating her misery, but she no longer attracted me, and the attempt was futile.' If we remain in the realm of external facts, Russell might be counted, like Wells, on the score of the latter half of his life as sexually promiscuous. But the spirit is utterly different; and this failure, because of his romantic nature, of normal youthful appetites, with the maximum of opportunity and legitimacy to stimulate them, is eloquent testimony. And the frustration felt here was mirrored in, or caused by, or was itself the cause of a painful intellectual frustration, when a hard day's thinking would leave him still

[32] Ibid., I, p.146.

with a blank sheet of paper before him. Meanwhile he wrote letters prais-
ing austerity and hair-shirts.

At the end of this long period, which must have seemed even longer in
the living, he was seduced by Lady Ottoline Morrell—he was too much
of a gentleman to put it like that—and had to confess this to Alys. When
Alys threatened to discredit Ottoline's reputation, he threatened suicide:

> I meant this, and she saw that I did. Thereupon her rage became
> unbearable. After she had stormed for some hours, I gave a lesson in
> Locke's philosophy to her niece . . . I then rode away on my bicycle,
> and with that my first marriage came to an end. I did not see Alys
> again till 1950, when we met as friendly acquaintances.[33]

It is a credit to his sense of justice as well as to his sense of the difference between subjective experience for different persons that he is not
afraid to print her quiet, uncomplaining letters written half a lifetime
later, which reveal the undying quality of her love. But here, the absurdly
inopportune lesson to the niece is a perfect symbol of separation of intellect and feeling. The flat, prosaic tone of the last quotation is as deliberate
and as characteristic as the heady romanticism of the earlier love passages.
It is as if he is here playing with the book's great theme.

Perhaps, too, there are times when he feels a grudge against the overwhelming strength of his passions; and seeks to take revenge on them
with a little witty worldliness. It is as if we are watching the most unlikely
of all transformations, of Shelley turned into Byron, when we find
comments like these:

> Ottoline could still, when she chose, be a lover so delightful that to
> leave her seemed impossible, but for a long time past she had seldom
> been at her best with me.[34]

And here he adds the trivial and telling little detail that she gave him
another chance, after telling him that she wished their relation to become
platonic, because he had been cured of pyorrhoea in America.

Or, choosing for a moment to view the passion of love from the stance
of a disinterested observer, he writes of his brother's second wife:

> very fat, used to wear green corduroy knickerbockers; the view of her
> from behind when she was bending over the flower-bed . . . used to

[33] Ibid., I, p.204.
[34] Ibid., I, p.213.

make me wonder that he had thought her worth what he had gone through for her sake.[35]

(This refers to his imprisonment for bigamy.) Or he tells us, almost with the smugness of Wells—which is, in Russell's case entirely misleading—how difficult it was in 1919 to arrange that two of his mistresses' times of arrival did not overlap. Probably he knows that our memory of his former agonies and intensities will prevent us from misinterpreting this. Nevertheless, the malicious delight in farcical situations is a real, though superficial, aspect of his character.

It would be easy to select quotations tending to show that he was self-righteous both in private and public affairs. And in the third volume, written in extreme old age, and much inferior in sharpness of self-criticism to the other two, this impression might even be said to predominate. But it would be a grave error to see the work as a whole in this light. It is offset by frequent touches of humorous self-deprecation, by honest records of his own inconsistency, and—most important of all—by poignant indications of desperate insecurity. The gifted, handsome aristocrat, admired friend of many of his cleverest contemporaries was easily rattled, even cowed, easily made to feel his own insignificance. We have already seen, in his confession of a wish to murder Asquith and Grey that his pacifism was linked to obscure passions, so that without fully understanding the matter, he felt uneasiness and a vague guilt. This made him extremely vulnerable to forthright criticism from a point of view unimaginably different from his own. This came, in devastatingly eloquent form, from D.H. Lawrence. The following is one of the most revealing passages in the whole work:

> He [Lawrence] always got into a fury if one suggested that anybody could possibly have kindly feelings towards anybody else, and when I objected to war because of the suffering that it causes, he accused me of hypocrisy. 'It isn't in the least true that you, your basic self, want ultimate peace. You are satisfying in an indirect, false way your lust to jab and strike. Either satisfy it in a direct and honourable way, saying "I hate you all, liars and swine, and am out to set upon you", or stick to mathematics, where you can be true—But to come as the angel of peace—no, I prefer Tirpitz a thousand times in that role.'

I find it difficult now to understand the devastating effect that this letter had upon me. I was inclined to believe that he had some insight

[35] Ibid., I, p.153.

denied to me, and when he said that my pacificism was rooted in blood-lust I supposed that he must be right. For twenty-four hours I thought that I was not fit to live and contemplated suicide.[36]

In the face of insecurity like this, his postures of superiority acquire a new meaning for us; they become almost endearing. Although he says he recovered quickly from this mood, and even found courage to answer Lawrence back, the wound was so deep that in a book published thirty-eight years after Lawrence's death, he did not excise the blistering criticisms which he had written much earlier. He called him his wife's mouth-piece, and his thought a mass of self-deception, and added 'Like Marx, he had a snobbish pride in having married a German aristocrat, and in *Lady Chatterley* he dressed her up marvellously.' The amused contempt which he shows for so many of the people he mentions, and even his tendency to portray his wives and mistresses as well-meaning children who failed to comprehend his profundity, need to be read with this in mind. His detachment, his jocularity, even his aristocratic poses all spring from a self-distrust and a power of suffering of unusual strength. His professions of hatred, too, which he boldly quotes from letters may have, in part, the same source. Their wild, sweeping quality (for instance 'I hate the planet and the human race. I am ashamed to belong to such a species' from a letter of 1916) testify to his own inner bewilderment. It is characteristic, perhaps, that when he has solid reason to feel personally aggrieved at being persecuted for seriously held opinions, he reverts to his style of light Augustan wit:

> At Trinity, meanwhile, all the younger fellows had obtained commissions, and the older men naturally wished to do their bit. They therefore deprived me of my lectureship.[37]

He thought that this was for his opposition to the war.

Love was the most awkward of all subjects to show forth his great principle of the conflict between thought and feeling. It required him to reveal himself in a harsh light, jealous himself while sternly rejecting jealousy directed against him. And he has to show the havoc caused in other lives. We do not doubt that this is really painful to him. There was nothing of the cad in him, though his actions may sometimes have made people wonder. This leads him to a profound analysis of the causes of his failure as a husband:

[36] Ibid., II, p.22.
[37] Ibid., II, p.33.

Underlying all occupations and all pleasures I have felt since early youth the pain of solitude. I have escaped it most nearly in moments of love, yet even there, on reflection, I have found that the escape depended partly upon illusion. I have known no woman to whom the claims of intellect were as absolute as they were to me, and wherever intellect intervened, I have found that the sympathy I sought in love was apt to fail. What Spinoza called 'the intellectual love of God' has seemed to me the best thing to live by, but I have not had even the somewhat abstract God that Spinoza allowed himself . . . I have loved a ghost, and in loving a ghost my inmost self has become spectral . . . my most profound feelings have remained always solitary and have found in human things no companionship. The sea, the stars, the night wind in waste places, mean more to me than even the human beings I love best, and I am conscious that human affection is to me at bottom an attempt to escape from the vain search for God.[38]

We read this as a final judgment on the complicated narrative of his loves, with its many painful and many comic incidents; and it rings true. He is truly accounting for himself, and his frankness elsewhere saves him from the reproach of taking refuge in high-minded justification for indefensible acts and omissions.

Russell's claim, a strong one in my view, to be a truly great autobiographer rests on passages like this, and especially on their felt truth as epitomes of the whole detailed narrative. We can do our own editing, and reject much of the third volume, though it has its moments, like the interview with the King quoted earlier. In general, it is insistent, even crude in its assertions. It seems to be written by a man who has forgotten the complexities of experience, previously so well understood. Sometimes, this issues in an amusing contradiction, as when he says:

No one can pretend to a liking for being imprisoned . . . It is a frightening experience . . . The worst is the general atmosphere, the sense of being always under observation, the dead cold and gloom and the always noted, unmistakable prison smell—and the eyes of some of the other prisoners.[39]

This imprisonment, in the 1960s, lasted only a week. He quite forgets that the much longer imprisonment of the First World War had been

[38] Ibid., II, p.38.
[39] Ibid., III, p.117.

described as one of the happiest times of his life, and that the warder had to remind him that prison was a place of punishment because he was laughing so much. But these are small matters. The loss of his great theme of opposition between mind and heart serves only to remind us how grand, in the main body of the work, it was.

VIII

The Quest

'tis a thing impossible to frame
Conceptions equal to the soul's desires.

(Wordsworth, *The Excursion*, IV, II, 136–7)

All men, to one so bound by such a vow,
And women were as phantoms.

(Tennyson, *The Holy Grail*)

And if you seek for any wilderness
You find, at best, a park.

(E.B. Browning, *Aurora Leigh*. First Book)

Facts revenge themselves upon the man who denies their existence.

(Leslie Stephen, *Hours in a Library*, III, p.245)

The things one says are all unsuccessful attempts to say something else.

(Bertrand Russell, Letter to Ottoline Morrell,
11 August 1918. Quoted in his *Autobiography*, II, p.90)

Do young men have these feelings still? . . . I take off my hat to myself. It was absurd if you like. But alas, what is later life, except the gradual breaking in of the soul to her prison?

(Autobiography of G. Lowes Dickinson, ed. by D. Proctor, p.67.)

THE LAST CHAPTER spoke of those who try to fulfil self by their influence on society. The next will speak of those whose aim is to find truth. Both groups might be called questers in a sense; but the essence of the quest as the word is used now is its privacy. The quester does not agree to test his aims or his opinions by any measure; he does not concede the onlooker any right to judge. He does not, as preachers of doctrines do, invite us to believe his message and follow his path. He is not writing to win agreement but to demonstrate his own uniqueness. The more successful he is, as a writer, the less shall we be inclined to believe that we are like him, and can imitate him.

Autobiographers are not inevitably egotistical; and it may well be true that most of us love ourselves too well to be autobiographers. But this particular kind of autobiographer can scarcely avoid conveying a proud separateness. He may be very frank about his failings, like Powys, or willing to make himself ridiculous like Ackerley. What he will not do is to admit that his case is typical.

It may seem at first sight surprising that most such accounts report the quest a failure. Sometimes this may be due simply to the writer's honesty; but just as often it is due to a dislike of finality. There may be a desire, hidden sometimes from the writer, to seek the unobtainable—'the light that never was on sea or land'. In some cases, the pains of searching are preferred to any conceivable point of rest.

The solitude of the quest may be a literal solitude, as it was for Havelock Ellis, all alone for a year in the Australian bush.[1] But others, like Haydon and Ackerley, are engaged in a search that entails constant contact with people. These are no less solitary within. The qualities they suppose to separate them from others may be high or low. A belief in his own genius sustained Haydon; a moral dread of sexual perversity inspired Powys. Kathleen Raine would count all other hopes well lost for the privilege of persisting in her quest. Ackerly eventually abandoned his with relief, tempered by a wry wonder that he had ever engaged in it. But all have in common a sense of being driven on by something stronger than their own will; and they might hesitate to say whether inspiration or fury or demon was the term to describe it.

No doubt there are some who are questers only for a time, and then think better of it. Chesterton's autobiography describes such a case. For him a search for religious truth took the place of the quest. Others retreat into ordinary concerns and ambitions. But this chapter does not speak of

[1] Havelock Ellis, *My Life*, Heinemann, 1940. Especially Chap. 4.

these, but of those who go on to the end, and greet failure as a tragic necessity and as a friend to their pride.

The quester's intense inner world tends to make him vague about times and seasons. When he turns his vision outwards, and describes the world he sees, he will find it unfriendly, or tedious or actively threatening, because it is the world that refused to take him at his own valuation. He may be inclined to blame it for his own decision to exclude it from his deepest concerns. He may show considerable satirical or comic powers, as several of those discussed in the following pages do. But he will not leave us in doubt that, however much he speaks of the world it is alien to him. It is composed of other people. And he always seems to be muttering under his breath what Oblomov said to his servant: 'You *dare* compare me to other people.'

(i) The High Quest: Kathleen Raine

In Kathleen Raine we find the quest at its most abstract. She is one of those who instinctively dislike the particularity of experience, who are uneasy that objects, people, tasks are all so specific. Such people are reluctant to accept anything on its own terms and for its own sake. They may be capable of ecstasy, but lack an enjoying temper; they are distressed by the quirkiness, the solidity and the earthiness of things. They want everything to mean something, and all meanings to be capable of being united into a grand, simple, though perhaps inexpressible meaning. To such, Plato will often speak powerfully; and his myth of the cave, in which all visible things are compared to shadows of objects out of sight will seem deeply satisfying.

The autobiography consists of three volumes.[2] In the early chapters of the first we have an evocation of a timeless world of childhood, that may remind us of Hudson or Muir. But only for a short time, because there is none of that wholeness and harmony which a child needs to create a paradise from the surroundings. She was early aware that her parents were pulling her in opposite directions. Her mother was 'poetic, not practical'. She was Scots, and the family's exile from Scotland was soon associated with exile 'from that legendary land which some call Eden, some Zion, some Tibet'.[3] Her father stood for progress, education and the future.

[2] Kathleen Raine, *Farewell Happy Fields*, 1973; *The Land Unknown*, 1975; and *The Lion's Mouth*, 1977. All pub. Hamish Hamilton.
[3] K. Raine, F.H.F., p.19.

But this plain opposition is modified by a religious difference which, to some extent, runs counter to it. The father had inherited an enthusiastic adherence to Methodism, where the stress was on conversion, and an open visible conflict between the forces of good and evil. The mother had inherited the Scots Calvinist tradition, which, working on such a temperament as hers, can produce a cheerful fatalism, allowing her to experience a oneness with nature, almost of a Wordsworthian kind. Such a result is probably rare, much rarer than the author appears to realize. But:

> I always had the impression with members of my mother's family, that their religion was extraneous to themselves whereas the songs and history and fairy-lore of Scotland expressed their true natures and real beliefs. To escape into that world of poetry whose people have no morality but only life and its many moods must have seemed for them —and was for me—like an escape into reality from the acting of a tedious part.[4]

But the father could only find value in songs and stories if they had a moral. By a sad, but perhaps common, irony, his sincerity and earnestness became embarrassing to the members of his family, until they came to seem like play-acting, and they were unable to give him the credit his genuineness deserved.

Even when the parents appeared to agree, for instance in supposing drunkenness to be the worst of all sins, the grounds of condemnation were perceived to be different. For her father it was the outward sign of the failure of grace in the great interior struggle of good and evil. For her mother it was the ultimate sign of loss of respectability. Her father was interested in the spiritual condition, her mother in the inherent nature, of a person. So much so that her mother's Calvinistic censoriousness was turned equally against inanimate things, and became a 'sinister animism'. For a sensitive child, the fact that these deep differences were not reflected in any official and clear-cut separation, such as occurs when one parent is a Catholic and the other is not, or when one is Christian and the other Jewish, can only have increased their eerie power. She felt that under the guise of an agreed teaching, she was being subjected to incompatible influences. As the differences were unconfessed or perhaps unrecognized, there was no relief or tension in taking sides; the child's tendency to solitude and secret thoughts was intensified. And, having two different moral systems to choose from, she came to feel that morality

4 Ibid., p.68–9.

was a matter of choice, or perhaps rather of intimate personal sensation. All through the account of adult life as well as of childhood she shows no awareness of moral standards as principles of objective authority. (This is perhaps only an aspect of her intense inwardness, her lack of awareness of the physical reality of things, the world of facts and events, in her ecstatic contemplation of their subjective value to herself. And in this, she shows herself a characteristic member of the 'Quest-school'.) Thus she can, later on, excuse herself easily and airily for quite serious moral delinquencies, but she is in earnest when she speaks of drowning kittens, which she did under adult orders, as murder. And were we not so sympathetic to her youthful intensities, because of the imaginative truth of her record, we might be inclined to smile at the breathless statement: 'So young, blood was already on my hands.'

The second way in which she diverges from those who celebrate a lost paradise is that she is soon striving and continues throughout all the future recorded years to strive for something incompatible with the primitive simplicities so lovingly recalled. For all her petulance against urban civilization, and modern sophistication, her resentment against Cambridge and all the other places where she learnt to be more and more different from her parents, she was seeking something for which all these later painful experiences were indispensable. She was searching for an esoteric wisdom, a key to the questions of life, which was to be found (she fancied) through books or wise philosophers. And yet we are inclined to doubt whether the contrast between this and the lost paradise of childhood is as plain to her as it inevitably is to us. She imagines, perhaps, that her strange personal way of seeing things, even in childhood, will partly bridge the gap. Of particular interest here is her account of the slaughter of the bull:

> Never in amphitheatre nor temple of the gods nor circle of stone menhirs did the fate of consecrated victim more totally absorb the minds and souls of the spectators; what the theatre only represented, the bull-fight simulates, this was.[5]

As this exordium will lead us to expect, she proceeds to interpret the event in mythic terms, as man's 'profound self-condemnation of his own animal nature'. But she continues the sentence in words that are very surprising, and which suggest that there are certain things about herself which she has not understood, and which three volumes more will show her still not understanding. She goes on:

[5] Ibid., p.59.

his own animal nature, still not extinct in men so primitive as to be securely rooted in the human principle to which on the Sabbath Day they aspired.

This is to confuse two interpretations. It may be (or it may not be) that the slaughter of the bull represents what she says, but if it does so, it cannot, as she goes on to imply, be because of the primitive cultural level of the participants, as though more sophisticated people could somehow escape from the body and its claims. The likeness between men and animals is not to be summed up in our loose use of words like 'brutal' to describe uncivilized behaviour. No one has ever been so highly civilized that he did not need to eat and sleep as animals do. To say nothing of the fact that this mythic interpretation she offers would never occur to any mind but a sophisticated, literary one.

In a sense, her confusion here is natural, and it is certainly revealing. There are two very different impulses at work, each so deep in her nature that she finds it impossible at this stage (and difficult always) to distinguish them. The first led her away from the censorious attitude of both her parents (different as they were) to carnal weaknesses, and led her to value the Catholic sense of community between saints and sinners, and the Catholic refusal to grade the unrespectable sins as worse than the respectable ones. This was clearly a strong factor in that incomplete and temporary conversion to Catholicism.

But the other impulse, though equally far from her parents' Protestant traditions, went dead against the Catholic impulse, It was the traditional search of the ancient mystery religions for release from the body, something rooted in pride and exclusiveness. It would even be true to say that when she received the sacraments as a Catholic, she received them with the expectations of such a devotee. She expected them to give her unique *experiences*; and approached thus, they must always be found unsatisfying. Hence her ambivalent attitude to the Catholic Church becomes intelligible. She always speaks in favour of its tolerance, its humanity, its inclusiveness, its deep instinctive comprehension of the parables of the wheat and the tares and of the good and bad fish. But she turns against it when it fails to provide her with esoteric mysteries, when it fails to offer a place in a select band of wise initiates who can afford to disdain the common herd because they find deep hidden meanings in writers such as Blake. The conflict is in a way all the more interesting because it is not fully articulated, but presented rather as if it were conflict of moods. It is really much more, a permanent conflict of principles.

And there is a further conflict in her own attitude to this slaughter of the bull. She took the bull's side; that is, according to her own mythic interpretation, the side of the animal in man against human discipline. This is opposite to her search for superhuman enlightenment. Or so it would seem. But she seeks to reconcile her attitudes by speaking of the 'innocence of nature' and by saying boldly, 'I was on the side of nature against man.' Perhaps then the superhuman wisdom was to be reached not by aspiring to lofty contemplations but by the merging of one's human status in a pantheistic vision of nature. But this, too, is a possibility she does not really pursue, and the sense of incompatibilities not fully understood remains.

With deliberate art she links the description of the death of the bull with the death of her cousin. The shock she felt at this was not the shock of bereavement; her affection for him was not strong. It was more like an affront to her dignity as a spiritual creature, so that the visible world, because it had been invaded by the death of one person, lost its reality for her. It was part of her impatience with everything provisional, subject to change and decay; her proud, almost insane (a word she actually employs herself) rejection of the necessary conditions of life as we know it. The solidity of things, to most people so deep an intuition that it would need a complicated philosophical argument to make them see how it could possibly be questioned, was to her obviously questionable. 'I was in terror,' she writes, 'even in broad daylight, of being alone, lest the gulfs of darkness should swallow me.'

Very close for her to her pursuit of esoteric wisdom was her sense of being a poet. It is more than a vocation; it is an absolute claim to subordinate everything, duty, happiness, the happiness of friends to a single peremptory claim. It is a revival, an intensification, of the highest claims made for the poet in the early nineteenth century. The poet is simply a different being from the inferior majority of the race; and no ordinary standards, intellectual or moral, can properly be applied to him. Nor can there be any argument about whether he is a poet or not, or whether he is a poet great or small. It is a simple matter of his own intuition. It is characteristic, perhaps, that though her second volume shows a wide acquaintance among her literary contemporaries, she shows herself unaware of her intellectual solitariness here. She does not stop to contrast her view of the poet with T.S. Eliot's (someone with a job to do, like a dentist). It is not so much that she is an archaist, consciously reviving a lost romantic world. Rather she lives imaginatively as an actual contemporary of Shelley, and dismisses the circumstances of the twentieth century as tiresome and irrelevant. It is very characteristic of her that she regards Cambridge as being reduced and contaminated because in her time it was no longer the preserve of the gentry, though well aware that, if it had been, she would not have gone herself. But her quarrel with Cambridge had much deeper roots. She protests against the materialism and the unreasoning belief in progress characteristic of the people she knew there.

We get a clear picture of her in these undergraduate years—estranged from the traditions of her parents, but much more deeply at odds with the slick modernism and emotional triviality of contemporaries, beautiful and desired for her beauty, but madly tempted to reject the very fact of being in the body. When we combine these dilemmas with the never-forgotten search for an ultimate traditional wisdom, we cannot be surprised at her moving in a Manichean direction:

> What has such love to do with the crude animal instinct by which the species is continued? The soul has other ends, another nature. As an animal, indeed, man is most detestable.[6]

There were only two ways to cut the knot, while she remained in this mind, solitude, which would perhaps have suited her best, if she had been strong enough for it, and a chaste, passionate love for a homosexual man. She chose the second:

> I saw in the kind of Platonic love possible between a homosexual and a woman a relationship free from the squalor of the body . . . I had always, as a student, been attracted towards such men, who were, indeed, so often physically beautiful, and of a fineness of feeling lacking in the others.[7]

And she continues with savage and (we may well think) excessive self-criticism:

> As to my body (as distinct from my beauty, which I thought of as something apart) my attitude towards it was of contemptuous indifference. It seemed no longer myself, or even mine. Like any prostitute I was able in this respect also to be what I would have called 'detached' —a cardinal virtue of scientific rationalism.

The close association of the incongruous ideas of prostitution and scientific rationalism is deliberate, and is an indication of her intense

[6] K. Raine, T.L.M., p.23.
[7] K. Raine, T.L.U., p.73.

distaste for the prevailing philosophy of Cambridge. (She is inclined to forget that though any person's circle of acquaintance in a great university may tend to a given world-view, there are hundreds of others representing many different views.) We may notice also that in her attempt to split body from person she was just as far in spirit from Catholicism as she was from scientific rationalism.

Yet her tribute to Catholicism is eloquent and deeply-felt; and it leaves us wondering whether she has really separated herself from it:

> ...Antonia White.* She it was whose influence chiefly led me to become a Catholic convert. I have since wavered and vacillated, finally (insofar as anything is final) unable to remain within the framework of the Church...Her steadfastness I honour; as I do those standards by which she measures all human conduct, those of the great Catholic Christian tradition. There is no better conscience in any human being than that tradition, and I am content to be judged...by that measure of perfection which offers to sinners like myself not any permissive condonation of what we have done but the possibility of the forgiveness of our sins. The Church knows, from its two thousand years of experience, that we are all sinners and that aspiring to perfection we but fall into spiritual pride.[8]

Who would dare to predict, in the case of a person still living, the ultimate outcome of the struggle between this truly Catholic spirit and Yeats's other course of taking Plato and Plotinus for friends?

(ii)   *The Quest in the World: a. De Quincey*

De Quincey's autobiographical writings, like most of his other writings are fragmentary, discursive, repetitive and occasionally contradictory. In the section that follows I endeavour to extract a general self-portrait, without paying attention to the interesting scholarly questions raised by the difference between various fragments. All quotations are from Masson's 14-volume edition of 1889.

De Quincey differs from Kathleen Raine in two very important respects. His quest is not a search for transcendent wisdom, but for an inner

---

* For Antonia White's account of her own reconversion to Catholicism see *The Hound and the Falcon*, 1965.
[8] K. Raine, T.L.M., p.3.

harmony and contentment. Thus, incongruously but not illogically, people, like his dead sister and the prostitute, Ann, and things, books and opium can all be taken at the same time as goals and as guides in his quest. The second difference is even more important. De Quincey is aware at one level of his mind that the quest is unattainable, a truth which never comes home to Kathleen Raine. Why this is so may be a matter of dispute. It could be argued that, as De Quincey remained, in his eccentric way, a Christian, he never lost sight of the gulf between any secular quest, however fascinating, and the ultimate search for God. Hence, the quest is not so much for wisdom—since religious truth has pre-empted this—but rather for experience. Or it may be said that for De Quincey, a true and extreme romantic, the idea of unattainability was itself attractive, and anything he could reach by definition disappointing. Perhaps both explanations are in their own way true.

At all events, very early in his narrative, when he is dealing with the end of his sixth year, he gives a characteristically powerful image of this unattainability. He records how the intuition came to him that 'Life is finished':

as bells heard from a distance on a summer evening seem charged at times with an articulate form of words, some monitory message, that rolls round unceasingly, even so for me some noiseless and subterraneous voice seemed to chant continually a secret word, made audible only to my own heart—that 'now is the blossoming of life withered for ever' . . . Yet in what sense could *that* be true? For an infant not more than six years old, was it possible that the promises of life had been really blighted? or its golden pleasures exhausted? Had I seen Rome? Had I read Milton? Had I heard Mozart?[9]

But what about the things he had already seen? He singles out the appearance of crocuses in early spring (remembered, so he assures us, from his *second* year). He regards the profound sense of pathos as inexplicable,

For such annual resurrections of plants and flowers affect us only as memorials, or suggestions of some higher change, and therefore in connection with the idea of death; yet of death I could, at that time have had no experience whatever.[10]

We are entitled, if we so wish, to interpret this as a hint that death, with

9 Masson, I, pp.28–9.
10 Ibid., I, pp.32–3.

all its immortal possibilities, was the real object of the quest all the time; if we adopt that view we shall see his whole complex and brilliant imaginative world as a kind of weary marking-time. The object of the quest is unattainable in this world, and its attainment will preclude any literary response at all. I do not press this interpretation. With such a chameleon as De Quincey it is very hard to know which hints lead to the centre of the labyrinth. But it is at least consistent with the main facts, his endless searching, and his rejection of everything found or wished for as in some sense inadequate. The failure does not appear as one of ill-luck or incapacity, but as inherent in the situation from the start. This is particularly striking as he shows the warmest appreciation of his family, of the Anglican church ('pure, holy and magnificent') and of his early environment. Like Carlyle, and like Disraeli's Sidonia, he finds in sooty Manchester an image of glory. Commenting on his memorable encounter with the *Agamemnon* of Aeschylus he says: 'Manchester was not Mycenae. No, but by many degrees nobler.' And speaks of 'the immeasurably profounder feelings generated by the mysteries which stand behind Christianity' as against the 'shallow mysteries' of Paganism.[11] Why then, if everything to which he was born was so admirable, did he wish to escape, both physically, by running away, and emotionally, by moving into a dream-world? He had, he says, a 'deep and gloomy sense of obscure duties that I never should be able to fulfil'.[12] And at the same time he had a sense of unknown powers and possibilities in human nature, powerfully excited by certain literary passages. The palpable world of home, and the loved pieties of the local church could not minister to these needs, because they were in a way too real.

His most powerful image of unattainability, more effective for the reader than all the lush landscapes of his opium dreams, is the missed person. We find this theme first in his account of Oxford, when he narrowly missed meeting his brother.

> This is felt generally to be the most distressing form of human blindness—the case when accident brings two fraternal hearts yearning for reunion, into almost touching neighbourhood, and then in a moment after, by the difference, perhaps, of three inches in space, or three seconds in time, will separate them again, unconscious of their brief neighbourhood, perhaps for ever.[13]

[11] Ibid., I, p.108.
[12] Ibid., I, p.71.
[13] Ibid., I, p.312.

This episode works in an unexpected way. It sounds like a familiar plot-device of innumerable melodramas, and detective stories and novels about spies. How different everything would have been if . . . But the point here is that if they had met, even though the consequences for the other man might have been as important as he supposed, the meeting would scarcely have been worth mentioning. By becoming actual it would have ceased to serve as an image of the unattainable. A common-sense response, as 'why do you think every meeting that never occurred so momentous, when those that did occur were not?' would evade the literary point. We cannot doubt that De Quincey was capable of strong responses to real things, to people, to doctrines, to landscapes and to authors. This makes his concentration on the things that never happened all the more significant.

All this will prepare us for the central position taken in his *Confessions* by the prostitute, Ann. He is intent on associating her with his opium experiences, and on associating both with the Impossible Quest. It is she, according to the late preface of 1856 to the *Confessions*, who 'coloured—or more truly I should say—shaped, moulded and remoulded, composed and decomposed the great body of opium dreams'.[14] Sometimes he uses phrases which could apply equally to himself or her, like, 'a momentary blindness', 'listening to a false whisper from his own bewildered heart', 'by one erring step', 'early sufferings in the streets of London'.[15] All these phrases actually refer to De Quincey himself but several seem particularly adopted as traditional phrases considered appropriate to street-walkers.

So Ann, especially after he has seen her for the last time and lost her forever, becomes a haunting image, of which the opposite is the immensity of London, and the strange, muted roar of its pulsating life. Both are, in different ways, images of solitude. And this solitude is associated with opium and with alienation from the self. It is not that in the ordinary sense he loves her, certainly not that he desires her. It is just that her misfortune, her obscurity, the impossibility of discovering her, the hopelessness of all enquiry establish her as the image of what he is seeking through opium, of what he cannot find. Perhaps he does not really wish to find it because if he found it, the unspeakable ultimate would only have escaped him once again:

[14] Ibid., III, p.222.
[15] Ibid., III, p.232.

To this hour I have never heard a syllable about her. This, amongst such troubles as most men meet with in this life, has been my heaviest affliction. If she lived, doubtless we must have been sometimes in search of each other—at the very same moment, through the mighty labyrinths of London; perhaps even within a few feet of each other—a barrier no wider, in a London street, often amounting in the end to a separation for eternity.[16]

He goes on to hope that she has found peace in death; and it is as if this hope is a foretaste of his own release first from tramping round London ('Oxford Street, stony-hearted stepmother') and finally from opium, from the romance of impossibility and from life. The poignancy is increased for him because their last parting was a casual one, made with the intention of soon meeting again.

Being human, Ann is a worthy image of his quest; and his tone in speaking of her is uniformly dignified and respectful, rising at times to emotion and eloquence. He is far more ambivalent about opium. He can speak of it at times as contemptuously as any of his unfriendly critics:

> happiness might now be bought for a penny, and carried in the waistcoat-pocket; portable ecstasies might be had corked up in a pint-bottle; and peace of mind could be sent down by the mail.[17]

At other times he paints a dignified and subtly self-adulatory portrait of the opium-eater as universal philosopher:

> many a time it has happened to me on a summer night—when I have been seated at an open window, from which I could overlook the sea at a mile below me, and could at the same time command a view of some great town. . . . The town of Liverpool represented the earth with its sorrows and its graves left behind, yet not out of sight, nor wholly forgotten. The ocean, in everlasting but gentle agitation, yet brooded over by dove-like calm, might not unfitly typify the mind, and the mood which then swayed it.[18]

But he is not so much, or so persistently the detached philosopher that he wishes to spare us a thrill of melodramatic horror:

> I was stared at, hooted at, grinned at, chattered at, by monkeys, by

---

[16] Ibid., III, p.375.
[17] Ibid., III, p.381.
[18] Ibid., III, pp.394–5.

paroquets, by cockatoos. I ran into pagodas, and was fixed for centuries at the summit or in secret rooms; I was the idol; I was the priest; I was worshipped; I was sacrificed. I fled from the wrath of Brama through all the forests of Asia; Vishnu hated me; Seeva lay in wait for me. I came suddenly upon Isis and Osiris: I had done a deed, they said, which the ibis and the crocodile trembled at. Thousands of years I lived and was buried in stone coffins, with mummies and sphinxes, in narrow chambers at the heart of eternal pyramids. I was kissed with cancerous kisses, by crocodiles . . . [19]

Memorable, though not, to my taste, very deeply impressive. But we are apt, perhaps, in reading it, to suppose that De Quincey is more completely under the sway of his own purple style than is really the case. For he is preparing for a climax that we do not expect. We are already within a few pages of the end of the *Confessions* and so far Ann has not reappeared. Now she does, but in an opium dream. She is perceived in two opposite ways, first as transformed into tranquil solemnity in the setting of Easter morning in Jerusalem then as she had been when he last saw her in London eighteen years before. Obviously, this is the climax of the whole book, and of all De Quincey's autobiographical writings. But it is an enigmatic climax. Does it, as the Easter setting (strongly emphasized) suggests, refer to the hope of heaven for them both? Or does the dream meeting, after so much anguish has been felt at the impossibility of the actual meeting, portend that the dream-world is superior to the real, because in it long-felt desire is at last attained? Or does it simply mean that we never get what we most want, but instead simply dream about it? Immediately after this, he records renouncing opium permanently. And this is enigmatic too. Was it because he had at last attained his object by recovering a shadowy image of Ann? Or is she a kind of guardian angel who signals his return from the semi-madness of opium to the ordinary ways of men? Whatever the answer, he showed good judgment in allowing her to return after the rhetoric of the cancerous kisses, and the eastern mystery. With her, he comes back to earth. And whether he intended it so or not, his last pages remind us that there was a very sensible man hidden away in the wayward and romantic genius. De Quincey in the end appears as a quester who could not deceive himself.

[19] Ibid., III, p.443.

(ii)   *The Quest in the World: b. Benjamin Haydon*

Alas, there was no sensible man hidden inside Haydon. But there was a
very honest boy, whom one cannot help liking, and who lived sixty years
without ever quite ceasing to be a boy. His first ambition, to be a great
classical painter, persists under all discouragements and failures, almost
unchanged to the end. He ended in suicide, an end which must have seemed
possible or even probable for so long that in the end it comes as a surprise. A man who has survived on the edge of a precipice for forty years
may well survive to die of senile pneumonia.

There are certain very obvious things about him which can become
subtly misleading, if not checked against less obvious things. He is
obviously megalomaniac:

> made a sketch of an idea that struck me while at Dover of a colossal
> statue of Britannia and her Lion on Shakespeare's Cliff right opposite
> the coast of France.[20]

or;

> I always filled my painting-room to its fullest extent; and had I possessed a
> room 400 feet long, and 200 feet high, and 400 feet wide, I would
> have ordered a canvas 399–6 long by 199–6 high, and so have been
> encumbered for want of room, as if it had been my pleasure to be so.[21]

It is equally obvious that he has a persecution mania:

> Every man who has suffered for a principle and would lose his life for
> its success ... who has incurred the hatred of his enemies exactly in
> proportion as they became convinced they were wrong—every man
> who, like me, has eaten the bitter crust of poverty, and endured the
> penalties of vice and wickedness where he merited the rewards of vir-
> tue and industry—should write his own life.[22]

But what exactly is this 'principle'? The odd and significant thing is
that, though Haydon is a vivid and eloquent writer, who is constantly
expounding the 'principle', we still end with a difficulty in answering
this simple question. Is it that antique forms of art can be effectively

---

[20] Journal, 19 Dec. 1808. *The Autobiography and Memoirs of Benjamin Robert Haydon*
(1786–1846), 2 Vols., Peter Davies, 1926, I, p.84.
[21] Ibid., I, p.293.
[22] Ibid., I, p.3. (Author's introduction.)

modernized? Or that genius is entitled to its reward? Or that the world has a duty to conform itself to one man's dream?

Perhaps Haydon himself would have answered with a more grandiloquent version of the first of these alternatives, but the reader of his book may be more inclined to the third. And here we find the absolutely essential point of difference from De Quincey. The dream-world of opium is in the head, and the things that De Quincey desired to find in the world were not impossible things. For Haydon only the world can validate his dream; yet the dream remains something distinct from ambition in the ordinary sense. The ambitious man wants something definite; if he is unrealistic it is because he ignores or undervalues the obstacles. But as the quotation given above (about the size of rooms and canvases) seems to show, Haydon's ambitions could not have been fulfilled even if he had really been, and been acknowledged to be, the genius he thought himself. Whatever success he might have attained, and he did attain some, would have been inadequate to the dream. Not only was it inevitable in the real world that the dream should be unrealized, he *needed* that it should not be realized.

One very significant point, which he mentions, but does not stress, is that he had very poor eyesight. 'It never occurred to me as an obstacle.'[23] He admits, forty years after, that this is odd, but shows no curiosity about the reasons. We may well feel that Haydon was a man of talent, but not for art. He had a talent for public-speaking and politics. He certainly had a talent for writing, which survives even its relegation to being at times a mere medium of complaint. He even had a talent for art criticism. Aldous Huxley, the editor of the edition from which the quotations in this chapter are taken, and the author of perhaps the best existing essay on Haydon, noted with delight his comment on West's classical pictures that: 'the venuses looked as though they had never been naked before,' and commented, 'there is nothing more to add; the last word on neo-classicism has been uttered'.[24]

To our considerable surprise, he was even capable of turning this sharp mockery against himself:

I dare say I talked rather more grandly to the artists; I suspect I looked down upon poverty. I did not relish the society of the middle classes; I thought their manners gross and their breeding hideous: I dressed

[23] Ibid., I, p.13.
[24] Ibid., I, p.xix.

better than usual; after a splendid party of Stars and Garters at the admiralty I thought an attempt in my own class a very dull affair.[25]

or again:

I now was a very great man in my own eyes. I had a notion at one time of wearing moustaches, but that went off.[26]

This power to detach himself, even momentarily and intermittently from his obsessions is in striking contrast to his extraordinary gift of maintaining, renewing and intensifying excitement. The following is typical:

Utterly disgusted at my wretched attempt . . . I passed the evening in a mixture of torture and hope; all night I dozed and dreamed of marbles. I rose at five in a fever of excitement.[27]

or on another occasion:

Full of the glory of resistance to injustice I went to bed and fell asleep. In the night I awoke and found myself standing in my cast-room, where I must have been a long time, half dead with cold, bewildered and staring at the head of Niobe. The glitter of the moon awoke me. The clock struck three and I became conscious I had been walking in my sleep.[28]

If Haydon could have brought all this into focus, could have given us a remembered synthesis of his passionate intensities and his cool, self-critical reflections, he might have been one of the greatest of autobiographers. Did he, we wonder, ever re-read? Did he ever feel, as we do, the incongruity between his feelings, genuinely sublime in their own way, and the objects of feeling? Was he ever struck with the contrast between his bravado and his analytical powers? Probably not, or he would have gone on to write differently. But there seem to be no clear stages in his life or in his work. He survived into the world of *Dombey & Son* and of Corn Law Repeal and Prince Albert. If life had the neatness of drama, he might have been expected to die young in some wonderfully romantic way, as Shelley and Byron had done. Or perhaps, he might have declined into a

[25] Ibid., I, p.85.
[26] Ibid., I, p.260.
[27] Ibid., I, p.67.
[28] Ibid., I, p.99.

respected and muted old age, like Wordsworth, or become a monument to shared memories of dead heroes, like Peacock. But he did none of these things. He persisted in attempting to preserve himself in a pose of heroic, youthful aspiration. And he perished a martyr to this insane grandeur.

(iii)   *The Quest in the World: c. John Cowper Powys*

The true pagan is a rare being in the modern world. The post-Christian agnostic liberal is commonly the very reverse of a pagan. As George Orwell pointed out, there are not many people who would be prepared to feed mullets on slaves; and (he might have added) those few would still be different from those who did it of old, because they would have difficulty in suppressing sensations of monstrous wickedness. Later we shall come to one, C.S. Lewis, who began but did not end by being something like a real pagan. Is Powys another?

A short answer might be, in the religious sense, yes; in the moral sense, no. At the very beginning of his long book, he seems anxious to persuade us of his true paganism:

> To get back that laurel-axe from that garden spinney at Shirley would now be to get back the full magical power of that timeless fetish-worship by the strength of which the quaintest, most ordinary object—a tree stump, a pile of stones, a pool by the roadside, an ancient chimney stack—can become an Ark of the Covenant, evocative of the music of the spheres![29]

Fetish-worship in various forms, especially the sexual form, is a leading theme of the book, and it is almost a point of vanity with him that he pursued his objects with more extravagant energy than anyone else could either match or tolerate. But within a few pages, with conscious art and with considerable insight, he gives the other theme, the eternal opposite of the first:

> I cannot remember a time when Conscience was not a trouble to me, ordering me to do what I didn't want to do and to refrain from doing what I wanted to do ... the grand struggle of my life has been between my Conscience and my impulse to live a life made up solely of and entirely of sensual-mystical sensations.[30]

[29] J.C. Powys, *Autobiography*, 1934. Quotations from MacDonald ed. 1967, p.3.
[30] Ibid., p.7.

And he makes no bones about labelling these 'my Viciousness'.

Refreshingly, perhaps, after the brilliant deviousness of De Quincey, who always leaves us to guess how much he really knew about himself, and after the sublime self-delusions of Haydon, we are back in a world of clear light and shade, as if we were in a clearing in a thick forest on a day of sun and heat. It is remarkable that his strong tendency to ecstatic description in rich, not to say over-lush prose, in no way inhibits this clear, antithetical vision, exact as a set of Augustan couplets.

And conscience to him is not alone a sense of responsibility for others. It contains also a passionate sense of purity. He endorses his brother Llewelyn, who was shocked by 'those symbols of pure lust on the sinister brick-red walls of the scoriac streets of ancient Pompeii' and speaks of entering little Byzantine churches in Rome to feel 'a rainy dew of cuckoo flower freshness' after the 'jaded sexuality of the ancient world'.[31]

His dominant vice, he says, was sadism. He cannot remember a time when sadistic thoughts did not intoxicate him. His whole life has been a struggle, in which he can report success, to restrain his sadism, which never, after very early years, issued in action. But in order to curb it, not only in action but in thought, he gave rein to a more ordinary kind of sensuality. He is very insistent on the notion that sadistic thoughts are evil in themselves, even when there is no question of actions in accordance with them. We expect him to relate this to the demanding conscience of which he has already spoken; we can scarcely doubt that it is the real source of his feeling. Does he feel perhaps that this would be over-obvious? Or is he worried because he finds it difficult to relate his strong moral impressions to any coherent religious or philosophical structure? Or is he here only (as he sometimes is) anxious to tease? For he goes off into a pseudo-magical theory, backed by a touch of arcane scholarship about Paracelsus, to show that evil thoughts produce 'magnetic vibrations' that contaminate the surrounding air.

At all events, there is no doubting the seriousness of his moral rejection of sadism. He was not afraid to write about it in his fiction (notably in *The Glastonbury Romance*); and here he finds a fellow-sufferer in Dostoevsky, who, he believes, sublimated and purified it by the power of the spirit. It would be interesting to know, but probably vain to ask, just what he meant by spirit. His cloudy pagan religiosity inhibits him from asking how this forthright and deeply-felt statement relates to those

[31] Ibid., p.35.

Christian doctrines from which he here borrows his terms. But on the moral side his statement is direct and unmistakable:

> What I am not 'allowed' is to write of sadists in such a way as to give myself, *and to other sadists* this ambiguous thrill . . . So inflexible is my Conscience in this matter that I would ten thousand times sooner spoil the 'art' of a book by keeping this deadly shiver out of it altogether than run the risk of providing fuel for this sinister flame. In this point I am in complete agreement—and I think Dostoevsky would be too— with the old ladies of the lending-libraries who think that certain modern books come straight from the Devil. The old ladies are not in error. That is precisely whence they come.[32]

No doubt there is a touch of bravado here. Just as a well-brought-up and obedient little boy will seek to prove his manliness by walking on the flower beds, so here the terrible Powys, who is about to give us 600 pages mainly devoted to the strange sexual by-paths down which he wandered, is out to startle, or even shock us, by identifying himself with the Puritan philistines, who (he knows quite as well as we do) would find little difference between his books and the Devil's brood. Yet in his own way he means it, though he has no idea what he means by the Devil. It is an example, which Newman might have relished, of the power of conscience, even when it lacks a validating principle, and stands forlorn, unable to be welded into any coherent view of life.

He is thus very different at heart from those pseudo-pagan high-priests of sexual gratification, with whom the unwary have sometimes been inclined to group him:

> Nothing has ever seemed to me so irrelevant as the championship of sex as something under the godlike auspices of earth and sun, a beautiful creative force full of life and joy. To me it has . . . been always a world of intense absorption, a world of maniacal exclusiveness, of delirious exaction of insane pursuit, a world existing parallel to the ordinary world of normal human activity, a world into which, when once you enter, and graze like a mad Nebuchadnezzar upon its fatal grass, the ordinary world appears completely dull, 'stale, flat and unprofitable', without lustre and without purpose.[33]

An intelligent and humane case-history of sadism might give us an

[32] Ibid., p.9.
[33] Ibid., p.34.

autobiography of value. But Powys has much more than that to offer. He is able to show a common source for his perverse and his normal tendencies. He finds it in an extreme degree of what is in itself ordinary enough —a proud individualism. With fine literary tact he finds for this what is at once a symbol and a poignant memory. As a schoolboy he had an intense desire to find a secret hiding-place where no one could ever reach him; he wanted 'to substitute a secret reality of my own for the reality created by humanity'. Here he finds the link between his sadism, in some ways the deepest presence in the book, but too tactfully handled to occupy much space, his sensuality, perverse, private and endlessly frustrating, yet innocent compared with the other, and what he calls his 'malice'. All issue from an unconscious resentment at the existence of other people, who, his insane egoism seems to whisper, have no right to be human as he is, moral agents as he is, to have joys and sorrows parallel to his.

He deplores the immorality and indeed the patent absurdity of this impulse. But sensation is sensation. And it is not certain that so strange and daunting a constitution is in the end inimical to the moral life of its (shall we say?) victim. Most of us, by instinct, perhaps, by early training, certainly, learn early to disguise our egoism in the dress of convention and public spirit. When the moment comes, as eventually it must, when a serious moral decision is unavoidable, we may find an unfamiliar conflict frightening. Powys, and those like him, will never be in danger of so being taken by surprise.

Of the two other tendencies which he finds dominant in himself, 'malice' requires little comment. Actually, the word tends to exaggerate what others might have called mischief or puckishness. It causes him to want to shock, upset or surprise other people. A temperament like this will find it hard to forget the artificiality of polite conventions, the oddity of our reticences about common and familiar things. And it will have an urge, half malicious perhaps, but half honestly derived from impatience with hypocrisy, to remind others of the pit from which they are digged. It seems to have been compatible with a fair share of kindness and friendliness, provided the inviolable personal independence was preserved.

His sensuality is altogether more complex; and he feels this so much himself that he proceeds to characterize it by a series of apparent contradictions, which are really artfully contrived to convey his meaning. A common feature of all is that they are boyish. He has both a boyish fastidiousness and a boyish coarseness. Descriptions of ordinary amorous scenes left him cold and disgusted. He detests 'the confounded linking up of humour with lust'. 'When you contemplate a bed of cuckoo flowers, do you,' he asks, 'go and proceed to spoil it by dragging in something facetious?' At the same time he revels with a kind of passionate, trembling purity, in delicate pictures of unclothed girls.

The cuckoo-flower comparison may be more revealing than he knows. The humour of sex springs from the tension between the objectively physical and the personal. If the objects of desire were not ordinary parts of the body to others, equally present to them when they are working or sleeping or reading, the humour would disappear. There is nothing funny about enjoyment of flowers. But Powys's attraction to the female form is so abstract and ethereal that he positively resents the fact that the female form is human and possessed by a personality as real as his own. He wants the girl to be as unaware of herself and of his interest as the flower is. A great deal of his history is taken up with the search for this impossibility:

> What I call lust is an intense, ecstatic contemplation of beauty. It is disinterested. It is impersonal. It seeks no advantage beyond to look and to enjoy![34]

The consequences of this lofty view can be paradoxical indeed. And he is able to achieve a grotesque, but still thoughtful, kind of humour in his awareness of the paradox:

> What I wanted were naughty puppets, incarnations of response to lust and *nothing else*; delicate, heartless, subhuman beings... One great discovery of mine was nothing less than those sordid-looking penny-in-the-slot machines that used to stand in rows, if you knew where to find them, in the New York of thirty years ago. They used to stand on either side of certain narrow hall-ways; hall-ways that always had a ghastly, sepulchral, and quite special kind of daylight in them, as if the cold codfish-eye of all the *two* o'clocks that have ever taken the heart out of a living day have been recaptured and imprisoned there. By turning the handles of these desolate machines and peering through a little spy-hole... I was privileged to play Peeping Tom while certain extremely unsylph-like ladies, of plump and matronly aspect, gravely and with no sign of coyness, removed their outer garments... I cannot recall that these machine-manikinesses of New York ever gave me *one single second* of real satisfaction. The *idea* of them, however,—and I

[34] Ibid., p.120.

remained a true Platonist, even in the matter of penny-in-the-slot machines—kept my hopes on the *qui vive*, I 'never *was*, but always to *be* blest.'[35]

The finest art may be made out of trivial and stupid things. Here, at his moment of lowest humiliation as a man, Powys achieves perhaps his highest point as an autobiographer. The impossible, self-defeating, self-refuting character of the quest (his own and that of many others) here attains a memorable symbolic expression. If he makes himself ludicrous he does so for a serious purpose. And the passage is subtler than it looks, because it depends for its impact upon the amazing contrast between the dirty-minded boy whose behaviour he is simulating and the literary artist who can endow the word 'Platonist' with a most delicate irony. For 'Platonist' means both idealizer, which in a curious topsy-turvy way the Peeping Tom is, and one whose love is not directed to sexual union, which in this most unexpected way he is also. At the same time we cannot but be impressed by the contrast between the claustrophobic self-absorption which alone could lead an intelligent and mature man to such behaviour, and the serene artistic detachment which is needed to give us such a memorable image of the poignancy of inevitable frustration. At moments like this, Powys can really be a great artist in autobiography.

When the encounter was with a real woman, his frustration was greater still:

> these Brighton wenches had minds very much like my own. What is called 'passion' had no existence for them, or for me. They were permeated with manias and riddled with superstitions, and so was I. They were profoundly coarse, but withal excessively fastidious, and such, I have a shrewd notion, is my own character.[36]

In fact, the quest, here too, just as much as in his solitary musings, landed him back in the prison of the self. The fine ambivalence of the whole book is that he both wishes to escape from that prison and wishes to remain in it. As I read the book—and I am aware that it could be read differently—the second wish is the deeper and stronger, and that image of the secret places he found for himself as a schoolboy is pervasive and even dominant.

Indeed, he not only resents people for not being himself, he resents facts:

35 Ibid., pp.469–70.
36 Ibid., p.241.

But what was worst of all to me was the idea of the reproductive processes. No one has ever lived who more devoutly wished that children
were born from trees or, like the warriors of Cadmus, out of dragon's
teeth sown in the earth.[37]

And he goes on to tell how once the mention of the male seed made him
physically ill.

He is well aware that his sexual nature is no isolated part of himself.
The need to interiorize, to remain alone, to create an infallible and eternal
church of which he is the only member (to adapt a comment of Chesterton upon Bernard Shaw) must have the same ultimate source. Widely,
though unsystematically, read in the literature of religion and philsophy,
he is a born syncretist.

> Every kind of religion touches me to the heart except those modern-
> istic forms of it where ethics take the place of angels and where the
> First Cause takes the place of Christ. I am as susceptible to religion as I
> am to the beautiful limbs of women. Communism appeals to me just
> because it excites the religious emotion. Catholicism appeals to me for
> the same reason; and for the same reason do all the traditional Hebraiz-
> ings of the Hebrew race.[38]

And for most of this time he was married. It is perfectly emblematic of
his story of self-absorption that he shows not the faintest curiosity about
the answer to the question that every reader is asking: What on earth did
his wife think about it all?

(iii)   *The Low Quest: J.R. Ackerley*

As soon as we open Ackerley's book,[39] we know we are in another
world. 'Nothing serious can happen here.' To signal this, he opens with
a skit on innumerable dull, factual memoirs; 'I was born in 1896 and my
parents were maried in 1919.' He seems to be saying all the time that life
is absurd, and he with it—and yet, after all, the pain is real. It is absurd
to be wounded in battle in the rump, but no doubt it hurts there too.
He was the son of a vigorous, dissipated and successful businessman,

---

[37] Ibid., p.223.
[38] Ibid., p.509.
[39] J.R. Ackerley, *My Father and I*, 1968. Quotations from Penguin ed. 1971.

and a vague, hypochondriac, complaining, colourless woman. The mother's role in the formation of the homosexual character, so often thought to be crucial, is here reduced almost to nothing. The only characteristic mother and son appear to share (no doubt selected with conscious literary intent) is a tendency to constipation; and it is characteristic of Ackerley to describe it as a martyrdom. The father kept two establishments, and attempted—for a long time successfully—to keep the fact secret from the members of both. It is not very clear why the mother eventually triumphed in the long, shadowy contest with her unseen rival. The father was carelessly generous, but subject to fits of furious resentment. The light tone does not entirely hide from us the author's sense of his own ingratitude.

Part of the book is taken up with his own researches into his father's past; and he supposes himself to have found a sexual temperament in some ways like his own in his father's early career, though no trace of it is seen in his father as he actually appeared to the son's memory. For autobiographical purposes, the only interest of this is to show how deeply his father's personality fascinated him, and perhaps also to hint that homosexuality can be hereditary.

And yet there are serious moments too, and when they come they are described in a taut, spare prose that is well-suited to the task. Two of them come in his account of school-life at Rossall:

> Teddy was the school whore; I can't remember whether he was expelled or departed more normally; at any rate, just before he left he took me aside and begged me, whatever I did, not to go the way that he had gone . . . I liked and admired him very much and if ever he had sat on my bed after lights out asking to be let in, I wonder if my life then and later would have been happier. Probably not; happiness of that kind, I suspect, was not a thing I was psychologically equipped to find. In any case he was in a different house. He was killed in the first few weeks of the war.[40]

The other comes only two pages later when a master to whom he sent to say goodbye warned him that pride would have a fall. 'I never forgot this shocking remark and think always with respect of the now anonymous man who troubled himself to make it.'

An unusual reaction to schoolmasterly moralizing; and it indicates, no doubt, his frustation at being cossetted, his obscure wish for standards of conduct, which seemed to be absent from the world of home, of school, and of the Bohemian literary world into which he soon drifted.

[40] Ibid., p.98.

Then follows a strange narrative of his repetitive and unsatisfying homosexual adventures. It is strange for several reasons. There is an extraordinary detachment, an overmastering weariness; but this is countered by a strong literary eye for incongruity and absurdity, a real surprise at the contradictions of his own personality and the futility of his life, and a serious intelligent curiosity about his own hidden motives. The result is an amalgam, unparalleled in books known to me, of patient analysis and black comedy.

When he arrives at a neat, epigrammatic statement of his condition, he is at once driven to question it:

> Unable, it seemed, to reach sex through love, I started upon a long quest in pursuit of love through sex. Having put that neat sentence down I stare at it. Is it true? At some point in the journey I would certainly have so described it . . . Street prowlers and male prostitutes, not many, were my first prey; of them strangely I remember nothing at all, but I find in my notebooks the following brief entry: No. 11 Half Moon Street, the kind of room in which one kills oneself.[41]

How many bewilderingly different attitudes there are in this brief and simply written passage, and how resolutely the author avoids contrasting and analysing them. The first sentence is statement full of deep implications; if we were to accept it as true, we could be much advanced in understanding the case. But then comes a casual-seeming retreat from it, which leaves us wondering what, if anything, is to take its place. Then can it really be true that he remembers nothing of the street-prowlers? Does he not rather mean that what he remembers is trivial and boring, and would detract from the classic dignity of his story? And what of suicide? On the whole, the book leaves the impression of a man who was inwardly very tough, who thought life rather absurd, but that it would be a weak way of going on to complain overmuch about this. In conventional, worldly terms, he seems to have been very sane. Does he mean us to think that the thought of suicide was an immature literary flourish, derived from bad romantic literature? Or did it show a real fear that the incoherence of his life might ultimately destroy his sanity, at which the elderly man who is writing the book can afford to smile, even though grimly? It is hard to say. At all events, by placing together thoughts separated by most of a lifetime, he achieves, in miniature, something like the bewildering, kaleidoscopic effect of the reversed revolutions and

[41] Ibid., pp.107–8.

recoveries in Conrad's *Nostromo*. There is conscious art in this; but at the same time he appears to be genuinely puzzled by himself. How was it that he always rejected the advances of those he liked and with whom he shared cultural interests? And did this only in order to continue to pursue the casual prey of streets?

The height of incongruity is reached when he tells how when travelling by train with his father he intercepted a signal from the waiter in the restaurant car, and 'excusing myself to my father for a natural need', followed him to the lavatory. For this is followed in the very next paragraph by:

> Yet in spite of these adventures, if anyone had asked me what I was doing I doubt if I should have replied that I was diverting myself. I think I should have said that I was looking for the Ideal Friend... Though two or three hundred young men were to pass through my hands in the course of years, I did not consider myself promiscuous but monogamous, it was all a run of bad luck, and I became ever more serious over this.[42]

Then he describes an attempt to achieve this 'monogamous' state with a young sailor. It was not monogamous even in inverted commas, because Ackerley was not faithful to him when he was at sea. Bu he was nevertheless sensitive about their joint domestic respectability, and tried to protect the sailor against the loose talk of his other homosexual friends. Another kind of writer with similar temperament and experience to Ackerley's might have made this episode, which could be portrayed as a serious attempt at disinterested love in a cottage, as central to his life. But, typically, Ackerley throws away his potential climax by calling the sailor a 'sacred cow', who must be protected against all contamination.

Describing how he became over-anxious and possessive, took a flat in Portsmouth to be near him at the end of his voyages, catered and cooked for him, he leads us on to the single quotation he gives of the words of the beloved:

> 'What, chicken again!' It is the only speech he ever made that has stuck in my mind. The end was clearly in view.[43]

Again we may be in doubt about the precise meaning of this. Does the triviality reveal a sadness too deep for tears? Or is the author just unwilling to miss the opportunity to make us laugh. In any case he soon

42 Ibid., pp.108–9.
43 Ibid., p.113.

follows this anecdote with a question that takes us to the heart of what the book seems to be saying.

> I sometimes wonder, though I cannot know, whether the remark . . . 'perhaps happiness is not your deepest need', may not be profoundly true, whether the hardship of it all was the very thing I wanted, the frustrations, which often seemed to me so starveling and wretched, my subconscious choice.[44]

Many romantic questers might be indignant or incredulous at being offered an interpretation from such a quarter, yet what is said here is near the truth about many of them.

As if to take vengeance on himself for such unaccustomed penetration he now shows his decline as more rapid and more sordid:

> I wanted nothing now but (the sad little wish) someone to love me. My last long emotional affair, in the torments and frustrations of which I wallowed for a year, was with a deserter, who became front-ally infected by a prostitute . . . he unbuttoned his flies to exhibit the proof, squeezing out the pus for my enlightenment. Twenty years earlier, I reflected such a performance would have dished him for me for ever; now I saw it as one of the highest compliments I had ever been paid.[45]

Then he takes leave of his parents with two characteristic touches of black comedy. Nursing his dying father, he has occasion to help him to make water. He associates this with the memory of all the other penises he has handled and with the thought that this one had 'shot him into the world'. His mother, as perhaps befits the pale, remote character with which the author has endued her, achieves a weak touch of pathos by becoming obsessed with, of all things, a pet fly. He speaks of her as 'ending up as I am with animals and alcohol'. His own old age is no less a subject of black comedy than theirs. From a querulous dog-denouncer, he became a passionate dog-lover:

> This bitch of mine entered my life in the middle forties and entirely transformed it . . . She offered me what I had never found in my sexual life, constant, singlehearted, incorruptible, uncritical devotion . . . From the moment she established herself in my heart and home my

44 Ibid., p.115.
45 Ibid., p.122.

obsession with sex fell wholly away from me . . . So urgent was my longing every day to rejoin her that I would often take taxis part-way, even the whole way, home to Putney from my London office . . . I sang with joy at the thought of seeing her . . . It was as though I had never wanted sex at all . . . the fifteen years she lived with me were the happiest of my life.[46]

There is considerable literary art, finely calculated, in the blank absurdity of this. Taken in the context of the whole sad book, it is perhaps the saddest passage of all. To show here that he understood this might be to mar the effect. Instead he gives his final, considered judgment in symbolic form a few pages earlier. Going through his mother's effects after her death, he comes to her holy of holies, a locked black bag, containing papers with the inscription 'Private. Burn without reading.'

At last! Beneath were sundry packages tied up in ribbon. They were full of wastepaper. There was nothing else in the bag. This was my mother's comment on life.

It is the son's also. And yet we may say that his way of saying *Vanity of Vanities* has attained to the dignity of memorable speech.

[46] Ibid., pp.190–1.

IX

Conversion

and, being dashed
From error on to error, every turn
Still brought me nearer to the central truth.

    (E.B. Browning, *Aurora Leigh*, Book First)

as once at a crash Paul,
Or Austin, a lingering-out sweet skill. . . .

    (G.M. Hopkins, *The Wreck of the Deutschland*,
                        1875)

Man lives that list, that leaning in the will
No wisdom can forecast by gauge or guess,
The selfless self of self, most strange, most still,
Fast furled and all foredrawn to No or Yes.

    (G.M. Hopkins, 'On the Portrait of Two
              Beautiful Young People')

THERE ARE USUALLY (not quite always) two aspects of religious conversion. There is change and growth of conviction; and there is a struggle to accept in the heart what has already been perceived and understood by the mind. The separation between these two processes may be sharp or may be so blurred as to be apparent only to an observer. Like all deep human experiences, conversion is liable to be more or less opaque to the subject. This is so both generally and in a special sense to which I return later.

Since expectations cannot but influence sensations, the general differences between Catholic and Protestant views of the matter is relevant. The Catholic view is that conversion is the beginning of a journey; or, perhaps better, a decisive change of direction, so that what before may have been a wandering journey becomes a journey with a goal. The Protestant view tends to telescope several different stages of Catholic experience into a unique, momentary action. The old Protestant question, 'Are you saved?' places in the past what the Catholic tradition sees as in the future. The state of certainty ascribed by Catholics to faith is extended in some strands of Protestant tradition to certainty about a personal spiritual condition. The objective and the subjective are merged; belief in truths of faith and hope of what God has already achieved in the soul of the believer are not clearly distinguished.

So, in an extreme case, like Bunyan's *Grace Abounding* (1666), the first stage, the growth of conviction, is practically absent. At the start of the book, when he considered himself to be leading a worldly and vicious life, his convictions are the same as at the end, when the conversion is complete. (Naturally, the words *worldly* and *vicious* must be understood in the sense in which Bunyan intended them. They do not imply dissolute behaviour as the world would judge, but rather a respectable life devoid of saving faith.)

During his worldly phase, he was convinced that the Bible was verbally inspired, that it was the key to salvation, and that each believer must wrestle alone to discover its saving message. He was convinced that God had chosen some and reprobated others, and that one could know for certain that one belonged to the first group if one had a particular series of experiences, beginning with conviction of sin, and ending with assurance of grace. He also believed—and the sense of anti-climax we may feel at this last would not have been intelligible to him – that it was wicked to take part in amusements on Sunday, since the Jewish law (which he nevertheless believed to have been abrogated by St Paul) forbade working on Saturday. It is an interesting question for historians how it came about that these comparatively new doctrines, which were

certainly questioned or denied by many of his contemporaries were as palpable to him as the air he breathed, even in his worldly phase. If he is
aware of any other doctrines—and he occasionally shows a vague awareness of the tenets of the Anglican establishment—it is only as views entirely
out of court from the start. He has no feeling of history. The knowledge
that presumably he must have had that sixteen centuries had elapsed since
the time of Christ arouses in him not the slightest curiosity about what
had formerly been believed, or about the source of his own ideas. Still less
does he require any reasons or arguments for doctrines which appear as
self-evident as time and space or as the consciousness of existence.

So the story of *Grace Abounding*, told with the incomparable vividness
of a literary genius, reduces itself to a single issue. Can he achieve certain
inner sensations which will assure him that he is saved? And can he, by
achieving these sensations, pierce the cloud of unknowing and assure
himself that his name has been written for all eternity on one list rather
than the other? The whole Christian life, conversion, vocation, discipline
and growth, together with repentance and charity are concentrated, as by
a remorseless and infinitely powerful pressure, into a single agonizing act
of will to control emotion so that he will actually have those feelings
which (he is convinced) will give him assurance of salvation. There is no
need to suppose that Bunyan was callous in his thoughts of those deemed
to be outside the reach of mercy. His state was probably very like Newman's in 1816 (in his short Calvinist phase): 'I only thought of the mercy
to myself.'

It is hard to find an image adequate to our sense of this emotional pressure which Bunyan so well describes. Astonomers, perhaps, can supply
us with one when they speak of a certain collapsed condition of a star in
which a matchbox full of its material would weigh many thousands of
tons.

Human feeling is wayward; it is impossible to force ourselves to feel
happy when we are sad or sad when we are happy. This truth of com-
monsense had been a corner-stone of an older tradition of spiritual writing, a distinguished exponent of which, in Bunyan's century was St
François de Sales. But Bunyan's doctrine required that it be ignored, or
rather, as experience decrees that it cannot be ignored, that it somehow
be ruled out of court. A state of feeling, which answered to the doctrinal
requirements must be created; and success or failure in the task becomes
very much more than a matter of life and death.

To guess at the psychic strain involved, we can only return to our
matchbox image. In the light of this, Bunyan's peculiar experiences, his

fear of the tower falling on him, his delusion that he had irrevocably abandoned Christ, his almost solipsistic sense of isolation are readily intelligible. It is wrong, I think, to suppose that Bunyan was an unbalanced genius of the kind dear to our romantic traditions. His other writings tend to suggest that he was extremely well-balanced, a shrewd, incisive countryman. If the style is the man, the verdict would be similar. A really unbalanced nature, like Carlyle's, will be likely, especially if gifted with literary genius, to reveal itself in the torturing of language into an unmistakable personal idiom. In Carlyle, and in those like him, there is a crazy recklessness of diction, an over-heating of the imagination, which are absent from Bunyan's work. He had a fine ear for common speech, a talent which entails a certain intelligent detachment. Though we are unable to say why he adopted the doctrines, we can surely say that it was the doctrines working on a steady temperament rather than a wild temperament simply that issued in these terrible experiences. And indeed, the literary grandeur of the monument he erected to these experiences in his book depends, in large measure, on this common-sensical quality, this power of sober detachment and exact description. If we doubt this, a glance at a contrary example of a really unbalanced mind, like Strindberg's diary, would be likely to convince us.

The intense subjectivism of all this needs no stressing. But there is a paradox here. The categories of subjective and objective are, in a certain sense, reversed. The creed, the object of faith, is transformed into a private experience; it is held to be impossible in any real sense to believe without feeling. To assent is to assent to one's own salvation, not to a scheme of salvation for all, or even for all those others who have been mysteriously excluded from reprobation. On the other hand, feeling, that unique, personal thing, that is different for each one of us, loses its autonomy. For the agonizing question is 'Can I make myself feel exactly what brother so-and-so, an approved model of salvation, reports that he felt?' The creed becomes subjective but the impalpable mystery of experience becomes a most exacting external standard.

But an important common feature in most Catholic and Protestant accounts is a complete emotional exhaustion preceding the actual moment of conversion. The prospective convert has been fought to a standstill. If he is a Protestant, this will be likely to take the form of agonizing doubt whether he is one of the chosen. For the potential Catholic, it is likely to be a sheer torpor of the will, an inability for a time, perhaps only for weeks or days, to grasp at what is known to be true and salutary. This is accompanied by a general sense of weakness and dependence. The emergence from this state is the point of special opaqueness to which I referred earlier. The convert, however articulate and analytical he may be, is unable to describe, or even remember, how or why he once again became able to reason, to decide and to act. An experience, or rather perhaps, a felt absence of experience, is intractable indeed if it totally defeats the formidable analytical powers of men like Newman and Knox, and yet is clearly of crucial importance to all their future lives. At most they grope for illustrative metaphors, like that which Newman used when he said that he was on his Anglican deathbed. The process of dying and being reborn takes its own time, it cannot be hastened or retarded, and the patient is far beyond the reach of medicines.

This is especially striking because a Catholic conversion is often, and certainly in many of the most notable autobiographical accounts, perceived as a process of reasoning. And this process does not differ fundamentally from the ordinary balancing of arguments and facts which provide the motives for secular decisions. There may, of course, be an emotional element, but this is more likely to appear near the beginning of the process and right at its end or after it is over. There may be an initial emotional appeal which first provides the motive for investigation, or, as in Newman's case, an entirely antagonistic emotion—what he called 'a stain upon the imagination'—may be very gradually overcome by argument and thought, and perhaps by the admission of new facts (like, in Newman's case, the Jerusalem bishopric). Either way emotional exhaustion sets in, and the former attraction or repulsion comes to seem to the weary mind infinitely remote, like an experience in a former life. A period of suspended animation begins:

> when, under ether, the mind is conscious
> but conscious of nothing

When this period is over it remains as unintelligible as it was while it persisted. The convert may be able to say that he wishes he had acted sooner, or that he cannot understand what delayed him; but he will not be able to say why the decisive moment came at one time more than another. But when it does come it appears as the practical enactment of something settled long before. It encapsulates a long process of thought, of weighing arguments, of rejecting old ideas and adopting new ones, or of developing old ideas in a new direction. Its momentary quality does not make it sudden. The thoughts that existed on the other side of the gulf of oblivion return, now vivid and operative, speculative no longer. A new life is waiting to be lived.

It is partly, no doubt, in respose to this gulf of oblivion that many accounts of conversion signalize emergence from it with a single memorable episode or phrase. Of this kind are St Augustine's recollection of the child calling 'Tolle, lege' in the garden, and Newman's 'Securus iudicat orbis terrarum.' The former preceded the moment of conversion by a few seconds only, the latter by years. Yet both have a similar function; they provide an objective equivalent, which the reader of the narrative can grasp, for something that cannot be expressed, even by the literary genius that each man undoubtedly possessed. They clutch at these phrases not only because they are relevant, not only because (we are not inclined to doubt) the record of hearing or reading them is substantially true, but because they are external. They represent an escape from that wordless prison of the self, which is not less but more terrifying if a Divine action is occurring within it. Here, they seem to say to us, is something you can understand, something whose meaning is agreed. It may be only a metaphor, but at least the metaphor was embodied in a fact, something palpable to ear or eye.

And yet, like certain complex symbols in imaginative literature (in *The Rainbow* of D.H. Lawrence, for instance), these recorded episodes may lack an obviously apparent meaning. The words would not have meant the same thing, or anything at all perhaps, to anyone else, or even to the same subject at a different time. Certain unimaginative readers have been inclined to grumble. *They* could perfectly well read 'Securus iudicat' without wishing to become Roman Catholics. They really didn't see . . . etc. etc. Such commentators are guilty not of an intellectual or theological but of a literary error. They forget that autobiography, even when its content is highly charged with theological arguments, is literature and not theology. The meaning of the phrases in the great works in which they are quoted is only to be found within these works, just as no one can understand why Lawrence's Gudrun frightened the bullocks who has not pondered on the whole of *The Rainbow*. Newman could have read (and probably did read) the words he quotes at any time before the actual reading of them, and responded to them only as a scholar noting an ancient theological view. Symbolic episodes like this may be likened to two pencil lines obliquely drawn across a page. There is only one point where they can intersect. When the point is reached the writer and the reader look back together over the distance travelled. If the image is well-chosen (to alter the metaphor) there comes a flash of light and the path traversed in darkness is revealed; and this moment alters also what is yet to come since, 'He who has seen a ghost cannot be as if he had never seen it.'

Since, as we have seen, the impetus of conversion can only come at the time appointed or appropriate, it may be provided by something familiar. Thus Vernon Johnson (in *One Lord, One Faith*, 1929) describes the effect upon him of a modernist conference held at Cambridge in 1921. He was at the time a seasoned and eloquent Anglo-Catholic preacher; he had known perfectly well for years that there was no fundamental agreement of faith among the Anglican clergy. He knew that some in high positions denied what were to him the essentials, as the Incarnation and the Trinity. Before, it had bothered him no more than other examples of the waywardness of human nature. Now, suddenly, and for no reason he is able to assign, he found that it cast doubt on the authority and hence on the Catholicity of the Church of England. Any of his friends and collaborators who was not affected in the same way might have replied that it was only part of the general human imperfection of the *ecclesia semper reformanda*, and could have pointed out that at an earlier time he would have agreed. Which was right is a matter of theological argument. But in terms of autobiography, Johnson's changed view is a unique, unanswerable event. To question it, provided we are quite sure (as here) that we are dealing with a truthful witness, would be as foolish as to say: 'You say you were born in 1886, and went to Oxford and were ordained in the Church of England; but lots of other people have been born in other years and have quite a different history.'

Johnson's moment of insight brought into question the nature of the body to which he then belonged. For Sheila Kaye-Smith[1] the corresponding moment came when she was forced to question the nature of her own commitment to that body. She was an Anglo-Catholic speaker and parish worker married to a clergyman of similar views, and she was a well-known novelist. They went on holiday to Sicily 'hoping to be appalled' by the superstitious backwardness, moral depravity and liturgical squalor of the religious life of Palermo. They found it, on the contrary, impressive in its persistence, practicality and ordinariness. Why on earth, a fellow Anglo-Catholic might have enquired, does that disturb you? According to our branch theory, the Roman church in Sicily is a true portion of the Catholic Church, just as we are in England. We ought to rejoice if it is sound and effective. But again, that would have been to miss the biographical point. What happened in Sicily was that Sheila Kaye-Smith came to realize why she had hoped to be appalled. It was because she had dressed up a very common English feeling of that time in the theological

[1] Sheila Kaye-Smith, *Three Ways Home*, Cassell, 1937.

robes of the branch theory. The inferiority that she desired to see, and did not see, was not the inferiority of one Catholic 'branch' to another. Indeed, it would have argued an inexplicable perversity of feeling if it had been; since the stoutest defenders of the branch theory would concede that the Roman branch was many times larger than the supposed English branch. The inferiority she wished to see was not essentially religious at all, but racial, national and social. The difference between what the Sicilians were and what she had expected them to be forced her to gaze into a mirror devoid of all power of flattering. And she saw a complacent, insular woman, quietly hugging herself at belonging to a small, privileged group, a class that ruled the country that rules a quarter of the world. But since her religious profession was sincere, she had only to ask herself, 'What has this to do with Jesus Christ and the gospel?' And by this question her adherence to the branch theory, and hence to Anglicanism was 'absolutely pulverized'. But only hers, and, as it turned out, her husband's also; someone who had adopted the theory on different grounds would not have been affected.

How subjective and personal the catalyst of conversion can be is well seen in cases where the decisive influence is ostensibly in entire opposition to the conversion which is about to occur. Thus Maurice Baring[2] was converted to Catholicism by reading Renan, because he revealed 'the astonishing fact that there was an early Church, of which the apostles were pillars'. Perhaps only those who have been prepared for confirmation in a famous public school can readily imagine the shock of surprise, and (for certain temperaments) the joyful awakening which this discovery of the obvious might cause.

More counter-suggestible still was Douglas Hyde, who had been for years a dedicated communist speaker and writer when he read Avro Manhattan's *The Catholic Church against the Twentieth Century*. These were the days when communist propaganda was largely aimed at helping people to forget the Nazi-Soviet pact and Stalin's admiration for Hitler by labelling all opposition to communism 'fascist'. Hyde, who already had a cynical understanding of this, might have been expected to be unaffected by what is, by any standards, a crude piece of invective. But it made him ask himself searching questions:

Against the twentieth century? Against the century of the atom bomb? . . . Against those beliefs which lead to people persecuting men

[2] See Maurice Baring, *Have You Anything to Declare?*, Heinemann, 1936, pp.127 & 133–4.

like Archbishop Stepinac and preparing a Red Terror against the Slo-
vak peasants? Why not? So am I?[3]

But this was only a preliminary. He still did not believe in God. What
followed illustrates very clearly how, in such cases, the unwilled and
unexpected predominates over the willed decision. He said to his wife,
whose thoughts were running parallel with his own:

> It is five to ten and we still don't believe in God as a living reality. In
> five minutes time, at ten o'clock, let's start. Let's act and think as
> though there really were one.[4]

They did, and for weeks nothing happened. He took to sitting alone at
the back of an empty Catholic Church in which felt replaced the stained
glass destroyed by bombing in wartime. 'One or two people came and
went. And I just sat.' He went many times, but still did not pray, until
one day he saw a worried Irish servant-girl:

> Through such light as managed to creep through the blacked-out win-
> dows and by the flame of the candle, I could see her busy with a string
> of beads, her hands moving, her head nodding every now and then . . .
> As she passed me again on her way out I looked at her face. Whatever
> had been troubling her had gone. Just like that. And I had been carry-
> ing my load around with me for months and years.

After this, faith came suddenly, and without further struggle. Unlike
many authors discussed in this chapter, Hyde is describing a complete
volte-face; and he needed two catalysts of opposite kinds. Who can say
why he reacted negatively to Manhattan's book and positively to the
Irish girl? Perhaps with another subject it might have been the reverse.
But, although Hyde presents his own conversion mainly as a complete
reversal of direction, which in most respects it undoubtedly was, yet even
here there was an element of continuity. Though sickened by the cynical
lying that communist propaganda demanded of him, he had originally
become a communist because he thought communism served the poor.
He came to see the oppressed Catholics of Eastern Europe as the image of
those oppressed proletarians of England of whom he had heard and written so much. And then he saw the same image again, not now as an idea
but as a visible reality. The Irish girl, because she obviously had no

[3] Douglas Hyde, *I believed*, Heinemann, 1950, p.249.
[4] Ibid., p.253.

property or social standing, was able, unconsciously, unaware that she was being watched, to present him with a new version, breathing and palpable of an abstract idea. He was converted by someone he had never met, whose name he never knew.

Douglas Hyde seems to have given little thought to worldly considerations. But there are some, heavily weighted with privilege and wealth, for whom they are very hard to forget. Such was Lady Herbert, the widow of a wealthy Anglican, whom she considered to be one of the best and noblest of men. As her Catholic convictions grew, she who had always been spoilt and cossetted, first by her father and then by her husband, was faced with the threat of losing the right to educate her children in a Chancery suit (or so she thought). She could not forget the Anglican church for the building of which her husband had given £30,000 (in the currency of the Victorian age) and in which he was buried. Her sense of inferiority to him, as well as her deep affection for his memory, could make her feel in certain moods that it was almost impious, after his death, to depart from his way. Cardinal Manning, who had been watching her progress, waited and tactfully withdrew. She went to live in Italy, and for a long time attended mass in Catholic churches without receiving the sacraments. Once again we find the period of mesmerized immobility, which feels as if it will last for ever. As her immobility was due to personal feelings and not to doubts, the usual dullness and desolation were intensified by self-reproach and self-disgust. One day she was watching the Host set in a monstrance, when she imagined Christ asking her why she waited. At the same time someone happened to touch her on the shoulder. Not a gifted writer, Lady Herbert achieved her one moment of eloquence when she simply added that she didn't go to bed that night.[5]

In these cases, and in many others that could be quoted, there is a subtle, intangible interplay between what is seen and what is thought and felt. The writer saw a common sight, or heard something that could be heard anywhere, or read a familiar passage. The inner movement of mind and heart had reached a point where the experience of something ordinary could be felt as unique and irreversible. But it would be superficial to ask, was the vision then only a symbol that was not really needed. And even more superficial to ask, was the vision only a literary flourish, divorced from real experience. It is through the external that human beings become aware of that 'selfless self of self' which introspection and analysis can never reach. And in many, perhaps most, such

[5] Lady Herbert, *How I Came Home*, C.T.S. pamphlet, 1894.

stories there is a further important element. Prior to his moment of vision, each writer is in a state of intense loneliness, whether the loneliness of solitude or the loneliness of the crowd. Humanity grows dim as he battles alone with God; and God too seems to have withdrawn. The moment of vision is often the awareness of another person. It may be Christ himself, as for Lady Herbert, but for her there was also an ordinary human presence, the touch on the shoulder. It may be an unknown child, or the words of St Augustine sounding across fourteen centuries or an Irish servant girl. Whatever it is, as in Wordsworth's vision of the blind beggar with the placard, humanity, felt before as a living absence, a mere mask or mechanism, or as a crowd powerless to help or understand, is suddenly restored to meaning, to solidarity and communion. It is as if God signals His presence by restoring to the sufferer an ordinary, but at the moment, infinitely precious, human presence. And the fact that the chosen vehicle of this is unconscious of his own significance, perhaps is not aware of the watcher to whom he means so much, may act as a strange endorsement of the idea that it is the finger of God.

*   *   *

In the above examples we have been dealing with the crucial later stages of conversion, which have a uniquely personal character in each case. It is much easier to generalize about the earlier, because they form part of a wide historical movement, the rejection of Protestantism. Why, we ask, was the mould in which England had been set for nearly three centuries to become so rapidly intolerable in the mid-nineteenth century and after? Anyone who undertakes a prolonged course of reading in autobiographies of the nineteenth and early twentieth century will emerge dazed with the sensation of listening to a jangling, long-drawn-out and infinitely lugubrious lament. 'They told us,' it seems to say, 'that it was wicked to play on Sundays, that cleanliness was next to godliness, that England was God's chosen race, that foreigners were wicked, that Catholics were idolaters, that the Bible was to be interpreted literally, but that we must on no account take the slightest notice of large parts of it (such as the early chapters of St Luke's gospel, or the sixth chapter of St John). They told us that the early church was Protestant, but did not even attempt to produce any evidence for this; they implied that Christianity died out before the end of the first century, and was then rediscovered in the sixteenth, but only in Germany and England. They told us that all ceremony was wicked, that we should worship without using our bodies, which were only fit for making money and getting on in the world. We can no longer accept this narrow and illogical conglomeration of myths, fallacies and half-truths. We are very desolate and what are we to do? Most terrible of all, we have nothing to love.'

And Protestantism could not or would not answer, even when the challenge was most plainly expressed, as it was, for instance, by Ruskin:

> In the first place, determine clearly, if there is a clear place in your brains to do it, whether you mean to observe the Sabbath as a Jew, or the day of Resurrection as a Christian. Do either thoroughly; you can't do both. If you choose to keep the 'Sabbath', in defiance of your great prophet, St Paul, keep the new moons too, and the other fasts and feasts of the Jewish law.[6]

It could not say why it reverenced the Bible but despised the Church from which it came; it could give no reason for its sabbatarianism. The early years of many people and the early chapters of many autobiographies were devoted to the painful discovery that the system was bankrupt. It had literally nothing to say for itself.

And yet, early teachings never completely fail to have effect. There is a residue of prejudice, all the more dangerous because unconscious. Dickens, so typical in so many ways, of his countrymen, illustrates this particularly well, making glorious fun of Podsnap's insularity, and then showing, in his continental letters, and in *Pictures from Italy*, that, when abroad, he was himself little more than a Podsnap uncomfortably gifted with genius. Newman spoke for very many besides himself when he wrote of a 'stain upon the imagination'.

Perhaps this has never been better described than by Dom Bede Griffiths:

> It is difficult to describe the fear with which the Roman Church filled me. It was, no doubt, partly the fear of the unknown. The Roman Church had always been for us as a family, as my father once expressed it, 'outside the pale'. It was something strange and remote and essentially foreign to English life . . . At Oxford a Catholic undergraduate was once pointed out to me (we were to meet years later when we were both Benedictine monks), but it was only a matter of curiosity to

[6] Ruskin, *Fors Clavigera*, 1871–84, George Allen, 4 vols. 1902–3, Letter XL, 1874.

me. I had never so far as I know spoken to anyone. And deeper than
this fear of the unknown there was an inherited family prejudice . . . I
remember my mother once said that nothing would give her greater
pain than that anyone she loved should become a Roman Catholic . . .
Behind this family feeling there was also a deeper feeling still, the prejudice which every Englishman inherits from the racial memory. The
breach with Rome is a psychic event in all our lives, something which
lies deeply buried in the unconscious, but is ready to erupt into consciousness, whenever circumstances force us to encounter it.[7]

This passage might easily have been written in the mid-nineteenth century by an early convert from the Oxford Movement. It is all the more
striking as a testimony of the strength of the feeling of which it speaks in
that it was written by a man who was at Oxford in the mid-1920s, not a
notably Protestant or insular milieu, and a man who had discarded Protestantism before he left school in favour of a pseudo-pagan acceptance of
romantic poetry as the philosophical guide to life.

One of the best-documented of all religious journeys is that from Anglo-
Catholicism to Catholicism. Leaving Newman aside for the moment, we
may note some general features, especially those that link it with the
sentiments described by Griffiths. Occasionally, it is true, we find a case
where the loss of Protestantism was not a factor. J. Britten, for instance,
was trained by his parents in ritualistic Anglicanism at St Barnabas, Pim-
lico, and never heard of Protestantism, never heard the Royal Supremacy
or the Thirty-nine Articles mentioned in the first eighteen years of his
life.[8] But it is clear that such a case is exceptional. Much commoner is the
case where the inner struggle of the Anglo-Catholic on his way to Rome
is strongly influenced by the Protestantism which he supposes himself to
have put away long ago. Sometimes this may take the form of disclaim-
ing one's own Protestant prejudices but pleading those of others. Some
flirt dangerously with the idea that the contrast between appearance and
reality in the Church of England is positively beneficial. Then the argument runs like this: 'The Church of England is a church which is really
in its inner being Catholic, but has usually had in history, and in some
aspects still has, the appearance of being Protestant. While objectively
deviations into Protestantism are to be regretted, and the loss to

[7] Dom Bede Griffiths, *The Golden String*, 1954. Quotations from Penguin ed. 1979,
p.96.
[8] See J. Britten, *Why I Left the Church of England*, C.T.S., 1894.

congregations of the sacramental and liturgical riches of the Catholic tradition deplored, yet in the given situation this may be providential. For the English people are so steeped in Protestant tradition, and especially in detestation of the Papacy, that the Roman Church will never be able to obtain a hearing. *We* can make them Catholics almost without their knowing it, under the respectable cover of very English things, the monarchy, the Prayer Book, the country vicar, with his Oxford degree, his children at a public school, his rejection of celibacy, his pleasant partisanship in the Boat Race. If he is really a priest, all these harmless disguises will enable him to bring a full sacramental faith and practice to those who may retain the shibboleths but will gradually discard the harmful substance of Protestantism. As for the awkward issue of schism, we will postpone that into some indefinite future.'

No one describes this state of mind better than Vernon Johnson. He shows how the idea of reunion with Rome by the whole Church of England was a necessary part of his Anglo-Catholic system, since to deny its possibility would be openly to delight in schism, which would be manifestly unCatholic. But the idea was relegated to a distant and unimagined future, where it could not harm present prospects. His emergence from this state was rather like the experience which George Eliot describes in *Middlemarch*, when Casaubon is forced to replace the platitude 'All must die' with the urgency of 'I must die, and soon.' Even more powerful than sentiments such as these, especially in the minds of dedicated men like Vernon Johnson and Ronald Knox, was the fear of parting with friends and of lost opportunities for work. This fear intertwined itself with tender memories of the rhythm of English prose in one of its great periods (in Prayer Book and Authorized version) and of places. Foremost of these for many was the English country church, parsonage and churchyard; the contrast with the English Catholic building, whether tin hut or sham Gothic, and the utilitarian brick presbytery was especially painful to those whose adoption of Anglo-Catholicism had been partly due to aesthetic motives. It was a common sentiment of Anglo-Catholics that foreign Catholics were to be preferred to English 'Romans'. In part this may have been due to natural rivalry with those nearest, in part to memories of previous defections, the great catastrophe of 1845, and many subsequent lesser ones, and in part to a (probably unconscious) racial contempt for the Irish. But perhaps another factor, less often considered than those just mentioned, is this: continental Catholics, like Anglicans, and unlike English Catholics, are the heirs of great ancient architectural traditions. More than we generally realize, our view of people's settings may determine in part our sense of what they are.

But all these feelings and sentiments, naturally, were not enough for serious and intellectual men like Knox and Johnson. The latter pinned his faith in the concept of episcopacy. Thus he was able to make an intelligible distinction between the Catholic branches (Roman, Greek and English) and Protestant sects. His insularity was extreme. He had never been to a Catholic service in England or abroad, had hardly ever left England before when, some forty years old, he arrived in Lisieux. By pure coincidence, apparently, it was the day of Therese's canonization in Rome. Asked to give an account of his faith, he said he put his trust in 'the universal episcopate'. 'Ou-est-il?' was the reply. This encounter was not quite wordless, like Hyde's with the Irish servant girl, but it was almost as brief and just as momentous.

Ronald Knox was the son of a thoroughly Protestant Anglican bishop, yet in him we find the residual influence of Protestantism at its minimum. He had abandoned it very early, and—this is important—without any sensations of revolt or loss of filial feeling. His father was affectionate, and there was a special bond between him and the six children, in their shared feelings about the mother, who died almost before Ronald, the youngest child, could remember her. The adoption of Anglo-Catholicism at the age of fifteen was painless. He was more conscious of continuity than of radical change. He had never felt Protestantism as a constricting system, and he was always grateful for having been taught a personal devotion to Christ in his earliest years.

The key to his story lies in his rationality, and his distrust of religious emotion. (This does not mean that he was unemotional; perhaps only people of strong feelings distrust emotion.) The following passage is very characteristic:

> on Saints' Days mentioned in the Anglican Calendar I used, for a time, to invoke the saint of the day while getting into bed. I gave up the habit because I came to the conclusion that my reasons for it were only superficial and emotional, without intellectual basis; then, as always, I dreaded the undue interference of emotion in religion.[9]

He does not give the date for this, but he was probably about sixteen. The rest of the story, lasting some twelve years, is an account of an extremely agile, witty and brilliant mind attempting to frame a theory that would satisfy him about the Catholic status of the Church of England. He did not feel the fear of Rome, which affected so many others,

[9] R.A. Knox, *A Spiritual Aeneid*, Longmans Green, 1918, p.42.

except in one very personal and peculiar way. He was a little vain of his exceptional argumentative powers. The anomalies of Anglican history, the stimulating challenge of showing that its Protestant stance was only a superficial appearance, appealed to the strain in him that enjoyed fantastically complicated conundrums and outrageously ornate rhyme schemes in comic verse. He loved paradox, not so much for its own sake as for its opportunities for the display of brilliance. 'To this day,' he writes, 'I am not certain that I should not have become a Catholic earlier if Catholicism were not so glaringly obvious.'[10]

It is a tribute to his fidelity to his principle of rationality that his theology was not in the least insular. Intensely English and home-loving by nature—the sort of person who could regret that he couldn't get *Punch* when travelling through the most beautiful cities in Italy—he never forgot the smallness of England in a map of the world. Nor did he allow considerations of England's still great secular power to influence his view of religious questions. In this, he stands in strong contrast to Vernon Johnson, Sheila Kaye-Smith and many others, including even Newman himself in the early years of the Oxford Movement. His struggle to find a theory for the Church of England was always a struggle to find a place for a small anomaly in a large system. It was very characteristic of him to find in the passage in the Acts where St Peter's shadow has a healing effect a kind of allegory of the relation between Rome and Canterbury.

This rationality, this devotion to system-making, could lead at times to bleak conclusions. Since Anglican bishops were cut off from communion with the seat of authority and the main portion of the Church, it seemed to follow that one need take no notice of what they said. They were simple ordaining and confirming machines. He even explained this principle to the bishop who ordained him, who, to his surprise, accepted it with the utmost kindness. The Church of England had been accused, not altogether fairly perhaps, of harshness to the original Oxford converts. It certainly worked hard to see that no such accusations would lie in the early twentieth century.

All this theorizing could not last for ever. He came to realize that all his loyalty to the Church of England was directed to a distant past (which was not, as it was for the early Tractarians, the seventeenth century, but the time before the Reformation) and an unknown future when reunion with Rome was presumed to have occurred. He came, gradually and very painfully, to realize that he had been relying on the Church of

[10] Ibid., p.57.

Rome as a safety net. 'If I fell, her arms were there to catch me.' Meanwhile he was trying ever more ingenious explanations of the Anglican formularies, and of current decisions of Anglican authorities, always shifting them, the latter certainly and the former probably, far from the intentions of the writers.

One thing he had forgotten. The effort to be always logical and to exclude emotion was bound to impose an intense emotional strain, because it was exercized, after all, over something for which he cared deeply and had made the centre of his life. When and how would the strain begin to show?

The moment came when he was attending his younger brother's first celebration as a newly-ordained Anglican priest. The two brothers had an exceptionally close affection. Instead of rejoicing as he had hoped, he found himself in a state of bitter uncertainty, and, perhaps for the first time, of some resentment. Perhaps, he thought:

> the bright vestments, the fresh flowers, the mysterious candlelight, were all settings to a sham jewel; we had been trapped, deceived, betrayed into thinking it all worthwhile; we had ploughed the sand, fought over a phantom Helen through all these years of conflict . . . there is no such bully as a logical mind; my intellect, thus peeping down the vistas of a mere doubt, forced my eyes open to the whole mockery it involved— and all the time I was supposed to be worshipping. So far was I, in this agony of realisation, from any holy thoughts, that at the last Gospel I found only a curse framing itself in my mind; a curse directed against Henry the Eighth.[II]

An extreme and excessive reaction, but he was right, as an autobiographer to present it in its full fury. It stands out in lurid contrast to what is, in the main, an extremely cool, lucid account, in which he never fails to speak generously of his Anglican friends and of the Church of England itself, of which, on the whole, his memories were happy. He had forgotten, perhaps, Newman's dictum that reason is but the map of the mind's progress; he had tried for too long to treat his brilliant logical powers as if they were somehow separate from himself. The Thirty-nine Articles had been like a set of intellectual hurdles, and 'somehow or other you are bundled over each in turn'. He had counted the intellectual but not the psychic cost of such experiences.

The rest of the story can be passed over, since it was only the gradual

[II] Ibid., p.197.

recognition of what he had tried to prevent himself from realizing, that he was at heart a Roman Catholic already. But he was an Etonian and the son of a bishop; and though he can by no means be called worldly, he was not without regret at leaving what (ignorant of the future) he could only suppose to be the church of official England. Revisiting Eton:

> I felt there more than anywhere else that what I contemplated would cut me off from the past—the official religion of England, which needs no Test Acts or disabilities to hedge round its inveterate Anglicanism; the world of school and university, of the worship that hallows national, civic, and municipal life.

Then he took the train for Farnborough Abbey, and as he passed Vauxhall:

> saw in panorama the twin towers of the Abbey [Westminster] nestling under the Houses of Parliament, and the solitary campanile of the Cathedral.[12]

It seems likely that this last passage was deliberately modelled on the celebrated passage near the end of Newman's *Apologia* where he recalls seeing the spires of Oxford from the railway.

The differences between the two passages, both very short, are indicative both of changed circumstances after the passing of more than seventy years and of differences of personality. Newman felt cut off from home, friends and the setting of his former intellectual life. Knox, who was later to return to Oxford for several years, felt cut off from the national life, of which the Abbey and the House of Commons appear as twin emblems. But the new factor, the tower of a Catholic Cathedral in central London, was emblematic of a long period of change and growth. Does Knox hint at an eventual reconciliation? Probably not, but simply saw the architectural emblems both of what he was leaving and what he was finding.

*   *   *

The ambiguity and the deep complexity of the word *world* is a Christian commonplace, rooted in the opposite meanings to be found in the gospels.

[12] Ibid., pp.236–7.

On the one hand, 'God so loved the world . . . '; on the other, 'I pray not for the world.' The long ascetic tradition proclaims the spiritual need to deny the world (in some sense). But in the nineteenth and twentieth centuries we find something which (so far as I know) is new. Since the industrial revolution there has been a movement, small in numbers but strong in eloquence, of rejection not of the world but of the modern world, not of civilization, but of this industrial civilization. Ruskin was its greatest prophet. As a sentiment it could be either religious or secular; in William Morris it was entirely secular. Ruskin's own case is a complex one. He experienced a kind of unconversion in the Protestant chapel in Turin, and wrote some of the most searching and fierce of all the denunciations of English 'Biblical' Protestantism. His later religious allegiance is a difficult question on which I am very willing to defer to Ruskin scholars. But there can be no doubt at all, I think, that the satirical bitterness of *Fors Clavigera* is informed by religious feeling of some kind. For our purposes all this is background. The two cases I select for closer consideration are those of Eric Gill and Dom Bede Griffiths, in both of whom Ruskinian sentiments about modern civilization were particularly strong.

I said just now that these sentiments were, in a long historical perspective, new. Griffiths might perhaps have questioned that. He wrote:

Now it was through the monastic life that the dignity of labour was restored to Europe. In the Roman Empire, which bears so close a resemblance in so many ways to our own civilisation, the significance of manual labour had been lost through slavery, just as it has been lost in the modern world through industrialism. But the monastic life restored it to its proper place in human life.[13]

The important difference, which Griffiths, in his eagerness to find a likeness between two distant historical periods, rather fails to stress, is that men like himself could look back to early monasticism, and Gill to the craftsmen of the great Northern cathedrals, but the early monks could not look back to any known society which represented their ideals.

Different as they are, Griffiths and Gill are alike in having trodden a very solitary path to Catholicism. Each feels that he came near to inventing it for himself, and then finding with surprise that it existed already. Gill approached all problems through the requirements of his work, first as a monumental mason and later as a sculptor. For the first he only

---

[13] Griffiths, op. cit., p.152.

needed technical skill (though that was always something he rated very high; and he never forgot, as many do, that 'technical' is a word derived from the Greek word for art). For sculpture, though, he needed a vision of truth. 'Religion was not only the world's first need, but *my* first need. The lettercutter might procrastinate; the sculptor couldn't afford to.'[14]

At first sight Gill's quest seems more philosophical than religious. He is seeking a truth which will validate his work. But this is slightly deceptive, and brings us to his memories of childhood. His father was a nonconformist minister, who later joined first the Countess of Huntingdon's connexion and then the evangelical wing of the Church of England. Though he had a rebellious, 'arty', agnostic period in his late teens and twenties, Gill was able to say:

> There has never been a time when I have not known or even when I have forgotten that the main lines of their [his parents'] teaching and example were the main lines of the road to heaven. They taught us nothing of the theology of poverty, they never even praised it. They did not despise the rich or riches, on the contrary they revered the rich as persons whom God had blessed. They had no political bias in favour of the poor . . . they made poverty holy—not in theory but in their daily lives.[15]

This is a very important testimony, which should be given its due weight alongside all the autobiographical attacks on the theory and practice of Protestantism summarized above. A little later, Gill goes on:

> if you have to be born into a morass, and that is everybody's fate today, it is far better to be born into the family of a poor parson than into any other; for the parson is by profession a dispenser of truth and even if, as it may come to appear later, his truth is not the whole truth and not nothing but the truth, even so it is the truth he is after.[16]

His complaint against his parents' view of life was much more against its secular than its religious aspect. He came to reject their narrow patriotism, their unquestioning belief in the British Empire and the police force. But he also felt that, admirable and genuine as his parents were, there was something lacking: 'no force, no sharp edge, no burning fire of

[14] Eric Gill, *Autobiography*, Jonathan Cape, 1940, p.165.
[15] Ibid., p.42.
[16] Ibid., pp.46–7.

Christ's word, no apostolate, no martyrdom—no power to bind or loose, no strength to hold even me, still less to hold all men'.[17]

Working in an architect's office in London, he gradually, after a year or so, gave up going to church, partly under the influence of the smart sneers of others in the office. He feels ashamed of this, because it arose from a vague lack of determination, not from thought or principle. But it is easy to understand how far away from his parents he was beginning to feel, like many others in the Edwardian age.

But his state of mind was not simple. His revolt against Victorian traditions was superficial compared to his revolt against a brash, new commercial civilization, which seemed to be losing what was best and eagerly developing what was worst in Victorian commercial practice. The issue of religious truth was inseparable from all the rest,—honesty, craftsmanship, respect for materials. Leaving the architect's office, and becoming a mason, he was immune from a merely nostalgic mediaevalism. The problem was practical and contemporary. In any case, there was in his nature a certain tough simplicity, an impatience with the pretences and frills, a determination to get to the heart of the matter, which is indeed very reminiscent of Ruskin in some moods. He could never have had the slightest temptation to be a decadent aesthete. But, cut off from Catholic contacts, and painfully impressed by the decline in Catholic art and architecture since the great days, he needed some link between his inner thoughts and the church:

> It was a long time before I realised that rationalism and humility and poverty were all in the same boat and longer still before I realised what that boat was. I do not blame myself for this, for I suppose nothing on earth is more completely and efficiently camouflaged than Peter's 'barque', which, from a short distance, looks exactly like the Ritz Palace Hotel.[18]

Much of Gill's nature, both what is most attractive and what is least lovable is adumbrated in this passage. There is a certain over-confidence, a certain excess of rhetoric, even if we recall that about 1910 the Church was in some parts of the world still closely connected with the powers that be. But there is a certain attractive bluntness, appropriate to a man who is in a hurry because he is so much in earnest. It is the voice of a man better educated technically than intellectually. His prose is almost that of

[17] Ibid., p.93.
[18] Ibid., p.92.

a journalist, but it retains a rough-hewn precision that journalists seldom possess. He writes as if with a chisel, striking through many resistant materials.

The catalyst he needed was provided by the plain chant at Louvain:

> After the slow procession of incoming monks and the following short silence when I first, all unprepared and innocent, heard: Deus in adjutorium . . . I knew, infallibly, that God existed and was a living God—just as I knew him in the answering smile of a child or in the living words of Christ . . . there is a palpable rightness in the things that God has made and that man is God's instrument for making. Emotion follows—of course, inevitably, but emotion is that which is suffered. It is the suffering that follows knowledge. We may, and often do, forget the knowing and wallow only in the emotion. It is better to forget the emotion.[19]

Again it is the craftsman speaking; and this sets him far apart from all those whose interest in liturgy is merely aesthetic or antiquarian. Always, he wanted to know and to do, not to feel.

There is a strong erotic strain in Gill's writing, and even more in his drawing, and in every way he forms a contrast to the more ascetic converts discussed in this chapter. He is erotic, but he is also a celebrator of marriage. Indeed, he would probably question the propriety of the word *but* in my last sentence. He would say it is only a bad convention that associates marriage with respectability and sexual joy with promiscuity. And he stresses the close connection between the sexual instinct and the inspiration of art. And it comes naturally to him to use sexual imagery in speaking of his devotion to the Eucharist. This is essentially different from the sexual imagery consecrated by great mystical writers like St John of the Cross, where an ineffable union is described in human metaphors. Gill is more like Coventry Patmore in finding a real likeness in the actual experience of two sacraments. Both were men who experienced the delights of marriage before coming to the Eucharist for the first time; and they mark themselves off both from cradle Catholics, who usually experience the Eucharist before puberty, and from ascetic converts.

> Just as physical love is the centre of our life as men and women, so the Holy Mass is the centre of our life as Christians. The Mass and the

---

[19] Ibid., p.187.

Eucharist are not only the centre of Christian worship they are also the centre of Christian merry-making.[20]

Very characteristically, this passage carries a footnote about the desirable circular shape of churches. But he continues eloquently:

the Real Presence which we affirm is the real presence of the man Jesus. Let no one suppose that because we adore him in spirit we do not adore him in our hearts. Very God, yes. And dear Jesus, too. He speaks to us and we speak to him. We kiss the hem of his garment, we also thank him for our bread and butter . . . He ordained the thunderstorms and the lion's voracity; he also blessed the daisies and the poor.

Conversion only intensified his hatred of commercial civilization:

A social order cannot in itself force anyone to do anything, but it can be such as to place many obstacles in the way of those who would live in a human manner. 'A man can be a very good Catholic in a factory' our parish priest used to be fond of saying. And he was very annoyed and called us bolshevists when we retorted: yes, but it requires heroic virtue, and you have no right to demand heroic virtue.[21]

On another occasion he made the sardonic reply: 'Yes, St Agnes was a very good Catholic in a Roman brothel.' In his eyes, there was little or no exaggeration in the comparison.

Gill died in 1940, the year the autobiography was published; and he is most unusual, in a mainly reticent period, in his outspokenness, sexual and political. Our dominant impression may be that there is a close connection between his natural independence and rebelliousness and his joyful submission to authority. He is ready to submit, eager to submit, but only to what he takes to be the voice of God.

Griffiths's story begins with a reverse conversion. The religion of his early training had not taken any strong grip upon him. His adolescent awakening to beauty in nature and romantic poetry seemed to separate him from it. The experience he describes is probably a very common one; it was exceptional only in its intensity, as all his later experiences were to be. More inward-looking than Gill, he made science and reason the chief butts of his early hatred. It is interesting that after two generations when people had been talking vaguely about 'the conflict between science and

20 Ibid., p.246.
21 Ibid., pp.214–15.

religion', usually without any clear idea of what they meant, Griffiths instinctively bundled science, rationalism, religion and conventional morality together as things to be hated and rejected. He was much nearer to Blake than to T.H. Huxley. At Oxford where C.S. Lewis was his tutor, he carried on a crusade against Dryden, Pope and the Age of Reason which 'had an almost religious fervour in it'. For such a temperament, Blake's attack on Newton's 'single vision' would naturally be a heady wine. The joy of nature and the joy of poetry were indistinguishable. To an eager young man, placed in one of the most beautiful settings in England (Addison's Walk in Magdalen College) sensation was enough for the moment. Friendship arose naturally out of the shared romance of poetry. Yet there was a certain chastity of imagination in a young man for whom November and February were loved above other months 'for the air of mystery with which they clothed the misty landscape'. He and his friends were at the opposite pole from the decadents and immoralists of late romanticism a generation before them. They were returning to early romanticism; and their revolt against morality was a revolt against legalism, and against everything that hinders the working of love. With all this intensity, naturally, went narrowness. On a visit to Ireland:

> It is characteristic that we never gave a thought to what might be the religion of the Irish peasants who received us so kindly and whom we so much admired. We were only interested in finding remnants of Celtic folklore among them.[22]

Clearly he was in an unstable state, because he had adopted a philosophy which will not last after early youth. 'Bliss was it in that dawn to be alive.' He began to emerge from it through reading St Augustine and Dante. He was not at first much interested in their conception of religious truth. He was fascinated by their passionate intellectualism; it was impossible after reading them to go on thinking of reason as arid logic-chopping. They trumped his literary romanticism by showing the desire for truth as engaging all the resources of feeling. At the same time Dante's treatment of Paolo and Francesca led him to think more deeply about the word *love*. The ambiguities of this word in English, which uses one word where at least five are needed, are favourable to adolescent confusions. Dante introduced him to the idea that one love can conflict with another, 'that it was not the fire of love which was evil but the passion that made one its slave'. And the *Purgatorio* 'stamped in my mind the fact

[22] Griffiths, op. cit., p.42.

that moral virtue is the transformation of passion and not its suppression, and so freed me for ever from the fear of Puritanism'.[23]

So far there is a certain inner logic in his progress. Dante was able to show him that his early revolt was due to a misunderstanding. But now his rejection of the modern world and of technical civilization, his determination to adopt a simple life—altogether a conventional path for the idealistic young from Coleridge and Southey to the present day—was crossed by something unpredictable and terrifying. He began to adopt a solitary life without any clear motive. He found it involved him in many things he had not contemplated:

> now something irrational seemed to be coming into my life. There had been the desire for fasting which, though I might justify it by reason to some extent, came upon me as an irrational impulse; and now this call to repentance had come, as an apparently irrational urge, and my reason rose up against it. Which was I to obey, this obscure instinct, this apparently irrational urge, or my reason and common sense? The conflict was the most intense that I had ever endured, and it was part of the terms of the conflict, that it could not be answered by reason, because it was precisely the place of reason in my life which was in question.[24]

The ordinary experience of those who try to lead a devout life was turned upside down for him. Most people who try to pray and fast need to discipline themselves, because they know that their ordinary inclinations may make them forget prayer and dislike fasting. For Griffiths, long hours of prayer and fasting, carried to a point that might be dangerous to health, appeared more like a temptation that had to be resisted, and ordinary innocent pleasures and avocations appeared as stern duties that he had to force himself to perform. We may link them, perhaps, with his early revolt against reason. He had, as it were, begun by standing on his head; and now the new and frightening things which were coming into view were seen upside down, and all the more vividly for that. He was afraid that if he spent whole nights in prayer, which felt, not like a duty but like an overwhelming urge, he would become unbalanced. He was doubly alone, for he lacked all guidance or authority, or any rule to live by; and the strange, contradictory state of his mind made it impossible to devise one. His strongest need was precisely the thing

[23] Ibid., p.61.
[24] Ibid., pp.103–4.

which his temperament and his whole history made him most anxious to reject, the sense of community.

The account so far given is one-sided, because it omits the influence of study and reasoning, and especially of reading Newman. But in the path of his theological thinking he was like many others; it was his experience that was peculiar to himself.

It was natural that such a man should find in monasticism one of the chief appeals of Catholicism. But here, too, there was an ugly surprise waiting for him. Visiting the Cistercian Abbey at Caldey, he found:

> The life had none of the attraction I had expected. It was not that there was anything wrong with the life itself, but simply that I had been beguiled by my imagination. I realised then that what I had been seeking was a fantasy under which my own self-will was disguised . . . I had followed my own desires for so long and worked out my own ideal, that it was difficult for me to see that the process had now to be reversed. But I began to understand why St Benedict had turned away from the extreme austerities of the early monks of the Egyptian desert, and had made humility and obedience the basis of monastic life.[25]

His entry into the Benedictine order followed his reception into the Church almost immediately; and in this too his experience was almost unique. And yet one of the most powerful influences upon him was an idea that is common to the generality of Christians:

> there was but one thing which could give any meaning to life, and that was the Crucifixion. The mass of human suffering would remain utterly unintelligible, if we did not know the one point in history, where the power of evil attained its greatest strength and human suffering was most acute, was also the point at which the love of God was most purely revealed.[26]

Like Gill, he remained unrepentant about his brusque rejection of contemporary Western civilization; and his later work *Return to the Centre* (1976) was written in India, and is strongly imbued with the sense of the superiority of the material simplicity of oriental culture.

*   *   *

[25] Ibid., p.135.
[26] Ibid., p.163.

C.S. Lewis dedicated his book[27] to Griffiths—a rare case of a tutor acknowledging a debt to a pupil. Though each began his search with an enthusiasm for romantic literature, their natures and histories were very different. The key to Lewis's story is well stated by himself: 'I have been a converted pagan living among apostate Puritans.'[28] Paganism, no doubt, is a word of many senses. Lewis does not mean that Virgilian *pietas*, the general sense of the pathos and dignity of human life, so finely described by Newman:

> his single words and phrases, his pathetic half-lines, giving utterance, as the voice of Nature herself, to that pain and weariness, yet hope of better things, which is the experience of her children in every time.[29]

His early rejection of Christianity was not, like that of so many others, a moral rejection of Puritanism, but a clear rejection of religion as such. He refers to God as an interferer, and this exactly expresses his early attitude in great things and small. He hated the idea of God, just as he hated going to parties and school discipline. His egoism was extreme, and modified only by a talent for intimate friendship with a very few like-minded people, beginning with his brother. He presents himself in early years as entirely without religious feeling and with no settled moral principles. What he did have was a strong sensibility to pain.

Clearly the death of his mother, which was one of his earliest memories, had a very special importance. He always believed that she had been a serene, comforting, happy person, while his father was nervous, emotional and at times wildly unreasonable. We can see the little boy forming a tough, protective shell against an unpredictable world which could deal such terrible blows. His egoism, his intellectual over-confidence, his inability to fit into any recognized group should all be seen in the context of this shrinking fear of the unforeseen. Very characteristic is his harsh reaction to the sight of his mother's dead body. Where many a child would have been overwhelmed with tender feelings and solemn vows, he was overcome with resentment, not only against death but against those kindly, mistaken people who had taken him to see her:

> I was taken into the bedroom where my mother lay dead; as they said, 'to see her,' in reality, as I at once knew, 'to see it'. There was nothing

---

[27] C.S. Lewis, *Surprised by Joy*, 1955. All quotations from Fontana ed. 1972.
[28] Ibid., p.60.
[29] J.H. Newman, *Grammar of Assent*, Longmans, Chap. IV, Sect. II.

that a grown-up would call disfigurement—except for that total disfigurement which is death itself. Grief was overwhelmed in terror. To this day I do not know what they mean when the call dead bodies beautiful.[30]

This passage is even perhaps more evocative than its author meant. That sullen word 'they' (reminiscent of its use in Edward Lear's limericks) is an instinctive return to childhood, of which the highly-literate and much-read mature writer was probably unconscious. He goes on:

The ugliest man alive is an angel of beauty compared with the loveliest of the dead. Against all the subsequent paraphernalia of coffin, flowers, hearse, and funeral I reacted with horror. I even lectured one of my aunts on the absurdity of mourning clothes.

To this experience he attributes (in part) his 'distaste for all that is public . . . a boorish inaptitude for formality'.

While many families (like the Knoxes above) have been drawn together by the loss of a beloved member, here the opposite occurred. His father's grief, issuing in wild, unemotional and sometimes unfair actions made the son draw away into a private world shared only with his brother. The pathos of a lonely man seeking companionship and comfort in his sons, and met with a wall of evasion and privacy is pathetic in the eyes of the mature writer, but could not be so to the estranged boy.

All these tendencies to solitary egoism were, however, less important than the 'joy' of the title, which is the book's main subject. He defines it as 'an unsatisfied desire which is itself more desirable than any other satisfaction'.

I call it Joy, which is here a technical term and must be sharply distinguished both from Happiness and from Pleasure. Joy (in any sense) has indeed one characteristic, and one only, in common with them; the fact that anyone who has experienced it will want it again. Apart from that . . . it might almost equally well be called a particular kind of unhappiness or grief. But then it is a kind we want. I doubt whether anyone who has tasted it would ever, if both were in his power, exchange it for all the pleasures of the world.[31]

Often the sensation was excited by reading, but it bore no relation to

[30] Lewis, op. cit., pp.21–2.
[31] Ibid., p.20.

literary quality, and only a vague and unpredictable relation to subject-matter. One of the strongest experiences was occasioned by a reading of *Squirrel Nutkin*, which inspired him with the impossible desire to possess autumn.

At this point, Lewis seems very near to the questers of Chapter VI. It is indeed highly probable that some of them began with experiences similar to his, though they have not left an equally clear account. In the end, he was to find himself in a position very far from them; and even at this early stage it is partly possible to see why. In the first place, these experiences were utterly separate from the rest of life. They could not form a way of life, because there was no known means of repeating the experience. Repeating the dose didn't work, though naturally it took him time to discover this. So at once there is a clear contrast with De Quincey's opium or Ackerley's sexual indulgence. He was reduced to longing for obvious impossibilities, like a return of a past moment. He was a boy and a man with at least a normal power of enjoyment of most things, and a particular zest for literary delights. He soon came to see that these were not the point. It was as useless to return to a literary passage to recreate the sensation it had originally excited as it would be to expect to see a remembered scene by looking again in another place through the binoculars with which one had seen it.

He was leading a double life, and he sharply illustrates by dismissing his own account—a very eloquent one—of the miseries of school, with the words, 'lies, lies! This was really a period of ecstasy . . . There were more leprachauns than fags in that House. I have seen the victories of Cuchulain more often than those of the first eleven.'[32]

He differed from the questers, too, in having, for a long time, no theory of life into which these experiences and the strength of the longing for them could be fitted. His intellectual life, that of the budding scholar of enormously wide reading, went on independently. He could no more fit his experience into his general view of the world than into the pattern of his pleasures and pains. He could no more reason from it than he could explain it. Meanwhile, the desired experience was becoming more and more rare, and seeking after it seemed to drive it away.

Naturally, in his reading he was on the lookout for authors who might have had experiences in the least like his own. About one of them, Wordsworth, he makes a significant comment. He says that Wordsworth failed to realize that the longing for the vanished vision was itself

[32] Ibid., p.97.

vision of the same kind. Whether this quite does justice to Wordsworth is a question we can leave aside. But it tells us something important about Lewis. The stock distinction between feeling and thinking people is not applicable to him. Questers are usually, like De Quincey and Powys, unable to present ideas in due proportion and order because of the sudden intensity of feeling. Lewis had an academic and analytical mind in a high degree; he is one of the clearest of scholarly expositors. For a long time, perhaps, in youth, joy and the desire to recover it were too overwhelming to the emotions to be coolly considered. But the time came when they were considered and then he could understand that the hopeless longing for the lost joy was the same as the lost joy itself. True, it was desire, and not possession. But so had been the original sensation. One can no more possess autumn than one can possess the past moment in which one yearned for it. If the two sensations were really the same, why did they not feel the same? Why was it such a difficult and long task to realize it? Because of the intrusion of egoism; because the first experience had simply happened, but the second was distorted by a straining of the will to force sensation into a desired pattern. To comprehend the likeness of the original longing and of the longing for the longing, he had to detach himself in thought, he had to accept things as they were. Here, perhaps, we find the very first stirrings of religious sensibility, the faint beginnings of submission to things as they are, which must include submission to the facts of one's own inner nature, and to the general conditions under which we feel and remember.

Rebellion is a familiar feature of the autobiographies of the last century and a half; but Lewis's had been of a peculiar kind. It was not rebellion against the father's authority or against Protestant repression, or even fundamentally, bitterly as he hated them, against schoolmasters. It was rebellion against life. At one point he speculates idly why he did not become a typical left intellectual of his generation, the generation of those who were boys or very young men in 1914. He gives his intense pessimism and scepticism as one reason. But the deeper reason he does not give, and perhaps does not fully see. Left-wing political views must envisage some desirable social state towards which political action may be directed. He was far beyond any such thoughts. Not only was he uninterested in society, but he was in revolt against his own being and the very laws of nature under which he held it. But joy was a mysterious anomaly, an unexplained exception to all this. How could he fit it into his view of life? He couldn't; and it was so dominating that he had to change his view of life to fit it.

Very characteristic is his strong preference for childhood over boy-hood. Boyhood is the time of gregariousness and conformity; or else of suffering at failure to conform. Very likely he was unlucky in his schools, and perhaps some of his teachers and contemporaries were as disagreeable as he remembered them. But the most humane and intelligent schooling would not have satisfied him. What he hated was being a boy; because boyhood makes it hard to remember and harder to respect the visions of childhood. Growing-up is a process that inevitably disturbs the disinter-estedness of the visionary gleam. And to recover it in maturity is not easy. So he is like Gray in reverse. Gray in his poem about memories of Eton generalized from his own experience to the conclusion that all schoolboys are happy, and all men miserable. Lewis was too pessimistic to reverse this exactly. Rather he says, all boys are miserable (and vicious); and some men may gradually escape from this vile condition.

Meanwhile his powerful but as yet very immature intelligence had been working to bring him to the stock late Victorian materialism. As is usual with clever boys working out their view of things from books, he adopted the clichés of the generation before, rather than new ideas. And the extreme romanticism and personal eclecticism of his literary taste made him slow to respond to the modern literary movement. Yeats is the only writer of the 1920s of whom he speaks with much enthusiasm; and he was appealing for two special and quite distinct reasons, because of the romantic dream-world of his earliest work, and because of his interest in magic and esoteric cults, which Lewis recognizes as one of his most intimate temptations:

> The idea that if there were Occult knowledge it was known to very few and scored by the many became an added attraction; 'we few' . . . was an evocative expression for me. That the means should be Magic —the most exquisitely unorthodox thing in the world, unorthodox both by Christian and by Rationalist standards—of course appealed to the rebel in me. I was already acquainted with the more depraved side of Romanticism; had read *Anactoria*, and Wilde, and pored upon Beardsley . . . If there had been in the neighbourhood some elder person who dabbled in dirt of the Magical kind . . . I might now be a Satanist or a maniac.[33]

But how, it may be asked, could this possibly fit into late Victorian materialism? Lewis's answer to this question is extremely characteristic:

[33] Ibid., p.142.

The two hemispheres of my mind were in the sharpest contrast. On
the one side a many-islanded sea of poetry and myth; on the other a
glib and shallow 'rationalism'. Nearly all that I loved I believed to be
imaginary; nearly all that I believed to be real I thought grim and meaningless . . . I was so far from wishful thinking that I hardly thought
anything true unless it contradicted my wishes.[34]

But there was one respect, and only one, in which this was not so.
Materialism made life meaningless, but it made it finite, terminating
with death. And as Mr Micawber said, no man lacks a friend who is in
possession of shaving materials. 'The horror of the Christian universe
was that it had no door marked *Exit*.' His emotional situation was the
exact opposite of that of spiritualists; he was far more eager to escape pain
than to achieve happiness.

I pass lightly over his encounter with idealist metaphysics, about
which I am not competent to speak. For our purposes the story becomes
interesting again, when most unwillingly, he has come to the conclusion
that 'God was God', 'the most dejected and reluctant convert in all England'. He was in a state which seems, in recent history, to have been very
rare; he was not a Christian nor an adherent of any other faith. But he
had an overwhelming sense of the reality of God, and of His unanswerable authority. 'If you ask why we should obey God, in the last resort the
answer is, "I am."' But he could still, for all his horror at this being
interfered with, have the comfort of being esoteric. His faith was one
that only a philosopher could possibly hold, and far away from 'popular
Christianity'.

The relation of this to the past history of 'joy' is of particular interest:

It may be asked whether my terror was at all relieved by the thought
that I was now approaching the source from which those arrows of
Joy had been shot at me ever since childhood. Not in the least. No
slightest hint was vouchsafed to me that there ever had been or ever
would be any connection between God and Joy. If anything it was the
reverse. I had hoped that the heart of reality might be of such a kind
that we can best symbolize it as a place; instead I found it to be a Person. For all I knew, the total rejection of what I called Joy might be
one of the demands, might be the very first demand.[35]

[34] Ibid., p.138.
[35] Ibid., p.184.

But he had already, while going up Headington Hill on a bus, experienced a moment of choice, without emotion, without threat or hope. He was aware of no motives. 'Perhaps a man is most free when instead of producing motives, he could say, "I am what I do." ' He felt like a snowman beginning to melt and disliked the feeling.

Only a few pages right at the end of the book are allotted to his conversion to Christianity, which clearly occurred at a level where this most articulate of men could not translate it into discursive thought. At most he gives a few hints. He had been studying myths all his life, and he knew the Gospels were not myths. 'And yet the very matter which they set down in their artless, historical fashion—those narrow, unattractive Jews, too blind to the mythical wealth of the Pagan world around them —was precisely the matter of the great myths. If ever a myth had become fact it would be just like this.' And he speaks eloquently of the uniqueness of the Person of Christ. But the struggle, once again, was to accept with the will what the intellect had found.

The real interest of his book lies in the gradual convergence of two streams of thought supposed to be flowing far apart towards different oceans—joy and thought. No one ever had a less naturally religious temperament or a firmer resistance, for a long time, to outside control. The struggle to discipline anarchic feelings is so bitter that the reader feels its pain and difficulty to the full. Most of us are not among the few, like Bunyan and Newman, for whom spiritual awareness is in the fibre of being. For the worldly majority, fully imbued with natural selfishness, the similar Lewis is an arresting case.

Like nearly all Newman's works, except *A Grammar of Assent*, the *Apologia* (1864) began as an occasional piece. Kingsley's attack, absurd though it was in itself, was important for several reasons. First it brought the mythology of what Bishop Hensley Henson was later to call 'the Protestant underworld' into the domain of civilized, literary life. However much of an ass he was, and however obstinately he persisted in a falsehood that had been proved against him to the perfect satisfaction of a Protestant public, Kingsley could not be ignored as a gutter pamphleteer. His position as popular novelist, favourite and friend of Queen Victoria and professor at Cambridge meant that an attack from him must be answered. This was important in several ways. It meant that Newman wrote his autobiography in defence of his honesty and of that of his fellow-Catholics. He wrote it at a low-spirited time, when but for the occasion given by Kingsley, he would not have thought of it; and he wrote it at an interim time, nearly twenty years after his conversion, but long before he had become a grand old man, and a national institution, as well as a cardinal. (It is true that the *Apologia* itself did much to ensure that he would eventually graduate as a national institution.) Most important of all, Kingsley concentrated Newman's attention, and that of his readers, upon a very complex issue, which Kingsley himself was far from understanding—the issue of continuity and change. Newman set himself to answer the question, how can I claim to be consistent when my faith and my allegiance have changed? And the very unusual nature of Newman's personal history, as well as his extraordinary lucid sense of the self as a primary, unchanging entity, meant that the question was an urgent, personal one. It rose up from the depths of his being, subtle and challenging to encounter a monstrous distortion of itself—yet not so monstrous as not to be recognizable—in Kingsley's crude polemic.

The point will become clear if we compare the tone and content of the *Apologia* with that of *Difficulties of Anglicans*, published more than ten years before, and specifically addressed to his old friends of the Oxford Movement who had remained Anglicans. He writes as a Catholic, pleading with others to follow him. He argues that they must follow him if they are to be true to the principles they first adopted; and he deals carefully with various objections that can be made to this thesis. But the *Apologia* is the account of a journey in which it is never possible to see far ahead, in which maps prove deceptive, in which the goal is for a long time unknown; in which signposts and indications are described according to the importance, often illusory, that they seemed to have at the time. In particular, he has to deal, and in the end triumphantly does deal, with the awkward question, how was it that many others, not very perceptive observers, sensed where he was going before he did himself?

I have called his personal history unusual, and obviously it was so in many ways; but especially in its chronology. It is not quite true, as is sometimes said, that all his history was a religious history, for he records how, at the age of fourteen, he was impressed with the plausibility of some of the arguments of Hume and Voltaire. But at fifteen he put all such thoughts behind him for good. The first stage of his journey, which he always regarded as the most decisive of all, was over at the age when most boys are still half children. The other two, the movement through Calvinism and liberalism to the doctrines of the Tractarians, and the movement from there to Rome, occupied nearly thirty years. He begins with a sudden reversal; he proceeds with infinite gradualness. In one sense he is changing; in another he is preserving continuity, unpacking unsuspected implications, even (he would have said) preserving, in the face of accidental errors, imperfections and omissions, the essential truth that he had perceived at fifteen.

No doubt the boy of fifteen was precocious and clever; but the experience he had was not an intellectual one, or not mainly so. His later development derives, in large part, from study and argument. Yet there are several reasons why this contrast is not felt so strongly as we would expect. His experience of ideas, and of historical personalities divided from him by many centuries, was unusually feeling. The word 'realize', a favourite with him, always means perceive feelingly, grasp in all its personal relevance. And then, partly because of this, long hours and weeks of thought and study are punctuated with moments of terrifying intensity, which he can only compare to seeing a ghost or to hearing a disembodied voice. These are literary images; he knew well that these moments welled up from the depths of his own mind, and he never believed that he had received any direct inspiration. Because his feelings were so strong he tended to distrust feeling; and after one of these precious or frightening moments of insight, he always returned to the 'sheer plod' of reading, analysing and arguing.

But feeling is much more than a disconnected series of emotional moments. There is also a general cast of feeling, personal to each man. Newman was naturally affectionate, retentive, reverent. His family affections, his patriotism, his love of home, first at Oxford and later at Birmingham, were all of exceptional strength. The well-known image of the snap-dragon on the wall at Trinity is characteristic, both in its visible, poetic character, and in signalling a determination to remain what he was and where he was, in an age when very few Oxford dons contemplated their life in Oxford as permanent. It is obvious that some features of his history and his book derive directly from this aspect of his nature. It is the source of his determination to obey his bishop's lightest word, a kind of obedience that Anglican bishops were very unused to receiving. It is the source of his valiant and ingenious, but hopeless attempt in Tract XC, to interpret the Thirty-nine Articles in a Catholic sense. That his primary loyalty, to Catholic truth, and his strong secondary one, to the Anglican Church, to Oxford and to all his own past efforts, could really conflict—this was not only painful, but for long almost inconceivable. Hence the slowness of his progress, and the interludes of static delay. Hence, too, indirectly, his fierceness of rebuke to some of those who were travelling the same path a little less painfully and a little more rapidly. It is almost amusing to see him fasten on the irrelevant question of O'Connell's politics as one of the few last strands in a rope that could no longer bear the strain. He did so, no doubt, because O'Connell was the predestined opposite of all his own loyalties and traditions, loyalties as Anglican, as patriot, as supporter of political authority. But the fierceness and unreasonableness of his reaction might have signalled to a perceptive observer that it was an emotional outburst only, which intellect and conscience would soon override. Indeed, the time would come when he would say that if he was an Irishman, he would be a rebel at heart.

But if this side of Newman, which may loosely but conveniently be labelled 'conservative' had been his whole nature, his life would have been very different. Against it, from the first, and noticed with admiration and alarm by Keble, Pusey and other friends, was a dynamic boldness, a readiness to encounter and state objections and difficulties in their full power. Thus he called the *Via Media* of Anglo-Catholicism, long before he thought of doubting it, a 'paper religion'. Or he writes of his sense, at the same period of his life, of the contrast between the 'triumphant zeal' of the early Church and the 'establishment . . . divided and threatened', and he goes on:

> I felt affection for my own Church, but not tenderness; I felt dismay at her prospects, anger and scorn at her do-nothing perplexity . . . As to leaving her the thought never crossed my imagination; still I ever kept before me that there was something greater than the Established Church, and that was the Church Catholic and Universal, set up from the beginning, of which she was but the local presence and organ. She was nothing unless she was this. She must be dealt with strongly, or she would be lost.[36]

His balance, his understanding of human nature, his wisdom were not easy achievements. They were born out of the clash of opposites. It was very characteristic of him both to say that he had a sense of God's existence as strong as of his own and to say:

> Of all points of faith, the being of a God is, to my own apprehension, encompassed with most difficulty.[37]

There is, of course, no contradiction; the question is being considered in two quite different ways. All the same, the opposition is startling, and very characteristic. So is the stark contrast between God's being and his

[34] J.H. Newman, *Apologia Pro Vita Sua*, Longmans, 1864, pp.94–5.
[37] Ibid., p.374.

absence from the world, introduced by the famous image of the mirror in which he did not see his face.

The *Apologia* has usually been read, very properly, as history and argument, and as a vindication of honesty. But to read it simply as autobiography for our present purposes is to realize that the story he had to tell endowed him with two perfect images for these two sides of his nature, the 'conservative' and the 'dynamic'. The Church of England naturally represented the first; because of family feelings, Oxford loyalties, academic attainments, early friendships consecrated and intensified by shared labour in a great cause, because, too, of English history and insularity, and the instinctive superiorities of an educated class. Aesthetic impressions, both literary and architectural, all told the same way. The idea of Oxford as a closed Anglican corporation appealed both to deep convictions and to more superficial Tory sentiments. On the other side, Rome was the interloper, requiring from him a theory of dynamic development, a living force, not a paper system. She was, in Protestant tradition, Anti-Christ, and had been once felt to be so in Newman's own mind. She was foreign, associated in history with the opposing powers of France and Spain, and in the present with radicalism, demagoguery, Irish nationalism and all ungentlemanliness. To Newman, subjectively, Anglicanism represented what was old and venerable, Rome with its baroque devotion what was brash and new. But this, naturally, was only at the level of personal memory and ordinary social life. When he went into his study, and went back to reading the Fathers, the position was reversed. Rome was the perennial; and her ancient voices seemed more and more to be speaking of the present day. Anglicanism seemed local and recent, unless one could ignore the Reformation, and believe, as for so long he tried to do, that its principles were those of the early Church. Thus the intense dislike of the Reformation which was so puzzling to most of their fellow-Anglicans was an absolute necessity of the Oxford men's position. As long as he could still believe that Anglicanism was based on antiquity, the tension between his 'conservative' and his 'dynamic' sides was controllable. The superficial traditionalism of Tory Oxford, of English gentlemanliness, the classical education, and Elizabethan liturgies could have as its basis the deep traditionalism of the Gospel and of Christian antiquity. And his dynamic side was engaged in his intellectual boldness, his efforts to achieve sanctity, the excitement of an influential movement that seemed to be clearing away the débris of many decades of self-satisfied worldliness.

When we understand this, we shall see how devastating an experience it was when Christian antiquity began to give a different report, when the shadow of the fourth century was found to be on the nineteenth, when 'the theory of the Via Media was absolutely pulverized'. It meant that the superficial conservatism of training and tradition and Anglican Oxford had come to lack its fundamental basis, or rather that the supposed basis was rotten. From then on, both the conservative and the dynamic aspects of his deeper mind and thought were on the same side, the side of Rome; and they were opposed by sentiments, memories, friendships and loyalties. These were very powerful; but in a man like Newman they could not triumph in the end over conscience and intellect.

So far we have spoken of a conflict of principles corresponding to a conflict within Newman's own nature. But there is something deeper, a man's own deepest self, below the level of all conflicts, that which is the precious but elusive goal of all classic autobiographies. Here, too, Newman as an autobiographer was fortunate, though that is too weak a word. He had a natural symbol for this also, whether we consider his book as a quest for the ultimate self, or as a vindication of honesty before the court of public opinion. From first page to last his book, as from age fifteen to almost ninety his life, was dominated by his desire to hold fast to and serve that Church which Christ founded. Of course, no one person can simply be identified with this, as Newman would be the first to say; but it can serve as an external, visible image of what is unspoken and unknowable, and that is something that most autobiographers lack.

The opposition of 'conservative' and 'dynamic' is one of several in Newman's nature, and thus in his literary style. He is intimate and spiritual, but he is also terse, practical and ironical. In his plainness and directness he is in the tradition of Swift and the great English plain style, yet some of his passages could only have been written by one steeped in Wordsworth and his contemporaries. The greatest merit of the *Apologia* autobiography reflects this; it tells the most intimate and subjective of stories through the medium of the most clear and objective things, doctrines, arguments, documents, dates and events.

X

Conclusion

Soul, self; come, poor Jackself, I do advise
You, jaded, let be . . .
(G.M. Hopkins, sonnet, 'My own Heart', about 1887)

As with all forms of literature whose aim is to describe reality the key question in the judgment of autobiography is that of truth. This is equally true of theology, philosophy, history and science. But there are few fields where the question is so elusive. The critic of autobiography must grapple with several different kinds of truth. The simple truth of accurate record of facts is clearly important; but as a rule this is overshadowed by other kinds. At the same time we are judging the autobiographer's central idea, the shape of his life as he sees it. The idea may be a simple one; in the great autobiographies it usually is. Thus Newman sees his life as a journey towards truth, and Russell as a fundamental incompatibility of truth and feeling. But the simple idea is embodied in a mass of detail, a vast complex of memory, document and interpretation. To judge how far the master-idea proves itself the right and inevitable form of all the detail is far from simple. The autobiographies we call great are those where the master-idea has its own momentous dignity, but at the same time is truly felt as working through the contingent and everyday. It is easy to think of a grand theme for an autobiography, but extremely difficult to convince the critical reader of its essential truth. Bad autobiographies are generally of two kinds; those that have no shape, but are only a random collection of memories, and those that fail to justify their theme because events and memories fail to rise to the level of the idea. There may be many reasons for this. Common ones are: egoism ('if only they had listened to me'), the pressure of multiplicity, failure to understand motives, and an inability to bring other characters to life. And all these are in addition to the ordinary causes of literary failure, which are found in this as in other forms.

But there is one difficulty in autobiography which is peculiar to it, and which springs from its inherent nature. Since the author and the subject are the same, we judge the style of writing in a special way. We do not only ask, is the writing clear or expressive or eloquent or imaginative? We also ask, is the personality conveyed by the style of writing recognizably the same as that described? In the great autobiographies—and once again Newman and Russell will serve as examples—there is a perfect unity here which goes far beyond any conscious intention, and which is a witness to the truth of the interpretation of the self. Even in one, like that of H.G. Wells, which is much less great, because much less intelligently discerning, we may be able to find this precious, indispensable unity between the describer and the described. In others (sometimes ones of great merit) it is absent.

It is not easy to find a close parallel in other literary forms. A biographer has no need to imitate his subject's idiom in order to give a just account of his character. We do not expect Gibbon to alter his style according as he is speaking of Constantine or Julian. Perhaps the nearest comparison— and it is not very near—is with dramatic poetry or dialogue in novels. But in autobiography the required empathy is with the self—empathy between the self as subject (the writer) and as object (the person described). This cannot usefully be striven for, nor is it a simple product of inner harmony. The man who speaks of inner conflicts, or has developed new beliefs and attitudes, may triumphantly possess it, while he who has changed little may fail to have it.

Perhaps the greatest autobiographies are those that fulfil both requirements. They are controlled by a leading idea, a pattern strong in its simplicity, but endlessly hospitable in receiving detail. At the same time, subject and object, the voice of the writer and the person described are experienced by the reader as a living unity.

Index

Ackerley, J.R. 148, 170–5, 205
Addison, Joseph 11
Aeschylus 157
Albert, Prince 163
Anactoria 207
Apologia pro Vita Sua 2, 194, 209–14
Apostate, The 53, 60–6
Ardath 61, 64–5
Arnold, Matthew 43
Asquith, H.H. (Lord Oxford) 92, 141
Auden, W.H. (quoted) 170
Augustine, St 3, 4, 182, 187, 200
Aurora Leigh 33, 147, 177
Austen, Jane 135

Babbage, Charles 36
Bagnold, Enid 37–8, 51
Balfour, A.J. 125
Baring, Maurice 184
Beardsley, Aubrey 207
Beauclerc, Lord Frederick 26
Beaufort, Duke of 27
Bedford, Duke of 138
Beer, Patricia 42, 47–9
Benedict, St 202
Bentham, Jeremy 127
Berners, Lord 76–9
Blake, William 139, 200
Bossuet, J-B 103, 105
Boswell, James 16–23, 24, 29
Brezhnev, Leonid 86
Britten, J. 189
Browning, E.B. 35, 147, 177
Bunyan, John 2, 11, 178–80
Burn, W.L. 121
Burns, Robert 38
Byron, Lord 16, 28–33, 105, 109, 142, 163

Capel, Mgr. 123
Cardus, Neville 54, 95–6
Carlyle, Thomas 49, 157, 180
Casanova, Giacomo 129
Catholic Church against the Twentieth Century 184
Chaworth, Mary 31
Chesterton, G.K. 5, 148, 170
Child in the Forest 95
Church, Richard 38
Clare, Lord 29, 31–2
Cobbett, William 135
Coleridge, S.T. ii, 201
Comte, Auguste 123
Connolly, Cyril 46–7
Conrad, Joseph 131, 173
Constable, John 20
Constantine, Emperor 217
Correlli, Marie 64
Craven, Earl of 23

Daily Telegraph 85
Dante 200
Darwin, Charles 130
Darwin family, 45
Defoe, Daniel 102
De la Mare, Walter 36, 38, 51, 88
De Quincey, Thomas 13, 39–43, 155–60, 162, 205–6
Dickens, Charles 12, 91, 102, 104, 109, 126, 131, 132, 163, 188, 208
Difficulties of Anglicans 210
Disraeli, Benjamin 157
Distant Prospect, A 76n
Domecq, Adèle 107
Don Quixote 106
Dostoevsky, Feodor 165
Dryden, John 200

Early One Morning 36
Einstein, Albert 129
Elected Silence 99
Eliot, George 123, 190
Eliot, T.S. 94, 153, quoted 181
Ellis, Havelock 148
Emerson, R.W. 43
Enchanted Places, 73
Enemies of Promise 47
Evolution and Ethics
Excursion, The 147

Far Away and Long Ago 55–60
Farewell, Happy Fields 53, 149–55
Farjeon, Eleanor 70–3
Fielding, Henry 11
First Childhood 76–9
Flaubert, Gustave 64
Foley, Winifred 95–6
Fors Clavigera 195
Francis of Assisi, St 59
Francois de Sales, St 179
Franklin, Benjamin 11–15, 119

Galton, Francis 123
Gaskell, Elizabeth 121
George, Henry 132
George VI, King 138, 145
Gibbon, Edward 33, 139, 217
Gill, Eric 5, 195–9, 202
Gollancz, Victor 82–8
Goncharev, Ivan 149
Gorst, Sir John 125
Gosse, Edmund 108–14
Gosse, Philip 108–14
Grace Abounding 178–80
Grammar of Assent, A 209
Granville, Lord 127
Granville-Barker, Harley 124
Gray, Thomas 207
Grey, Sir Edward 141, 143
Griffiths, Dom Bede 35, 188, 195,
  199–203
Guardian, The 97
Guiccioli, Teresa 32

Hare, Augustus 88–92
Harrison, Frederick 123

Have You Anything to Declare? 184n
Haydon, Benjamin 13, 148, 161–4, 165
Hegel, G.W.F. 140
Helsinger, Howard 119
Henry VIII, King 193
Herbert, Lady 186
Hitler, Adolf 86, 93
Hobhouse, John 32
Holy Grail, The 147
Homer 101–2
Hopkins, G.M. 177, 211, 215
Hound and the Falcon, The 155n
Hours in a Library ii, 147
Hudson, W.H. 54, 55–60, 67, 149
Hume, David 33, 210
Hunt, Leigh 12
Huxley, Aldous 162
Huxley, T.H. 123, 134, 200
Hyde, Douglas 184–6, 191

Ibsen, Henrik 86, 94
Importance of Being Earnest, The 12
Irving, Edward 49

James, Henry 64
John of the Cross, St 198
Johnson, Samuel 3, 18–19, 22, 23, 49,
  84, 127
Johnson, Fr. Vernon 183, 190–2
Jones, L.E. 41–2, 43–4
Julian, Emperor 217

Kaye-Smith, Sheila 99, 183–4, 192
Keats, John 5, 61, 93–4
Keble, John 212
Keynes, J.M. 114
Kingsley, Charles 209–10
Knox, Mgr. R.A. 181, 190–4, 204

Lady Chatterley's Lover 144
Landow, George P. 119
Land Unknown, The 149–55
La Touche, Rose 100
Lawrence, D.H. 144, 182
Lear, Edward 204
Lewis, C.S. 35, 65–6, 164, 200, 203–9
Liddon, Canon H.P. 123
Life of Samuel Johnson 16, 18

Lion's Mouth, The 149–55
Little Dorrit 102
Lloyd George, David 92
Lowes Dickinson, G. 147

Macaulay, Lord 17n, 140
Macbeth 12
McTaggart, J.M. 140
Manhattan, Avro 184
Manning, Cardinal H.E. 123, 186
Marchand, Leslie 29
Martineau, James 123
Marvell, Andrew 77
Marx, Karl 144
Maxwell, Gavin 6, 37, 49–51
Merton, Thomas 99
Middlemarch 190
Mill, J.S. 4, 8–10, 82
Milne, A.A. 73–6
Milne, Christopher 73–6
Milton, John 156
Mind at the End of Its Tether 5–6
Modern Painters 81, 99
Montgomery, Robert 89
Moore, Thomas 28
Morrell, Lady Ottoline 142, 147
Morris, William 195
Mozart, W.A. 156
Muir, Edwin 4, 54, 55, 66–70, 71, 149
Murray, John 32
Mussolini, Benito 86
My Apprenticeship 121–9
My Dear Timothy 83–8
My Father and I 170–5

Napier, Priscilla 46
Napoleon 129
Newman, Cardinal J.H. ii, 8, 10, 13,
    82, 179, 181, 182, 188–9, 193–4,
    202–3, 209–14, 216
Newton, Sir Isaac 139, 200
North and South 121
Nostromo 173
Nursery in the Nineties, A 71–3

O'Connell, Daniel
Old Curiosity Shop, The 91
Omphalos 110

One Lord, One Faith 183
Our Partnership 124–9
Over the Bridge 38
Owen, Wilfrid 94

Paradise Lost 64
Pascal, Roy ii, 2
Patmore, Coventry 198
Paul, St 85, 178, 188
Peacock, T.L. 164
Pickwick Papers, The 91
Pictures from Italy 188
Planck, Max 129
Plato 149, 154–5, 169
Ponsonby, Lord 24, 26
Pope, Alexander 28, 78, 169, 200
Portal, Lord 138
Potter, Beatrix 205
Potter family 122
Praeterita 100--8
Prelude, The ii, 54
Pringle, Sir J. 21
Prufrock and Other Observations 94
Pusey, E.B. 212
Powys, J.C. 148, 164–70, 206

Rainbow, The 182
Raine, Kathleen 6, 53, 148, 149–55,
    156
Raverat, Gwen 44–6
Reformation of the Eleventh Century, The
    ii
Reid, Forrest 53, 54, 55, 60–6, 67, 72
Renan, Ernest 184
Return to the Centre 202
Robespierre, Maximilien 11
Rob Roy 12
Rousseau, J-J. 22
Ruskin, John 43, 72, 81, 99, 100–8,
    109, 113, 118, 188, 195, 197
Russell, Alys 141–2
Russell, Bertrand 6–7, 114–20, 128,
    135–46, 147, 216
Russell, Dora 7
Russell, Lord John 137

Scarlet Pimpernel, The 48
Scoop 55n

Scott, Sir Walter 24n, 25, 58, 101–2
Sewell, Elizabeth 4
Shaw, G.B. 124, 170
Shelley, P.B. 135, 139, 142, 153, 163
Sitwell, Osbert 7–8
Southey, Robert 3, 201
Spencer, Herbert 86, 121–3, 127
Spender, J.A. 92
Spender, Stephen 92–5
Spiritual Aeneid, A 191–4
Spurgeon, Rev. C.H. 123
Stalin, Josef 129–31, 132
Steele, Sir R. 11
Stephen, Leslie ii, 147
Strindberg, August 94
Surprised by Joy 65, 303–9
Swift, Jonathan 214
Swinburne, A.C. 207

Tait, Katherine 7, 14
Taylor, Harriet 4
Taylor, Jeremy 91
Tennyson, Lord 61, 94, 147
Thackeray, W.M. 96
Three Ways Home 99, 183
Thurber, James 118
Times, The 71
Tirpitz, Admiral Alfred von 143
Tolstoy, Count Leo 60
Traherne, Thomas 53

Trevelyan, G.M. 140
Trollope, Anthony 8, 102
Tyrrell, George 37

Victoria, Queen 209
Victorian Boyhood, A 41
Virgil 84, 203
Voltaire, F-M. 33, 134, 210

Wagner, Richard 86
Waugh, Evelyn 55n
Webb, Beatrice 120–9, 133
Webb, Sidney 127
Wells, H.G. ii, 5–6, 120, 124, 128,
   129–35, 141, 216
Wesley, John 110
White, Antonia 155
White, Joseph, Blanco 10
Whitefield, George 110
Whitman, Walt 135
Wilde, Oscar 207
Wilson, Harriette 16, 23–8
Woolf, Virginia 128
Worcester, Lord 27
Wordsworth, William ii, 9–10, 40–1,
   51, 54, 60, 75, 94, 147, 150, 164,
   187, 205–6, 214
World Within World 92

Yeats, W.B. 207